CW00922657

Strategic IT Management

Inge Hanschke

Strategic
IT Management

A Toolkit for Enterprise
Architecture Management

 Springer

Inge Hanschke
iteratec GmbH
Inselkammerstr. 4
82008 München
Germany
Inge.Hanschke@iteratec.de

Figure Drawings by Frank Fischer, Ottobrunn

ISBN 978-3-642-05033-6   e-ISBN 978-3-642-05034-3
DOI 10.1007/978-3-642-05034-3
Springer Heidelberg Dordrecht London New York

Library of Congress Control Number: 2009939716

ACM Computing Classification (1998): K.6, J.1, H.4, C.0, D.2

© Springer-Verlag Berlin Heidelberg 2010

English Translation from the German edition:
Strategisches Management der IT-Landschaft
Ein praktischer Leitfaden für das EnterpriseArchitecture Management
by Inge Hanschke © 2009 Carl Hanser Verlag München
All Rights Reserved.

Cover design: KuenkelLopka GmbH, Heidelberg

Printed on acid-free paper

Springer is part of Springer Science+Business Media (www.springer.com)

Preface

Changes in business models and faster-paced innovation and product lifecycles pose a big challenge to IT managers – who are already tasked with keeping operations running reliably. You have to anticipate the impact of changes taking shape ahead, and take decisions rapidly, backing your choices by solid fact. To do this, you need an overall perspective of how business and IT interact.

This is exactly where a toolkit for strategic management of the IT landscape can help, by building greater transparency into the current IT landscape and making explicit its contribution to the business success of the enterprise. The enterprise strategy and business requirements are cascaded into requirements for IT: an ongoing process that entails building a picture of the target architecture, designing implementation plans and managing the process for taking plans into action.

Right from the start, the toolkit must enable management of the enterprise from a helicopter viewpoint and accommodate every aspect of the enterprise architecture: business and IT structures, processes and organisation, as well as software support. Yet it also has to be introduced in achievable stages that deliver tangible success. Senior management, business departments and IT teams all have to be convinced by success. Only if its value is apparent will the concept be given the go-ahead for further investment.

So how do you arrive at a workable toolkit? How do you go about it, and what investment and effort can you expect to make? What is the payoff?

The relevant literature investigates a number of approaches. Yet information is patchy and lacking real-life application for many of the relevant aspects. Inadequate documentation and lack of standardisation both leave their mark, making it difficult for IT and business managers and their teams to navigate this challenging territory.

Motivated by the challenge of assembling a comprehensive, practicable toolkit for the strategic management of IT landscapes, I set to work on this book. It condenses the experience of many projects with customers, and insights from many hundreds of hours of discussion with experts from client companies, consultancies and academia. The book takes a holistic view of the IT landscape management process, above all giving specific guidelines on how to establish and how to roll out strategic IT landscape management in the enterprise and ensures it becomes established practice.

This book will help you embark successfully into strategic IT landscape management and evolve it effectively. The first step is what matters. There is rarely a second chance.

Munich, August 2009   Inge Hanschke

Acknowledgements

Many thanks to my team at iteratec and colleagues at other companies for the productive exchanges, especially in the course of the design and development of the EAM tool iteraplan.

Thank you to my discussion partners, reviewers and supporters, whose valuable comments and feedback have greatly contributed to this book: Karsten Voges, Gunnar Giesinger, Andreas Feldschmidt, Matthias Häring, Margarete Metzger, Irene Weilhart and others who did not wish to be named, but whose contribution is much appreciated.

Last but not least, thanks to Frank Fischer for the graphics expertise and to Marion Bonleitner, Alice Golja, Svenja Altwein and Luisa Kunze for the editorial assistance and Hannah Lea for the excellent translation.

And a special thank-you to my family, who kept me going and encouraged me with their feedback.

Contents

Chapter 1
Introduction

Every morning in Africa, a gazelle wakes up.
It knows it must run faster than the fastest lion or it will be
killed.
Every morning a lion wakes up.
It knows it must outrun the slowest gazelle or it will starve to
death.
It doesn't matter whether you are a lion or a gazelle.
When the sun comes up, you better start running.
Thomas L. Friedman: The World Is Flat, 2005

Against a backdrop of globalisation, mergers, mounting competition and accelerating innovation cycles, organisations are forced to review and adjust their business models more frequently than ever before. Organisations need their IT solutions to implement these altered business requirements – simply, quickly and affordably. So, right in line with the morale of Friedman's story, IT has to be made ready for the next big run.

Figure 1.1 shows the scenario common in many organisations. Permanently changing business requirements have over time spawned landscapes of such

Fig. 1.1 A common situation

I. Hanschke, *Strategic IT Management*, DOI 10.1007/978-3-642-05034-3_1,
© Springer-Verlag Berlin Heidelberg 2010

heterogeneity and complexity that cost-efficient and above all speedy action is virtually impossible. The IT landscape resembles a patchwork of systems, home-grown processes, technologies, methods and standards. Yet taken individually, every component was originally a good, solid, technically mature performer – and well up to its job. So where exactly is the problem?

In many organisations, the IT landscape has evolved organically over decades. Once in place, systems or interfaces would usually be left well alone unless intervention was absolutely essential, the golden rule being "never touch a running system". When extensions were made, they were bolted on haphazardly rather than being cleanly integrated. This creates nonessential interfaces – and technological diversity where none is required. Pressured by the need to deliver quick answers to business requirements, developers all too often resort to the easier option of a new standalone solution. The tough option – to consolidate the landscape – is the IT equivalent of open-heart surgery. Unsurprisingly, enterprises tend to steer clear of such undertakings, because even minor changes to such complex systems can have disastrous impact.

New technology, legal requirements and tougher security and compliance legislation exacerbate the situation. Fresh technologies are often introduced without retiring an equivalent volume of legacy technology. But the older an IT system or interface gets, the more difficult it becomes to service or replace: technology moves on, knowledge on the details of the implementation grows stale as time progresses, the employee who knows the system leaves the company, and the documentation – if any – exists only in rudimentary form.

If you want to take charge of your IT costs and be prepared for your next "big run", you'll have to tidy up the patchwork landscape. Strategic management of your IT landscape helps you do precisely this.

1.1 Strategic Management of IT Landscapes

Strategic management of the IT landscape creates an overview of the structures that exist in IT and the interactions between IT and the business. Framed by the parameters of strategic IT management, it provides a toolkit for planning and directing the evolutionary development of the landscape. The key elements of this planning toolkit are IT landscape management and technical standardisation (see Fig. 1.2).

IT landscape management embraces all the processes for documenting and analysing the landscape and for governing and controlling its evolution in line with strategic business objectives. It promotes better understanding of the enterprise as a whole – and of how IT helps drive forward the enterprise's business success. It also creates a common language between business and IT, forging links between business structures – processes, functions and products – and the structures in IT such as information systems and interfaces, and rendering explicit the complex interdependencies that exist between and within these domains. This enables you to identify trends, pinpoint where action is needed, and where there is potential

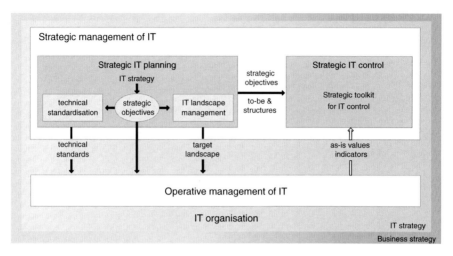

Fig. 1.2   IT management

for improvement. The resulting transparency helps satisfy the need for information from multiple perspectives and creates a solid basis for decisions.

By working with technical standardisation – i.e. by defining technical standards and managing compliance – it is possible to provide reasonably priced IT support which is custom-tailored to business requirements.

Corporate strategy, IT strategy and operative business requirements are all channelled into designing the future IT landscape and choosing technical standards. These strategies and requirements set the framework for evolutionary development of the IT landscape on the operational IT management level.

A key input for strategic IT control is transparency: clarity on the interdependencies that exist in the landscape, a clear statement of progress made toward goals, and the extent to which planning and business requirements have been enacted. Progress toward goals is measured by comparing the as-is values with targets on indicators from operative IT management.

1.2 Navigating This Book

The structure of this book reflects the patterns that exist in strategic management of IT landscapes (see Fig. 1.3). The starting point is strategic IT planning, where the strategic goals are defined (Chap. 2). Taking into account the structures predicated by the enterprise architecture (Chap. 3), these goals inform the design of the target landscape (Chap. 4) and choice of technical standards (Chap. 5). Moving beyond the planning stage and into practice, implementation is underpinned by embedding the practices in the organisation and by applying an array of control levers, tools and governance entities (Chap. 6).

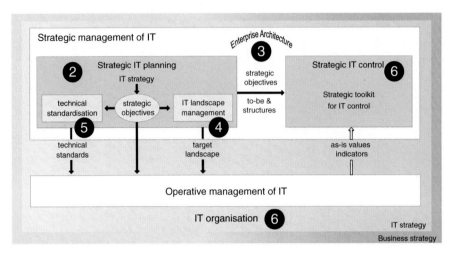

Fig. 1.3 Suggested path through this book

You can read the chapters in the given order, or dip in and out as you wish. Each chapter is a cohesive unit.

Chapter 2 surveys the components of strategic IT planning, focusing on IT strategy development and how this interacts with strategic management of the IT landscape. As the key "takeaway" from this chapter, you gain a good all-round idea of how strategic goals draw a framework around IT landscape planning.

Chapter 3 introduces the nomenclature and structures of Enterprise Architecture Management (EAM) and provides guidelines for adopting your own enterprise architecture.

Chapter 4 explains how you can ensure the evolutionary development of your IT landscape proceeds in alignment with your strategic business goals. The chapter provides an explanation of content and processes, and pointers on how to embed IT landscape management practices in the organisation. It also includes guidelines on how to adapt IT landscape management to your particular needs.

Chapter 5 introduces the process of technical standardisation and its components. The guidelines and "how-to" roadmap will help you introduce technical standardisation into your enterprise.

Chapter 6 contains a set of measures for embedding IT landscape management in your enterprise and directing the evolutionary development of IT.

Each chapter contains numerous references for recommended reading to deepen your understanding of the subject under discussion.

1.3 Who Should Read This Book?

This book is intended for anyone in business or IT involved in documenting, designing and planning the IT landscape. The following stakeholders in particular will receive answers to key questions:

- CIO and IT managers and IT function units
    - How do you render explicit the interdependencies and connections that exist within and between business and IT structures?
    - How do you recognize that action needs to be taken, and how do you identify potential for optimisation in IT?
    - How do you unearth interdependencies and the impact of changes in IT?
    - To what extent is your IT landscape standard-compliant?
    - How do you effectively steer the evolutionary development of your IT landscape?
    - How do you make apparent the contribution of IT to the business success of your enterprise?
- Business managers and stakeholders from process management or business process optimisation
    - How do you scope out the need for action and potential to optimise IT support for the business?
    - How can you tell whether the IT landscape is future-proof, simple and robust, or complex and unstable?
    - How do you reveal where interdependencies exist and scope out the impact of business changes?
- Managers of business transformations such as mergers or restructuring
    - How do you identify sections of business and IT which are loosely or tightly connected?
    - How can you analyse and appraise the potential impact of restructuring?
    - How can you evaluate and compare planning alternatives?

1.4 Scope of This Book, Further Reading

This book touches only briefly on issues relating to operative IT management. A detailed treatment can be found in [Blo06], [Buc05], [Buc07], [Fer05], [Foe08], [GPM03], [Krc05], [Mai05], [Rom07], [Tie07] and [Zin04]. Likewise, you can find further information about IT controlling in [Ahl06], [Blo06], [Hei01], [Küt06], [Küt07] and [KüM07].

This book makes no explicit differentiation between strategic and tactical IT management, since no clear boundary can be drawn between the two, and nor would such a distinction make any difference to the guidelines and toolkit which the book presents. The distinction between strategic and tactical levels is dealt with in literature such as [Mül05].

Operational infrastructure planning is not addressed in detail in this book; interested readers might like to refer to [Joh07] and [itS08].

I have included only brief references to tool support. You can find a comparison of commercial EAM tools in [Seb08]. You might also like to investigate the Open Source product iteraplan (www.iteraplan.de), which helps enterprises make a quick, easy start to strategic management of their IT landscape.

Chapter 2
Strategic Planning of IT

Do today what others will not think until tomorrow – because nothing endures but change

Heraclitus, 450 B.C.

Against a backdrop of globalisation, mergers & acquisitions, mounting competition and accelerating innovation and product lifecycles, organisations are being forced to review and adjust their business models more frequently than ever before. With IT that is in gear with their business requirements, organisations are far better positioned to beat their competitors to market with innovative products and chart a pathway into new domains.

Strategic planning of IT has a key role to play here. The objective of planning IT strategically is to align it with overarching corporate goals and business requirements and make it agile enough to deal with constant change in the company and its environment. By creating a holistic understanding of the business model, corporate strategy, strategic positioning of IT and IT itself, strategic planning of IT codifies the planning assumptions and precepts on which IT decisions are based (see Fig. 2.1).

Key to strategic planning of IT is the process of developing the IT strategy (see Sect. 2.5). This process stakes out general directions and purposes, defines technical standards and the target ("to-be") picture of the landscape, creating the signposts in the overall roadmap for IT development (see Fig. 2.1). IT strategy development makes use of IT landscape management (see Chapter 4) to define the landscape toward which the enterprise is working. The technical standardisation process (see Chapter 5) serves to define the technical standards – technology and also bought-in products such as databases – that will best fulfil the strategic objectives of the IT strategy roadmap.

Questions answered in this chapter:

- What is the difference between strategic and operational planning of IT?
- How do I find out how IT is currently positioned in my enterprise? How do I determine the present performance potential?

I. Hanschke, *Strategic IT Management*, DOI 10.1007/978-3-642-05034-3_2,
© Springer-Verlag Berlin Heidelberg 2010

- How do corporate goals translate into goals for IT?
- What principles and strategies are appropriate for me?
- How do I define the future standing of IT and its future performance potential?
- What's in an IT strategy? What does an IT strategy document look like?
- How do I arrive at an appropriate IT strategy?

Fig. 2.1 Scope of strategic planning of IT

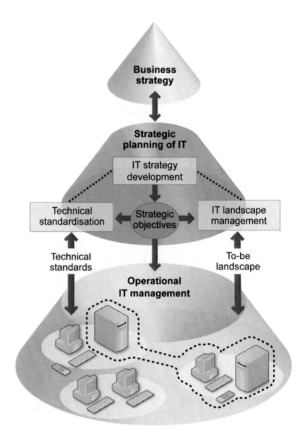

2.1 Scope and Definition

In planning IT strategically, you align it in strategic terms with your business model, and lay down an authoritative framework to guide and inform how IT is managed at the operating level. You also decide on technical standards and medium-term and long-term target views of the enterprise architecture. This provides a basic set

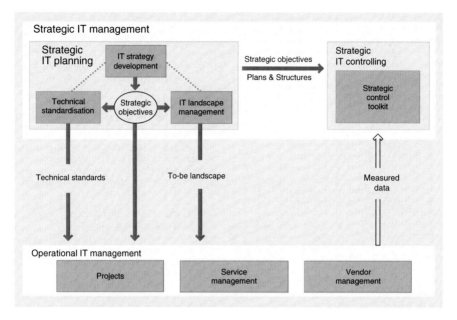

Fig. 2.2 Strategic and operational IT management

of metrics for projects and for service management and vendor management (see Fig. 2.2).

Over time, the strategic parameters are fleshed out (for instance during projects or maintenance activities) until they are detailed enough to form a basis for implementation. It may be more appropriate at operating level to deviate from these basic parameters. By benchmarking real-life values from operational-level IT management against the outcomes you originally planned, you can keep tabs on any discrepancies. Such benchmarking is part of the strategic control toolkit (see Sect. 6.3).

Compared to what is used at operating level, the information and indicators in strategic-level IT management are very coarse-grained. However, drilled down to operating level, the information is far more detailed. Table 2.1 illustrates the various granularities.

Important:

- Be sure to create clear links between strategic-level information and the more detailed information from operational IT management. Without a clear view on how the goals cascade down, you will not be able to benchmark current "front-line" values against the strategic targets you have set for relevant indicators.

Table 2.1 Examples of different granularities

Strategic IT management	Operational IT management
Process map and business processes on value chain level	Business processes on activity level (EPCs) and detailed process descriptions
Business objects such as customers or contracts	Data models
	Entities and attributes
Big-picture view of IT landscape	Details on all IT systems and their interaction
	Requirements in terms of business operation, e.g. detailed SLAs
Applications, e.g. SAP	Deployment packages, class diagrams, configuration items (CMDB)
Coarse-grained operating infrastructures such as vendor integration infrastructure	Components of IT systems, hardware units such as servers and network components, their interaction and topology
	Configuration items (CMDB)
Effectiveness indicators – "doing the right things" e.g. strategy and added-value contribution, business criticality, compliance with standards, strategic alignment	Efficiency indicators – "doing things right", e.g. SLA fulfilment, including availability, response times and reliability for the various IT systems
–	Scores on operating indicators and current values compared with targets

Derived from corporate goals and business requirements, the strategic direction is an overarching concept and also scopes and guides individual projects. The scope clearly stakes out the leeways for projects and maintenance activities (see Fig. 2.3). These strategic parameters are defined in IT strategy development. Usually the strategy is rolled forward annually, but major projects may also require parameters to be reviewed more frequently.

Fact file:

- The overarching strategic direction, technical standards and vision of the future IT landscape creates an authoritative scope to guide and inform the actions of IT management.
- Be sure to use appropriate granularity at each planning level. Strategic planning of IT requires a big-picture view. If you amass too much detail, you won't be able to see the wood for the trees!
- Changes – the practical interventions that enact the strategy – are usually implemented through projects and maintenance activities. Projects can take various forms, for example organisational, software engineering and infrastructure projects.

- Establish a strategic control toolkit to measure progress toward targets and compare as-is with to-be values (see Sect. 6.3).
  You won't know where you stand unless you can identify the gaps between the current situation and your strategic targets

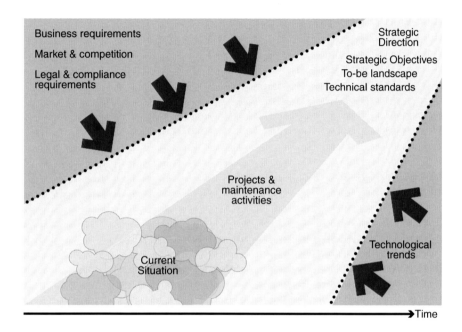

Fig. 2.3   Strategic alignment of IT

2.2 Role of IT in the Organisation

To set realistic targets, strategic planning of IT has to use the real-life situation in the enterprise as its starting point. You can determine the standing of IT – how it is positioned in your company – by asking "What part does your IT play in the enterprise?" and "What is the current performance potential of IT?"

What Part Does Your IT Play in the Enterprise?

The standing of IT can be described in terms of four levels of significance (see Fig. 2.4 and [Her06]):

- **IT is a cost factor**: IT is merely an internal provider of IT commodity products – for instance, it is seen as a provider of peripheral equipment. Alongside other

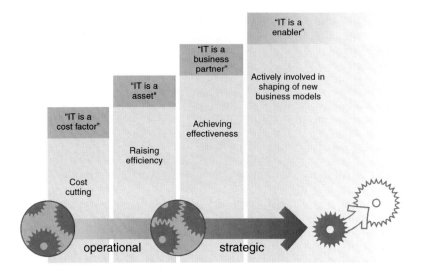

Fig. 2.4 Standing of IT

internal service providers like finance accounting, IT is seen as a necessary evil, with considerable nuisance value, and should be as cheap as possible. IT has no impact on the business.

- **IT is an asset**: IT solutions are regarded as integral to core business processes and essential for enacting security and compliance requirements mandated by law. The target for IT is to deliver operational excellence, and the focus is on raising efficiency and quality in the business and IT by enhancing business processes and decision-making. IT must provide a reliable, cost-efficient operating base, and can advise the business on ways to step up efficiency. This is IT's contribution to value proposition of the company.

- **IT is a business partner**: IT is perceived by the business as a contributor not only to value proposition but also to the enterprise strategy. As well as enabling reliable, cost-effective business operation, IT makes a key contribution to effectiveness by helping the enterprise enact its strategy. IT is expected to deliver valuable input for business decisions and to raise operational effectiveness (e.g. through standardising IT business process support). Part of IT's role is to render explicit the impact and interdependencies that exist between ideas in business and in IT. Business requirements have to be actioned swiftly and cost-effectively on the basis of IT structures which can be flexed forward into the future and sustain the enterprise on its chosen path.

With IT planning and business planning so tightly intermeshed, managers can be certain that IT investment decisions will be taken in terms of value to the business, and deliver business-oriented IT products with SLAs designed to support the company's various functions adequately.

- **IT is an enabler**: IT is seen as an enabler when business managers perceive IT as actively involved in shaping new business models. Strong business orientation and an ability to anticipate future demands give the business fresh impetus through new technology, and flexible, sustainable IT structures give the enterprise the agility it needs to adapt quickly to change. IT has to see itself as integral to the business, able to generate new business ideas through skilful application of existing and innovative technologies.

If your IT is regarded as little more than an internal service provider for commodities (a box-provider), its influence within the company will be minimal. Services could just as easily be sourced from an external provider. IT is a cost factor, and related decisions are taken solely with cost targets in mind. In this situation, you're likely to see IT budgets being pared down with every year that passes. Nonetheless, IT is expected to offer services at prices that match market benchmarks. If cost metrics are all that matters, the influence of IT and its creative freedom will inevitably shrink. Over the long term, IT is likely to lose its ability to innovate altogether.

If this is the position you're in, you have to break the vicious circle. To increase the standing of IT, be sure to get the people from business departments round the table with you when you're planning IT solutions and projects. This is the only way you're going to change the way other people think about your IT.

Raising the standing of IT will be a long process of change in the enterprise. You will have to stay committed and tenacious as you edge forward with changes. IT has to be close to customers, learn to speak their language, be familiar with customers' problems and know what they want. IT teams can keep a constant lookout for opportunities to enhance business processes and feed ideas back into the business. Major value can be added by simplifying and standardising business processes, for instance: just by documenting business processes and their IT support, you can identify startpoints for change.

Only if people perceive your IT is closely aligned with the business – and has proved itself valuable – will IT be able to assume a more active role. IT has to deliver a demonstrable contribution to the company's value-added.

The greater its standing, the more influence IT will have. The more useful it is, the more opportunity it will have to shape the direction of the business. For example, IT can assist decision-making by providing valuable input on outcome scenarios (for business and IT), perhaps even take part in business planning as a partner or "shaper" of the business.

Before embarking on the change process, first make an accurate appraisal of where you are right now. Senior management buy-in is essential for any change: they have to agree with and communicate your appraisal of the situation. Table 2.2 lists typical indicators of the various levels, helping you determine what standing IT has in your company.

Table 2.2 Determining the standing of IT

IT is ...			
Cost factor	**Asset**	**Business partner**	**Enabler**
Product and service portfolio			
Commodity IT, such as provision of peripheral equipment and operating standard software	Securing business operation through reliable, cost-effective basic IT Fulfilment of security and compliance requirements	Business-relevant IT products e.g. focused on business processes or the enterprise's products Reliable, cost-effective basic IT	Impetus for business through new technologies and business-relevant IT products Reliable, cost-effective basic IT
IT planning focuses mainly on. . .			
Reactive planning	Operational IT planning based on business planning	Business planning and IT planning intermeshed	Business planning and IT planning intermeshed
Decision on outsourcing or in-sourcing	Transparency of IT landscape Technical standardisation	Strategic planning of IT landscape	Anticipatory planning, e.g. future scenarios
Efficiency in IT; no risky projects	Efficiency in business through IT	Efficiency and effectiveness	Effectiveness, sustainability and efficiency
IT controlling focuses mainly on. . .			
Cost reduction	Cost/benefit and operational excellence Benchmarks	Contribution to value-added and cost/benefit	Contribution to value-added and strategy, and cost/benefit
IT organisation			
Stand-alone service provider or profit centre	Department or business unit in the company Benchmarkable Service-IT IT consulting and advisory services	Department or business unit in the company Organised into business IT and service IT; Business-IT is organised to reflect the business Corporate functions for strategic planning of IT	Business unit in the company Organised into business IT and service IT. Business IT is organised to reflect the business Corporate functions for strategic planning of IT and innovation management integrated into business planning
Position within organisational hierarchy			
–	IT manager reports to member of executive board	IT manager on executive board	IT manager on executive board
IT cost accounting			
Entire IT costs redistributed as flat-rate contribution	Systems for internal service charging Cost centres and in part cost units	Systems for internal service charging Cost units, e.g. projects	Systems for internal service charging Cost units, e.g. projects

What is the Current Performance Potential of IT?

Another key task is to determine the current performance potential of IT to under-pin the appraisal of its standing in the enterprise. This is largely about estimating whether and to what extent IT is a competent service provider to the company's departments. One measure of this is the extent to which IT actively advises users and implements their business requirements with appropriate, cost-effective IT solutions in line with the strategic objectives. Ultimately, the objective is to ascertain how well IT fulfils the following core tasks:

- **Ensuring business operations stay up and running**
  Is IT operation adequately reliable and secure? Does it enable problem-free operation? Can it deliver compliance with statutory and regulatory frameworks?
- **Appropriate, cost-effective IT support**
  Is IT support adequate for enacting business requirements? Do benefits outweigh costs? Is IT support cost-effective compared to external providers?
- **Securing the future viability of the IT landscape**
  Does strategic planning of the IT landscape take place, aligned with the corporate strategy? Have technological standards been defined to frame evolutionary devel-opment of the landscape? Are these appropriate to sustain the company along its chosen path (see Chapter 5)?
- **Optimising and enabling the business**
  Is IT contributing to optimising business support? Does it deliver fresh impetus to the business through IT innovation?

Important:

The current performance potential should be appraised both by IT itself and by external stakeholders (users and management), to determine whether self-perception and external views match up. If they do not match-up, you will have to take a more active stance in marketing, and communicate more clearly the added value of IT.

The current performance potential of IT can be appraised on the basis of prod-uct/service portfolio and structure. The example in Fig. 2.5 shows the IT portfolio, mapping the importance of IT for the various business segments and the relative effort undertaken in IT. Also part of the portfolio are consulting services (e.g. for issues relating to security), IT operation, IT infrastructure provision, and support services (see also Sect. 2.5.3).

Analysing the significance of IT for business segments and their value chains can help stake out the product and service portfolio (see [Por85]). The elements in the portfolio can be grouped by organisational areas in IT, as Fig. 2.5 shows (see Sect. 6.2).

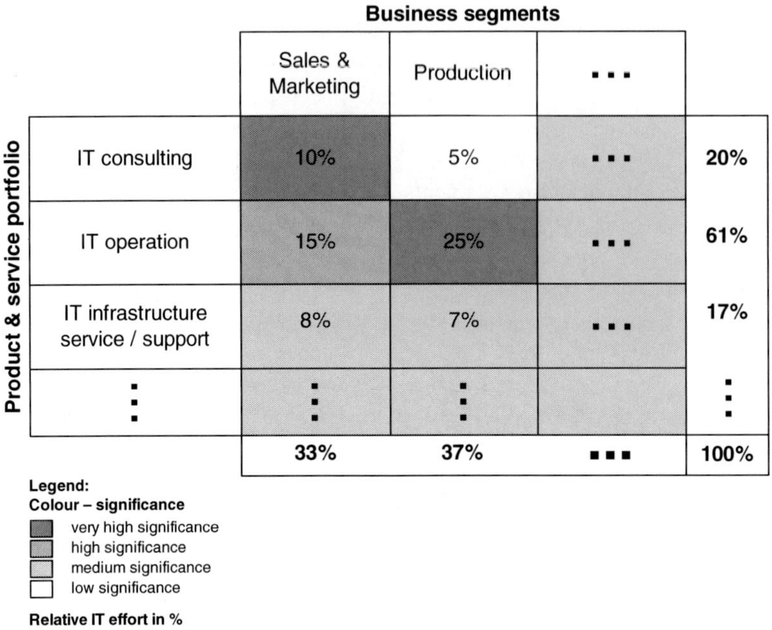

Business segments

	Sales & Marketing	Production	...	
IT consulting	10%	5%	...	20%
IT operation	15%	25%	...	61%
IT infrastructure service / support	8%	7%	...	17%
⋮	⋮	⋮		⋮
	33%	37%	...	100%

(left axis label: **Product & service portfolio**)

Legend:
Colour – significance
◼ very high significance
◼ high significance
◻ medium significance
☐ low significance

Relative IT effort in %

Fig. 2.5 Current performance potential of IT

To obtain a realistic estimate of potential performance, you have to appraise every IT service. It is advisable to use standardised models such as Cobit, ITIL or CMMI (see [Her06], [Joh07], [Foe08] and [Zin04]), since this will enable you to benchmark yourself against other enterprises – and you also gain a baseline for ongoing monitoring.

This product and service portfolio provides a basis for naming and also pricing IT services in the company (see [Küt06]).

Fact file:

The standing and potential performance of IT has to be appraised correctly, since this is the basis for its strategic positioning. You can use Table 2.2 as a guide for your appraisal. You should determine the potential performance on the basis of your product and service portfolio and use standardised models to help.

2.3 Strategic Positioning of IT

"Where Do We Want to Go" or "How Does IT Wish to Position Itself in the Future"?

IT has to be clear what standing it wishes to attain within the organisation. Then, armed with appropriate arguments, IT people must make a case to senior management that this is the way to go.

The big but: how do you find the right arguments? For a start, it is advisable to back your presentation with solid facts all the way, detailing precisely what contribution IT makes to value-added and strategy. As shown in Fig. 2.6, IT can contribute in a variety of ways to the present and future business models (see also [Kag06] and [Bre06]):

- **Stand out from the competition through individualisation or cost leadership**: Powerful, efficient and/or flexible IT solutions and good provision of business information can make a key contribution to differentiation. Supplying information effectively is all about providing meaningful business intelligence

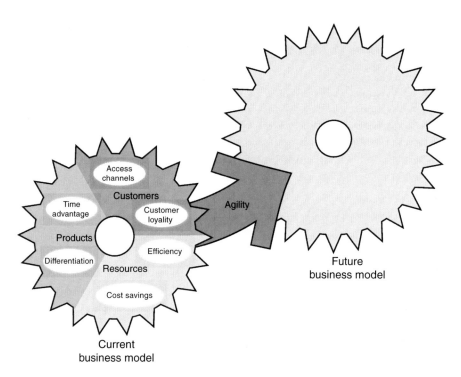

Fig. 2.6 Contribution of IT to corporate success

promptly about markets, customer requirements, competitors and their products, the cost and benefit of your customers' products, and what alternatives exist for sourcing.

- **Be faster than competitors**: Being faster than other players means relentless focus on business innovation, quicker product development and quicker time to market. Information technology can help carve out this time advantage through strategic planning to scope out future opportunities, through flexible and robust enterprise architectures, and technical innovation.
- **Create and optimise access channels for customers**: IT can make a sizeable contribution to creating easier access to your organisation for customers: self-service portals, for example, can act as sales channels and service access points which are precisely tailored to customer requirements.
- **Make customers more loyal – and more dependent**: Affordably-priced IT solutions that can be tailored to the organisation's needs will give a major uplift to its core business, greatly simplifying and streamlining operations. Extra ease of use, particularly in routine tasks, increases customer satisfaction and emotional loyalty. Individualised solutions also tie customers more closely to the organisation by increasing dependence – just think of automated integration of suppliers in just-in-time production workflows!
- **Efficient assignment of resources**: If IT is helping business processes run better – with leaner or automated workflows, with networked supply chains or electronic collaboration via portals, or simply by keeping workflows digital end-to-end – the organisation will enjoy substantial efficiency gains in business workflows.
- **Cost savings**: Standardisation or homogenisation of IT landscapes open up enormous opportunities for cost savings, not least through economies of scale. Expertise can be focused, IT can concentrate on its own core services (complementing these by outsourcing), and generate major potential for cutting costs.
- **Agility to change the business model**: Becoming and staying agile – having the ability to adapt swiftly to changing environments and new market situations – is one of the most important business challenges of all. Yet innovative solutions keep an organisation ahead of competitors only until the other players catch up. In terms of importance, how fast a company can transform itself now ranks equally with its business model. Powering virtually every modern business process, IT plays a key role here, and its reaction speed and flexibility feed directly into the success of the business. With flexible, robust enterprise architecture, the organisation is better positioned to respond swiftly to changes.

Important:

Work out which of these aspects of value-added are or could be relevant in your case, and from there build your case for raising the standing of IT in your organisation.

You might find it useful to run through the following questions when analysing how IT can and wishes to position itself in the future:

- **What contribution can IT bring to new business models?**

  Can IT contribute to making products and services more appealing, or to accessing new target segments or regions?

  Example I: family insurance and other new insurance products can be created simply and flexibly by bundling existing products via a product configurator.

  Example II: a broker portal to integrate field staff more tightly into the organisation.

- **How can IT contribute to making the enterprise more agile?**

  Can IT help give the organisation time advantages over its competitors? Can IT accelerate corporate transformation?

  Example: flexible IT architecture based on standardised interfaces such as SOA with components which can be orchestrated flexibly into the landscape.

- **How can IT raise the efficiency of business processes and deliver optimal support to the current business model?**

  Can IT contribute to reducing costs in its own domain or the business? Can it demonstrably increase business value or benefit?

  Example I: use virtual reality technology for creating marketing collaterals.
  Example II: identify redundancies and media discontinuity in processes.

- **What contribution can IT make to reducing business risks?**

  Can IT contribute to reducing business risk to an acceptable level, or help fulfil compliance, business continuity management and security requirements?

  Example: make transparent the risks inherent in processes and applications.

Ultimately, your organisation's management will have to decide on the basis of the business case you put forward how IT will be positioned – in other words, whether it will be regarded as a cost factor, asset, partner or enabler. However, by highlighting the present and potential performance of IT, you can substantially influence this decision. A compelling business case from IT professionals can raise the standing of IT in the company.

Still, IT managers alone will not be able to achieve a major turnaround of opinion. It takes people at top management level to champion the issue and stake out precisely what role IT is to play. Importantly, senior management must communicate where decision-making powers and responsibilities on key issues lie. There have to be clear groundrules on who takes decisions on IT investments and on prioritizing of business requirements, and what channels are to be followed. Likewise, procedures at the touchpoints between business and IT have to be codified (see Sect. 6.2).

Important:

If the role of IT is not championed and communicated by senior management or if procedures are not explicitly codified, such questions will inevitably be left to the operational level. Without clear parameters staked out, IT will fail to exert any sustained impact on the business, and nor will it be possible to steer and direct it as required. This is exactly the line taken in the following extract from the Economist Study Business 2010 (see [Kag06]):

> The question of whether or not IT is a commodity becomes redundant – it will be a commodity for companies with poor business models and organizational processes and a competitive advantage for those companies that use it to support and execute on a strong business model.

Once defined, the strategic positioning should be documented in the mission and vision of the IT strategy. A mission is the driving purpose of an organisation; a vision is the long-term goal and direction to which the organisation's entire activities are aligned.

Example:

Vision: to be a partner of the business
We work with IT customers to identify opportunities for raising efficiency, growing the business and avoiding risks.
We underpin the operational excellence of the enterprise.
We are a team of highly qualified IT managers, business-function architects, software architects and infrastructure experts with a broad network of competent consultants.

Mission: for IT to deliver measurable value contribution
We generate benefit that shows through on financial statements, delivering return on investment for our shareholders at a level to sustain a fair, long-term alliance.

For our employees, we provide a challenging work environment that ensures individuals are highly motivated and have opportunities for continued professional development.

What Performance Potential can IT Deliver in the Future?

Once you have your strategic positioning statement, give it some weight by specifying the levels of performance you expect IT to be providing in the future. This entails defining your future IT service and product portfolio consistently with its strategic positioning. With the present portfolio as a starting point, you can then analyse what changes will be required and successively engineer these changes.

Figure 2.7 illustrates this process. Beginning with the current portfolio (see Sect. 2.2) the growth arrows show the changes in the IT product and service portfolio.

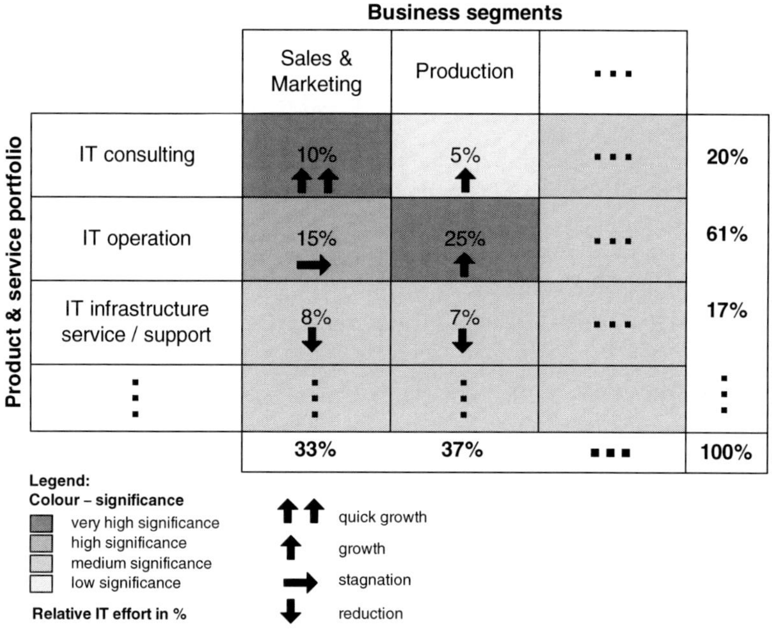

Fig. 2.7 Future IT performance potential, example

Alongside general support and resilient operation for core applications, the future portfolio could include items such as consultancy services, framed by wider issues such as process modelling. And, on the product side, technical software products might be complemented by business process-oriented products such as all-round on-site service support for field sales staff.

Fact file:

- Make sure you are clear what role and position IT is to have in future.
- The IT performance you are aiming for must be in alignment with the strategic positioning and must also be attainable.

  Take care neither to underestimate nor to overestimate potential, because this leads to false expectations among users.
- With the planned product and service portfolio as your basis, map out what performance IT will be able to deliver in future.
- Make your business case to your organisation's senior management by staking out the contribution of IT to corporate value-added and strategy, thus taking it to a higher standing within the organisation.
- The strategic positioning of IT – whatever its role – needs the buy-in of senior management and must be clearly articulated throughout the company. This is the only way IT will have a firm footing.

2.4 Strategic Objectives

The repositioning of IT is framed and informed by strategic objectives. Guided by the strategic positioning of IT, these objectives are developed on the basis of the corporate strategy and business requirements.

The strategic objectives are binding – both on strategic IT management level and at operational level. They create the metrics by which you measure progress on implementation. The key elements of strategic objectives are:

- **IT goals**: The IT goals describe the status you are aiming for. They should be formulated such that you can measure the degree of goal attainment. Be sure to set goals with care: IT goals should be SMART, meaning Specific, Measurable, Achievable, Realistic and Time-bound. (There are also other terms for this common acronym, aimed more at the "people" aspect: Stretching, Motivating, Ambitious, Rewarding and Tangible, for instance.)
- **Principles**: Principles are specific, binding policies for action: make-or-buy preferences, for instance, or best-of-breed.
- **Strategies**: A strategy is the plan of action you decide on to achieve particular goals. As such, a strategy makes a statement on how goals are to be attained. Strategies in IT can include the application portfolio strategy, a strategy for sourcing or for innovation.

The following sections provide guidelines for deriving IT goals and best practices for principles and strategies.

2.4.1 Deriving IT Goals

The process of deriving goals for IT from the overarching corporate goals is fundamental to strategy development. The connections between corporate and IT goals must be transparent, enabling you to verify that goals are consistent with corporate strategy. Figure 2.8 shows a best-practice derivation process; this is described in the following.

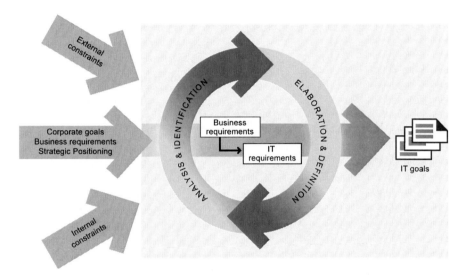

Fig. 2.8 Deriving IT goals

The IT goals take shape in an iterative process comprising two stages, Analysis & Identification, and Elaboration & Definition. What you do is this:

1. Look at the corporate goals and strategic positioning, identify and analyse what is driving the business. Put together a list of current business requirements.
2. Drill down the definitions of business drivers and requirements until you have a clear-cut statement that is specific enough to formulate "SMART" IT goals.

Helpful hint:

Break down business requirements along functional dimensions – business processes, products, business functions, business data and organisational structures. Analyse what interdependencies exist and what possibilities there are for IT support.

Example:

Corporate goal: to reduce the new-product development time by one third.
Step one in goal refinement: to reduce NPD time, the business process "research & development" and subprocess "series release" of the "production" business process must be investigated further.

3. Identify and document the requirements for IT: analyse all the IT assets in terms of dependencies and opportunities for IT support. These IT assets include the IT service and product portfolio, the application landscape, current technical standards, operating infrastructure, external and internal resources.
4. Refine and evaluate the requirements for IT, and use these requirements to formulate SMART IT goals. Costs and benefits should be your key evaluation criteria.

Important:

- In many cases the corporate strategy will not exist in written form. You will therefore have to make assumptions, document these assumptions and obtain feedback, for example, by staging workshops with representatives of senior management.
  It is crucial to have corporate goals documented explicitly. Without a clear statement on where the enterprise is headed, value-based management of IT will be impossible, because it will not be known what its benefit to the enterprise actually is!
- Maintain clarity on how corporate goals are cascaded into IT goals.
  An Excel spreadsheet is a good way to document the links and ensure connections can be traced back.

Example for Deriving IT Goals

ALPHA, a manufacturing company, has set itself the goals of increasing sales volume in product segment X in Europe by 20% and reducing service costs by 30%. These two corporate goals are described in Tables 2.3 and 2.4.

These goals have already been broken down along functional dimensions, i.e. steps one and two are not necessary here.

Table 2.3   Sales volume goal

Corporate goal	To increase sales volume in product segment X
Context	An ease-of-use campaign to drive up European sales in product segment X
Content	To optimise product segment X to bring it more closely into line with European usability requirements and thus to raise sales volumes in Europe in product segment X
Impact	To become the biggest player in Europe in product segment X
Metrics	To raise sales volume in Europe by 20%

Table 2.4   Service cost goal

Corporate goal	To reduce service costs in product segment X
Context	More economical delivery of services for products in product segment X
Content	To reduce on-site service calls by engineers in product segment X in Europe
Impact	To have service costs in Europe in product segment X comparable with competitors
Metrics	To reduce service costs by 30%

Step three is about seeking potential "quick-win" points for raising sales volume and reducing service costs in product segment X. The applications that support this segment are analysed, as are the current technical components. The investigation reveals a few opportunities: personalised self-service portals, for example, could increase customer loyalty, thus raising sales volume and reducing service costs. An analysis of the service and product portfolio shows up other options: it might be possible to introduce usage-based charging for software components and to expand products in segment X to include virtual reality software as fixed, configurable elements of products.

These opportunities are then evaluated by expected effort, benefit and various other criteria. The idea of a personalised self-service portal then takes shape as a specific proposal (see Table 2.5).

Important:

Refine your IT goals with enough detail to define metrics with specific values. For more information on metrics and performance measurement systems, please refer to Sect. 6.3.

By ensuring clear connections between IT goals and the metrics at operational level, it is easier to verify in the course of strategic controlling whether corporate goals are being achieved and business requirements fulfilled.

Table 2.5 IT goal: personalised self-service portal

IT goal	Personalised self-service portal for product segment X in Europe
Content	Provision of a portal infrastructure with easy user interface enabling end users to download new software statuses and information about products in product segment X
Impact	To be the first provider of self-service solutions in product segment X on European market
	Less on-site service by engineers is required.
Metrics	I 30% reduction in on-site service in order volume
	II At least 2,000 customers via self-service portal
Contribution to corporate goal	*Increase sales volumes in product segment X*
	Metric II has no direct correlation.
Contribution to corporate goal	*Reduce service costs in product segment X*
	Metric I has correlation with proportion of on-site service in service costs.

Fact file:

- There must be transparent connections between corporate goals and IT goals. Only then will you have evidence of IT's contribution to business results.
- Break down IT goals to the extent needed to operationalise them.
- To monitor goal attainment, each IT goal must have metrics for which specific targets can be defined.

2.4.2 Principles for Strategic Guidance

Principles are a set of high-level statements which establish a general direction or a policy for IT-related decisions. An organisation might have principles to guide the selection of software solutions, for instance, project evaluation, roadmaps for IT landscape or software rollouts. Where principles exist, their application is essentially mandatory, and there must be good reasons for any non-compliance. Principles are in themselves enduring, they are not impacted by rapid pace of change in technology or products.

Note:

The term "guidelines" is often used instead of "principles". However, guidelines do not have the same binding character as principles; as the name suggests, they merely provide orientation. Whether you decide to apply principles or guidelines is very much contingent on the specific situation in your enterprise.

You document a principle by specifying its name, a brief description of what the principle is about, the requirements for applying it, the context in which it is used, and any notes on how to apply it (see Table 2.6).

Table 2.6 Template for describing principles

Principle <name of principle>	
Description	<Description of principle>
Reasoning	<Explanation; i.e. why do we have this principle?>
Prerequisites	<Prerequisites for application>
Context of usage	<Which contexts are specifically included, which are excluded, e.g. restriction to organisational matters>
Notes for usage	<Special notes on applying the principle, e.g. essential follow-up activities>

Table 2.7 Make-or-buy principle, example

Principle preference for standard software (make or buy)	
Description	If business requirements can be fulfilled adequately by bought-in software, standard software takes preference over own development
Reasoning	As a rule, time-to-system and SLA fulfilment are better with standard software than with own development
Prerequisites	For business requirements to be considered adequately met, the current version of the software at the time the decision is taken must overcome all K.O. criteria, meet all core requirements and comply with technical standards. K.O. criteria and core requirements must all be defined and documented prior to the evaluation
Context of usage	No restrictions
Notes for usage	Access to source code must be secured upon concluding the contract (to future-proof the investment)
	The manufacturer must estimate and underwrite the fulfilment of open requirements

In deciding how to proceed on make-or-buy issues, you would normally consider questions such as competitive differentiation, whether the organisation has the resources and capabilities to develop software in-house, and what sourcing strategy it operates. A common statement is: standardisation where possible; variation where necessary.

Principles are essential for framing your decisions on IT assets and on strategic and operational IT management tasks. Here are a few examples of widespread and/or tried-and-tested principles (see also [Boa99], [Bur04], [Der06], [War02], [Wei04]) and others):

- **Selecting software solutions**:
  - **Best of breed (cherry-picking)**: The Best-of-breed approach entails selecting
    the best software solution or product for each area of application according to
    a predefined raft of criteria. The "cherry-picked" solutions and products then
    have to be integrated into a unified entity.

> **Important:**
>
> The risk of the best-of-breed principle is that you can end up with an unman-
> ageable patchwork of products, a situation exacerbated by frequent release
> changes and the need to juggle a variety of vendors. Therefore, introducing
> best-of-breed solutions can generate significant workloads for adjustment of
> interfaces.

  - **Make or buy**: The make-or-buy principle determines the organisation's
    preference for bought-in software or own developments (see example in
    Table 2.7).

- **Guidelines for selecting and appraising projects**:
  - **Prioritise core business**: Projects focusing on securing core business are
    prioritised.
  - **Infrastructure projects first**: If a software project will entail major changes
    to IT infrastructure, the infrastructure adjustment must be managed in a
    separate project upstream of the software project.
- **Design principles**:
  - **Avoid heterogeneity**: Consolidate redundant technical components and
    applications through technical standardisation and homogenisation (see
    Sect. 5).
  - **Technical structure follows business structuring**: Applications should be
    organised by business criteria such as business components or functional
    domains. Related principles include "clarity of data ownership", "clarity of
    process ownership" or "probability of change".
  - **Avoid redundancy**: Effort should be taken to avoid redundancy in IT support
    and in technical standards. This means not having more than one application
    performing the same business function, and having a single lead system to
    manage master data.
  - **Only the lead system can modify master data**: Be sure to define a lead
    system for master data. The master data may only be modified by this system.
  - **Single point of distribution for master data**: Master data which is required
    by more than one system must be distributed by a single, central point of
    distribution, e.g. via a master data hub.

- **Procedures and principles in strategic IT planning**:
  - **Divide & conquer**: Break problems down into smaller units to resolve separately. Once you have your subsolutions in place, you can reassemble them into an integrated entity.
  - **Tuning**: Optimise and stabilise the present application landscape before investing in new solutions. For every new application you are considering, investigate whether it might be more opportune to expand or modify the resources you already have in place.
  - **Housekeeping** (also known as the survive strategy, opportunistic development or quarantine approach): The principle here is to survive with the IT landscape as it is. This means a halt to development, or reducing to a minimum all evolutionary development or expansion of the existing IT landscape. The focus is emphatically "must-have" development only.

    The IT landscape should be kept alive by quick-and-simple devices such as culling and consolidating master data, improving IT service organisation accessibility, centralising IT procurement, reviewing licences and maintenance contracts, bug patching in operational applications and making sure financial reporting can be completed as required.

    This principle is commonly applied to road-test new business models. For instance, if it is uncertain whether the business model will work, the organisation will decide to postpone fresh investment in a new target landscape until it can see its way ahead.
  - **One IT approach**: This approach entails consolidating the application landscape by introducing an all-in solution (bought-in or developed in-house) for a particular business segment. The "One IT" solution must adequately deliver the core functionality required for the business in question.

    This principle is commonly applied – albeit in modified form – in mergers and acquisitions. The IT solution of the stronger partner is wrapped around the acquisition target, and the data of the acquisition target is migrated to the selected IT solution. This generally means master data has to be consolidated. The One IT approach is also much in evidence driving decisions to buy standard software, the idea being to "stretch" the software to fit as many business segments as possible.
  - **Tried and tested over new**: Business systems with a proven track record should be favoured over new systems.

Important:

- Rolling out a new application tends to take considerably longer than changing the existing landscape, and there is greater implementation risk (particularly in migration). Such risks can only be justified by the business perspectives afforded by the greater design freedoms.

- You are unlikely to find a one-stop solution for all your needs. Even if you elect to use standard software, you will often need to make adjustments – in effect compromising the "One IT" principle.
- In general, product rollout projects of extended duration will pursue a "survive" strategy.

  – **Replacement strategy** (also renewal strategy): This entails a deliberate push to replace legacy systems.
- **Approaches for introducing new applications**:
  – **Big-bang**: New applications are introduced in one go, without intermediate stages. This is a way to make sweeping changes rapidly, but there is a greater risk of things going wrong.
  – **Evolutionary approach**: New applications are introduced incrementally. System renewal takes place step by step, with introducing intermediate solutions. This approach entails more effort overall than a big-bang rollout, but keeps the implementation risk down.
- **Increasing technical quality**:
  – **Flexiblizing**: Development of the business systems landscape over time focuses on keeping things flexible – by orienting development to components and services, ensuring integration ability and standardisation.
  – **Deconvolution**: Systems should be organised according to business criteria into loosely coupled components. The reasoning here is that convoluted connections between components and a lack of modularisation can make conducting projects in mature landscapes a highly fraught process.
  – **Decoupling**: Systems and loosely dependent components are decoupled via a broker or ESB.
  – **Encapsulation**: Specific application areas are segregated by introducing interfaces and standardisation.
- **Efficiency in operation**:
  – **Virtualisation**: Operating infrastructure units can be scaled using virtualisation technologies.

Important:

With enterprises being so different in terms of business models, corporate cultures or strategic direction, there is no single "right" way to do something. Select the principles which best fit your requirements. You should define principles for all IT assets and for all IT management tasks.

2.4.3 Strategies to Underpin Goal Achievement

A strategy is the plan of action you decide on to achieve particular goals. As such, it makes a statement on how goals are to be attained. Strategies can be aggressive, moderate or defensive.

Strategies serve to guide and limit IT decisions. As a rule, a strategy is implemented in the context of a project. You can define strategies to support the decision-making process pertaining to each of your IT assets. For more information, please refer to [War02].

Important:

Principles and strategies must all be clear and comprehensible. They must be articulated and codified. As a rule, it is better to apply just a few selected core principles and strategies. By keeping the number down, you will be better able to measure progress towards goals and steer a clear direction in implementation.

The following types of strategy are discussed in relevant literature (including [Ber03-2], [Boa99], [Nie05], [Rüt06], [War02] and [Wei04]):

- **Technical standardisation strategy**: A technical standardisation strategy is likely to frame definitions of standards for the technical implementation of software, hardware or network components. This strategy helps you reduce costs and avoid uncontrolled proliferation of components and systems in the IT landscape. See Sect. 5.
- **Application strategy**: An application strategy defines a framework and guidelines for deploying applications effectively and efficiently to support the business. The strategy guides and informs actions for adding value (e.g. software solutions to promote sales, or increase customer loyalty through CRM), for enhancing day-to-day operations and making the enterprise more agile (e.g. through introducing service-oriented architectures).
- **Innovation strategy**: An innovation strategy determines the enterprise's policy toward new technologies. For example, the strategy might stipulate that new technologies are to be appraised proactively with a view to potentially introducing them into the enterprise. See Sect. 5.4.2.
- **Investment strategy**: Investment decisions must be consistent with the enterprise's investment strategy. Decision criteria such as cost, benefit, strategy and value contributions are often visualised in a project portfolio.
- **Sourcing strategy**: The sourcing strategy answers the classic make-or-buy question: which IT services can or should an enterprise perform itself, and which should it source from other providers? A sourcing strategy appropriate to the needs of the business helps improve the cost structure, reduce operating risk, raise flexibility and give the enterprise more control over its IT.

- **Vendor strategy**: A vendor strategy helps the organisation select and manage its vendors. For instance, some organisations will operate a "preferred vendor" strategy, the idea being to avoid proliferation in the number of vendors, to reduce costs and secure vital expertise for the organisation.
- **Data strategy**: A data strategy essentially comprises guidelines and policies on data ownership, compliance, data protection and security, as well as statements on data quality requirements and how these are implemented.
- **Other examples**: Partner alliance strategy, integration strategy, open source strategy, network/hardware strategy and disaster prevention and recovery strategy.

There is considerable interdependence between these strategies – the technical standardisation strategy, for example, will determine how the application strategy is formulated.

Important:

Take care to select strategies consistent with your strategic positioning, IT goals, and the principles you are pursuing. Strategies must also be consistent with one another.

Given the importance of application strategies in strategic IT planning, we will now investigate various application strategies which have been tested and proven in enterprise use. You can choose the strategies which best fit your situation.

Application strategies can usefully be presented with portfolio diagrams. These give an at-a-glance overview of how applications are positioned relative to one another. Portfolio analysis is a method used in strategic management; portfolio management is a simple yet structured approach that helps the IT organisation roadmap its medium-term planning. It serves to categorise, evaluate, prioritise, cluster and manage control objects such as projects or applications, and create communicable units out of the resulting deliverables.

IT portfolio management is all about developing and strategically managing portfolios of items such as projects or applications. A portfolio creates a framework for appraising projects, applications or other control objects according to predefined criteria such as potential benefits, costs, strategy and value contribution, and risks, and for presenting them in diagram form.

Portfolios can be used to map the as-is status of the landscape, its to-be or planned status or both, according to various criteria. They help organisations develop planning scenarios to roadmap development of the IT landscape.

Portfolios improve the quality of communication between IT specialists and business management; as such, they are a vital tool for building acceptance of IT as a strategic partner. Portfolio management has gained widespread acceptance among business managers, not least because it pulls together salient information in concise form – a welcome change for managers who are already inundated with data and information.

The following best-practice approaches for application strategies all have proven track records:

- Application strategy dependent on business process classification
- Application portfolio "strategy contribution and value contribution", based on Ward/Peppard [War02]
- Application portfolio "technical quality and business value", based on Maizilish/Handler [Mai05]
- Application portfolio "business value and technological appropriateness" (see [Buc05])
- Application portfolio "business value and risk"
  This portfolio has strong similarities with the portfolio "technical quality and business value" (see [Buc05])
- Application portfolio "strategic fit" and "landscape management fit" (see [Krc05] and [Krc90]). See Sect. 4. We are going to investigate the first four strategies in greater detail. For more information about the other best-practice approaches, please refer to the stated literature.

Important:

Portfolios are an excellent way to present strategies in visual form. The visual presentation is arguably one of the reasons why portfolio management has attained such overwhelming popularity in organisations. Portfolio diagrams do not inundate managers with information, and help present salient facts with at-a-glance visual clarity.

Application Strategy Dependent on Business Process Classification

The business processes are classified in a portfolio (see Fig. 2.9) according to their competitive differentiation and change rate. Business processes are considered to be high differentiators if they play a key role in sustaining or expanding the business. Business processes have a high change rate when they must constantly be adjusted to changes in the competitive environment or other external conditions.

Each quadrant denotes a typical strategy – in this example the four quadrants are titled "automated and integrated", "agile", "automated & standard" and "manual & standard". Each application is placed in the quadrant containing the business processes which it supports.

Business processes that contribute to differentiating the organisation from its competition (these are placed in the "automated & integrated" and "agile" quadrants) help improve the position of the company on the market. Typically, these are

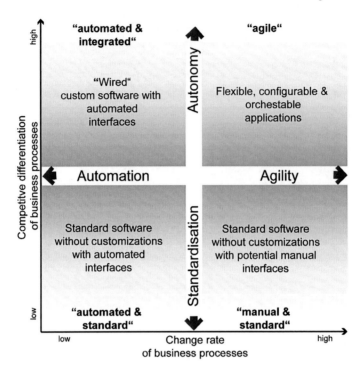

Fig. 2.9 Application strategy dependent on business process classification

sales and marketing processes directed at acquiring new business, but can equally include processes to prevent customer churn and improve the enterprise's image equity on the market. Call centres, for example, an Internet-based information system or a data warehouse can all contribute to raising the standing of the organisation in this way.

Differentiator-type business processes have to be as unique as possible – which typically entails using custom-developed software. Where such processes are subject to slower rates of change, they (and by association the interfaces between systems and partners) should be integrated and automated as tightly as possible. Sequences and procedures can be hardwired in this way, because the rate of change is relatively slow and the efficiency gains through automation will usually outweigh effort for making isolated changes. Such processes can build tightly-integrated connections with business partners, and the resulting boost to efficiency will reduce costs. This is the type of process in operation at organisations which integrate their suppliers into just-in-time manufacturing.

Differentiator-type processes with rapid change rates have to be designed so as to maintain agility of response to changes. A good example here is product management at telecom providers. These organisations set exacting benchmarks for their applications, needing systems which are flexible to configure and orchestrate. This requires component-oriented designs and flexible infrastructure such as SOA.

Landscapes can consist of a blend of suitable bought-in and custom-engineered components.

Business processes such as payroll, accounting or HR management are less subject to rapid rates of change, and are less likely to be a factor differentiating the organisation from its competition. As such they belong in the "automated & standard" quadrant. These processes should be conducted as cost-efficiently and with as much standardisation as possible. Recurring tasks can be automated, as can business partner integration. This helps raise process efficiency.

When it comes to business processes which do not add competitive value, the enterprise should try to use standard software. Automation can be introduced to drive efficiency in processes which are not subject to frequent change. This can mean having hardwired processes. However, if more flexibility is required, overly complex IT systems are not the solution. What matters is to deliver basic operation for the main business transactions as cost-efficiently as possible. Other, nonstandard transactions have to be performed manually.

There are also alternative portfolio dimensions to classify processes (see [War02], [Wei04] and [Wei06]). Alongside differentiation and rate of change, other common classifications are strategy and value contribution, risk estimate and cost.

Application Portfolio Matrix "Strategy Contribution/Value Contribution", Based on Ward/Peppard [War02]

This application portfolio is based on the concept proposed by McFarlan (see [War02]). It is in widespread use. Its concise presentation of how IT contributes to present and future business success makes it a good tool to aid communication between business managers and IT professionals on plotting the future direction of the application portfolio.

Like the model discussed above, this application strategy also maps the portfolio to a diagram. Applications are classified according to their value contribution and strategy contribution. The value contribution indicates the extent to which a system supports business processes which create competitive advantage for the organisation – e.g. in sales and manufacturing. The strategy contribution indicates how the system contributes to enacting corporate strategy, in other words, its part in the future business success of the enterprise. Section 6.3 provides further details on metrics.

The portfolio's four quadrants (see Fig. 2.10) are described below:

- **High potential ("WILDCATS")**: Wildcats have the potential to play a pivotal role in the future business. Systems of this nature include tryout projects which are heavy on IT but short on actual business context (e.g. SOA infrastructure projects). With their benefit in terms of actual business contribution being so hazy, projects like this are as far as possible "quarantined" from the operational application landscape. It is also essential to keep close tabs on their costs. If costs run out of control or the project seems to be going nowhere, the organisation should have no compunctions about cutting the project short.

Fig. 2.10 Application portfolio "strategy contribution and value contribution"

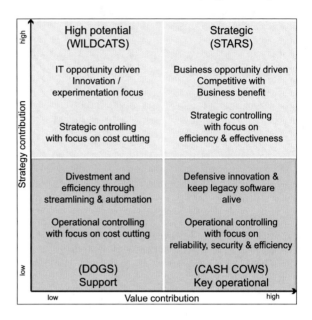

- **Strategic ("STARS")**: Applications that contribute strongly both to value and strategy are the "stars". They sustain both the present and the future business of the organisation. Through relentless business-oriented innovation, the enterprise can ensure these applications address strategic goals (see Sect. 5.4.2). Stars offer effective, efficient business support and have tight vertical integration (which means tying business partners into workflows).
- **Key operational ("CASH COWS")**: Unlike stars, cash cows just keep the present business going. All business functions (billing, for instance) must work reliably, efficiently and securely. Risks should be avoided, which means no technical experiments.

    Cash cows are often the legacy software in the organisation. The question here is how much effort to invest in order to keep legacy software alive – do you want to invest defensively? You have to decide whether permanent revamping is worth the effort, or whether complete overhaul or new buy/build might be better.
- **Support ("DOGS")**: Dogs are the applications that support non-differentiating business processes such as payroll or HR administration. These applications must be efficient and above all inexpensive in operation. Leverage whatever opportunities you can identify to streamline and automate these applications. New projects on these systems will usually only be undertaken when the organisation is forced to make changes on account of statutory frameworks or compliance requirements.

Table 2.8 lists questions to ask for classifying applications and allocating them to the most appropriate quadrant (see [War02]).

Figure 2.11 shows an example application portfolio. Alongside the classifying attributes "strategy" and "value contribution", the chart also presents information about the cost and health of the applications.

Table 2.8 Guidelines for classifying applications

	High potential	Strategic	Key operational	Support
Does clear competitive advantage accrue for the business through this application?		Yes[1]		
Does the application support a specific business goal and/or a critical success factor?		Yes[1]		
Does the application eradicate a business disadvantage of the organisation compared to competitors?			Yes	
Does the application prevent a foreseeable business risk from escalating into a more substantial problem in the near future?			Yes	
Does the application contribute to raising business productivity, or can it help achieve sustainable cost reduction?				Yes
Does the application assist fulfilment of formal requirements?		Yes[2]		
Can the application lead to future benefit or value for the company?	Yes			

[1] If the business benefit can be clearly articulated and it is understood how this can be attained; otherwise high potential.
[2] Where non-compliance could lead to significant business risk; otherwise support.

By adding planned applications, arrows, and an indication of which systems are to be replaced, IT managers can create a clear picture of development trajectories. Future applications have either "planned" or "to-be" status. Planned applications are those which are already framed by projects and have taken more specific shape. By way of contrast, a to-be application has not yet been planned so specifically – for instance, an organisation might have decided to introduce a new sales application, but has not yet determined whether to use standard software or develop its own.

Useful hint:

Assign a timestamp for each planning status of your application portfolio. This gives you a clear record (which you can trace back if necessary) of which as-is status (e.g. on January 1, 2009), which planned status (e.g. project portfolio on January 1, 2011) and which to-be status (e.g. roadmap 2015) were used.

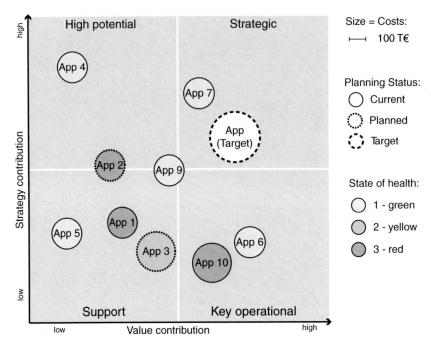

Fig. 2.11 Example of application portfolio: strategy and value contributions

Application Portfolio Mapping "Technical Quality" Against "Business Value", Based on Maizilish/Handler [Mai05]

In this application strategy, the applications are classified into four quadrants according to technical quality and business value. The technical quality takes into account both the status of the application along its lifecycle and the extent to which performance, security or other quality requirements have been implemented. The technical quality largely determines what effort will be involved in evolutionary development of an application. The business value comprises the contribution which an application makes both to strategy and enterprise value (Fig. 2.12). For more information about these metrics, please refer to Sect. 6.3.

The integrated presentation of business and IT aspects makes apparent at a glance whether core business operability is in any way jeopardised. Which quadrant an application is placed in determines the strategy to be pursued in its future development:

• **Question marks**: Applications in this quadrant have strong technical quality but little business relevance.

    All applications in this quadrant are under observation, and the quadrant must be reviewed regularly to decide which applications should go, which should stay,

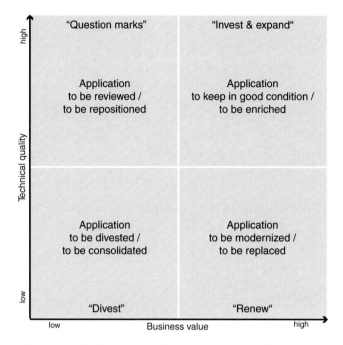

Fig. 2.12 Application portfolio "technical quality and business value"

and which might appropriately be enriched with more business content, enabling them to be repositioned.

As a rule, the applications in this quadrant tend to be tryout-type applications which are heavy on IT, or sub-applications which have been rendered superfluous owing to changes to the business model. An example: reports generated for a purpose which is no longer current, and which have never been removed.

- **Invest and expand**: Applications in this quadrant are the archetypal "ideals". Technical quality and business value are both high. Care should be lavished on these applications, with every effort taken to ensure they maintain their superior technical quality. Where possible and feasible, the applications should be enriched with more business functionality.
- **Renew**: These applications are of material importance to the enterprise's core business, but their technical quality is low. Outage of these applications will jeopardise the enterprise's business continuity. Accordingly, they urgently need modernisation or, if this is not possible, they must be replaced by other systems with high technical quality.
- **Divest**: Applications which are neither important for the current or future business nor technically viable should be divested, and their functionality shifted to other applications with better technical quality.

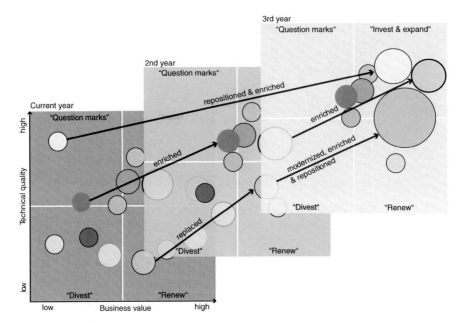

Fig. 2.13 Roadmap for strategic evolution

Beginning with the current application portfolio, the organisation can draft out its roadmap for developing the application landscape over the coming years (see Fig. 2.13). In accordance with the strategies the enterprise is pursuing, applications are then "divested", "expanded", "repositioned & expanded" or "renewed".

Important:

An application portfolio can present just the applications which are already in productive operation; it can also include planned or to-be applications. Arrows, or a sequence of version portfolios (roadmap), can be used to map changes over time.

**Application Portfolio "Business Value/Technological Appropriateness",
Based on [Buc05]**

In this application strategy, based on [Buc05], applications are classified according to their business value and technological suitability (or appropriateness). Instead of four quadrants, this portfolio works with five areas.

The technological appropriateness dimension encompasses the technical quality, modernity (how "state-of-the-art" an application is), complexity and age of both the application itself and the operating infrastructure on which it runs (Fig. 2.14). It also includes an appraisal of the application lifecycle and available IT resources.[1] For details on metrics, please refer to Sect. 6.3.

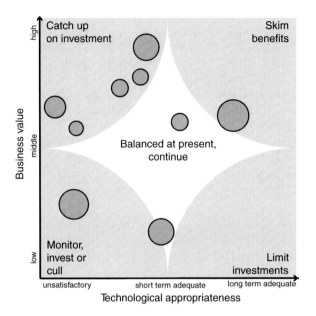

Fig. 2.14   Application portfolio "business value and technological appropriateness"

The relative positioning of applications within this matrix shows up the areas that cost reduction measures could feasibly target without jeopardising the overall sustainability of the applications.

   Which quadrant an application is placed in determines the strategy to be pursued in its future development:

- **Catch up on investment**: The applications grouped in this area have high business value but inadequate technological appropriateness. Since these applications are critical for the enterprise, they must be monitored carefully. IT deficits must be mitigated or eradicated altogether; an alternative is to replace these applications by others with higher technological quality and equivalent ability to perform the business functions in question.

---

[1] Including specialist expertise such as Assembler programming.

- **Skim benefits**: The applications in this area are appropriate in terms of both technology and the value they deliver to the business. Enterprises should fully skim business benefits of these applications, where feasible also rolling them out at other locations.
- **Balanced at present, continue**: The applications in the centre of the portfolio strike a good balance between business value and technological appropriateness. These applications can include IT systems for support processes such as accounts management or HR administration. Accordingly, no action need be taken pertaining to these applications.
- **Limit investment**: The applications in this area are technologically appropriate but have only low business value. Accordingly, investment should focus on functional extensions that raise business value.
- **Monitor, or invest and cull**: The applications in this area deliver only little support to the business and moreover are technologically inappropriate. Keep a close eye on any applications here – it may be appropriate to retire certain of them and introduce replacements.

Each of the application portfolios and associated information strategies discussed above has a proven track record in real business operation, having been applied successfully for strategic planning and management of the application landscape in multiple organisations.

Helpful hint:

At the initial, early stage in landscape appraisal, it is fine to use an essentially pragmatic approach to classifying applications. Organise a workshop with participants from business departments and IT, and have the participants classify the applications. The discussions this engenders, and the process through which stakeholders move toward consensus, are usually an efficient way to reach an agreement on classification.
In practice, this approach will seldom produce divided opinion!

Fact file:

- There are different types of strategy, e.g. innovation strategy or application strategy.
- There are numerous best-practice approaches for application strategies. You can use these to develop your own strategy customised to the concerns you wish to address.
- Portfolios are a useful tool to visualise strategies.

2.5 IT Strategy

> Good business leaders create a vision, articulate the vision and relentlessly drive it to completion.
>
> Jack Welch

Aligned with the corporate strategy, the IT strategy maps out a vision for the medium-term IT development trajectory. It forges connections between the current state and the essential innovations in the future. The IT strategy documents the current situation (the terms of reference), the strategic positioning and strategic objectives. It sets out a formal, mandatory framework and planning assumptions for strategic and operational-level IT management. As stated in [Coe03], [Dic85] and [Win03]), an IT strategy provides answers to these questions:

- Current situation: where are we now?
- Goal and to-be status: where do we want to go?
- Routes to the goal: how do we get there?

An IT strategy is reviewed regularly, often every year, and adjusted as necessary. As such, it creates a robust framework for target-focused planning and management of IT and for IT service delivery.

2.5.1 Content of an IT Strategy

The key elements of an IT strategy are represented in the strategy "house" (see Fig. 2.15). The IT strategy is derived from of the corporate strategy and business requirements, taking into account external and internal constraints and conditions such as statutory requirements, but also the availability of resources.

The strategic positioning and objectives form the "roof" of the IT strategy house. The major IT assets are the horizontal "beams":

- **Service and product portfolio**:The sum total of IT products and services that the IT unit provides for its customers.
    Example: application hosting, infrastructure provisioning, also support services for business process modelling
- **Application landscape**: The sum total of all business applications in an enterprise. Applications are code units with cohesive business logic which provide functionality that can be used in the course of business processes.
    Example: application "SAP R4.7"
- **Technical standards**: By establishing technical standards such as a particular database or runtime environments, an enterprise can drive forward technical homogeneity and standardisation within the IT landscape. In general, technical standards are assembled into a standardisation catalogue, or blueprint, which

serves as a mandatory framework for projects and maintenance, and for taking applications into productive operation (see Chapter 5).

- **Operating infrastructure**: The operating infrastructure essentially comprises the hardware and network infrastructure on which the applications run. The operating infrastructure must be appropriate to ensure availability, scalability reliability and security of IT support as required by the business.

- **Vendors & employees**: Employers and vendors are the IT resources. The organisation will conduct its IT tasks either in-house or commission external providers, depending on what core capabilities it has for performing the work. The capabilities and numbers of resources ultimately determine the quality of service delivery.

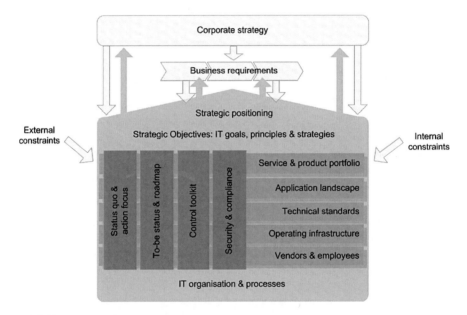

Fig. 2.15 IT strategy house

The aspects relevant to strategy are presented in the IT strategy house as vertical bars:

- **Status quo and action focus**: Having taken stock of the current situation and summarised it clearly,[2] the next step is to determine the strategic position (see Sect. 2.2). The analysis of the current status helps you zero in on the points you need to address in order to operationalise requirements and strategic objectives.

---

[2] Stocktaking of all IT assets might be necessary, i.e. the product and service portfolio, application landscape, technical standards, operating infrastructure and resource situation.

- **To-be status and roadmap**: Depending on what points have emerged as your action focus, the next step is to define objectives for all IT assets, e.g. for the future technical standards and target landscape, together with a roadmap for implementation. The strategic objectives and planning must be embedded in systems for measurement and control and be clearly articulated within the organisation.
- **Control toolkit**: Performance indicators, embedded in a measurement and control system for IT (e.g. balanced scorecard, cockpit), help the organisation monitor and direct its strategic IT planning.
- **Security and compliance**: Security and compliance are important aspects with far-reaching impact. Shortfalls in IT security or less-than-assiduous observance of compliance requirements can have harsh consequences for the entire enterprise.

  Take care to consider all relevant compliance-related and statutory requirements (e.g. SOX, Solvency II, Basel II, BDSG (German Federal Data Protection Act), KonTraG (Controlling and Transparency in Business Act) or labour law) and also ensure confidentiality, integrity and availability in accordance with corporate security policy and directives.

Cutting through both the strategy aspects and IT assets are the IT organisation and processes. Putting IT strategy effectively into practice hinges on having clearly delineated roles and responsibilities, with clearly codified IT organisation and decision-making processes. The IT organisation and processes form the foundation of the IT strategy house.

There is no one-size-fits-all approach for deciding on goals, principles and strategies, or for choosing a control and measurement system to monitor progress. Rather, this depends on the scope for performance development of IT, its strategic positioning, and the size of the enterprise or the complexity of its business model; there can be substantial differences between solutions.

2.5.2 IT Strategy Document

An IT strategy document should be as brief (approximately 20 pages) and as succinctly formulated as possible. The key aspects, particularly the objectives, must be described clearly and unambiguously. The following structure for the IT strategy document has proven a highly viable approach (see also Fig. 2.16):

- **Chapter 1 – Management summary**: Summary of strategic positioning and the salient content of the document; intended for business managers and senior management.
- **Chapter 2 – Requirements to the IT**: Brief summary of the corporate strategy, business requirements and internal and external constraints (e.g. statutory requirements) determining what is required and expected to deliver from the IT. An important element of this section is a statement of compliance and security requirements.

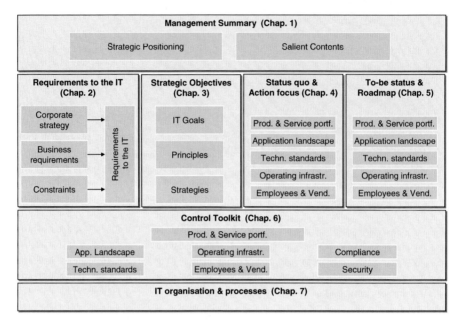

Fig. 2.16 Structure of an IT strategy document

This summary will ideally answer the following questions: how does the company earn its money? Which markets, regions or customer segments does it address? In what way is the enterprise expecting to change its business model in the future, and over what timeframe?

- **Chapter 3 –Strategic objectives**: This section documents the medium-term and long-term IT goals, and the authoritative principles and strategies which the enterprise has elected to apply, taking into account the current capabilities of IT and the internal and external constraints.

- **Chapter 4 –Status quo and action focus**: This section documents the present product and service portfolio, the IT landscape as it now stands (application landscape, technical standards and operating infrastructure) and resource aspects (employees and vendors).

    It also provides a statement on action focus points, derived from the strategic objectives and the statement on the requirements IT is expected to fulfil.

- **Chapter 5 – To-be status and roadmap**: A description of the officially agreed to-be status of IT assets and a roadmap for implementation.

    The IT strategy document should also state what direct and indirect interventions will be required to move ahead on the roadmap. Alternative planning scenarios can be recorded in intermediate versions of the IT strategy document.

- **Chapter 6 – Control toolkit**: This section describes performance indicators as a scorecard system/cockpit and decision criteria for planning and directing IT service planning and delivery for the IT service portfolio, all IT assets, and for planning and directing compliance and security aspects.

This section must clearly document what control tool has been selected – e.g. a Cockpit and/or measurement and control system such as the BSC – and articulate precisely which operating data is to be channelled into the system. This section is a key part of the IT strategy document.

- **Chapter 7 – IT organisation and IT processes**: Who participates in which IT decisions, and who has overall decision-making authority in each case? This should be clarified for issues of strategy, investment, projects, architecture, infrastructure, security and risk management.

  This section also indicates what internal and external resources (employees and vendors) will be required to implement the IT strategy. In addition, you should describe the financing model for IT service provision (for instance, cost centre or profit centre?) and make a statement on usage-based service charging models for business departments.

Important:

- The IT strategy should include at least a broad-brushstroke outline of the corporate strategy, business requirements and internal/external constraints. Without this, it will be difficult to demonstrate where the requirements for IT have come from.
- It must be clear how IT goals have been cascaded out of corporate goals. If you have clear links between the deducted goals, you will later find it easier to document and articulate IT's contribution to achieving these corporate goals.
- Be sure to formulate the key statements succinctly. The IT strategy document must be read and understood by all IT employees.
- Make sure you have procedures in place to verify compliance with objectives: working along the principle "what gets measured gets done", this way you can be sure the IT strategy will genuinely be implemented.

2.5.3 Guidelines for IT Strategy in Practice

This section provides guidelines on elaborating your IT strategy to fit your particular situation. In general, IT strategy development is initiated by the CIO. The CIO ensures that, following its initial development, the strategy is regularly reviewed and brought into alignment with changes in the internal or external environment. Updates are usually made annually, and IT strategy development is a process which generally extends over several months. The various strategy aspects are successively developed in a series of strategy workshops, in some cases with different participants each time. Participants should be selected and geared up mentally to the task such that as a team they address the issues under consideration systematically, creatively and in a disciplined manner, with a common language and a common understanding of the strategy.

Both the IT strategy development process and the people you choose to engage in this process must be selected as befits your enterprise's organisation and culture. It should be clear upfront of the process which stakeholders have to be consulted when, and for which steps.

> **Important:**
>
> You should involve a least one representative of senior corporate management, and all IT managers for all IT core areas.

You can use the following guideline in both initial and rolling strategy development. It comprises largely two phases, analysis and design:

- **Analysis**: In the analysis phase, collect and consolidate statements on what is required of IT, and what constraints and conditions need to be observed. Define and document the status quo, and use this as a basis for appraising IT (see Fig. 2.17).

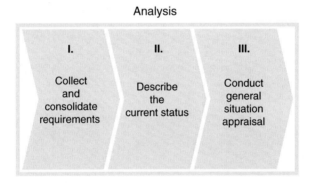

Fig. 2.17 Activities in the analysis phase

- **Design**: Define the position of IT, draw up strategic objectives and planning frameworks. Make provisions for implementation (see Fig. 2.18).

The activities in the two phases are described in detail below:

Design

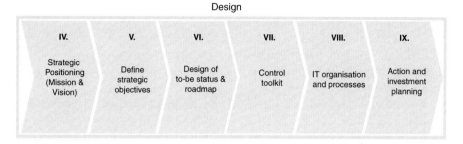

Fig. 2.18   Activities in the design phase

I. Collect and Consolidate Statements on What Is Required of IT, and What Constraints and Conditions Need to Be Observed

You should pull together and consolidate the following information to help you in your appraisal of IT:

- **Key aspects of the corporate strategy**: Find out and document the major aspects of the corporate strategy. Of key importance are the corporate goals and business drivers. These form the basis for deriving the IT strategy.

Important:

- If the corporate strategy does not exist in written form, write down your own assumptions on what it is – particularly the business drivers and corporate goals. This enables you to document how the IT goals were arrived at, and you also have a basis for discussion with senior management.
- The requirements for IT have to be discussed and agreed with senior management and the business departments concerned.

- **Current business requirements**: Solicit feedback from IT customers and departments on their current business requirements. Business requirements describe in business terms what services IT must deliver, cascaded down into issues pertaining specifically to IT. Business requirements can be both operative and strategic – for example, round-the-clock service for field sales staff.
- **Internal and external constraints**: Find out what external constraints exist. You should consider statutory and compliance requirements as well as the IT market and competitive environment, and also complete a trend analysis – this will help you map future technical scenarios to frame an outlook for IT and the business.

   When analysing internal constraints, look at the capabilities, core competencies and resources of IT and its performance potential.

For more information about methods for analysing internal and external constraints, you might like to refer to literature such as [Win03], [War02], [Ber03-1] and [Ber03-2].

Based on your findings, you can then identify and appraise opportunities and threats, strengths and weaknesses.

II. Describe the Current Status of All IT Assets and Document What Action Needs to Be Taken

Document the product and service portfolio, the present application landscape, the technical standards you use at present, operating infrastructure, the current resource situation (employees and vendors), and indicate any points where it is already clear that action is necessary.

You might find the ideas in Chapter 4 useful to help you capture and analyse the current landscape. Chapter 5 provides guidelines on how to create a record of the technical standards which your enterprise currently uses.

III. Conduct a General Situation Appraisal

• Identify the performance potential of IT as it is now, and its standing in the enterprise (see Sect. 2.2).
• Determine the maturity of IT processes using standardised models such as CMMI (see [Zin04], [Joh07] and [Foe08]).
• Document your appraisal in the IT strategy document.

IV. Strategic Positioning

Define the performance potential and standing you are aiming at (see Sect. 2.3). Formulate the mission and vision of IT.

Helpful hint:

• The more concisely you formulate your mission or vision, the more likely it is that the content will engrave itself on people's minds – and the easier it is to transform into goals and strategies.
• Be sure to involve key stakeholders in development and formulation processes right from the outset! This is the only way to ensure buy-in from stakeholders – essential to take plans into action.

V. Define the Strategic Objectives (IT Goals, Principles and Strategies)

Derive your strategic objectives from the corporate strategy, business requirements and external and internal constraints. The strategic objectives largely comprise IT goals, the principles and strategies (see Sect. 2.4).

Using the strategic positioning of IT as your starting point, formulate the IT goals from the business requirements, and continue to refine goals until you have a set of transparent, practical interventions with operational-level granularity. By ensuring you have clear links between operational-level measures and the corporate and IT goals, you can maintain clarity on how you arrived at the outcome. Guidelines for deriving IT goals are provided in Sect. 2.4.1.

Define principles and strategies. These frame and inform the decision-making process in IT management. Guidelines on how to select appropriate principles are provided in Sects. 2.4.2 and 2.4.3.

Principles and strategies must each be clear and comprehensible. They must be articulated and codified. As a rule, it is better to apply just a few selected core principles and strategies. By keeping the number down, you will be better able to measure progress towards goals and steer a clear direction in implementation.

VI. Design the To-be Status and Roadmap for Implementation

Revisit your analysis of the current landscape status with a view to operationalising the requirements for IT and achieving strategic objectives. In this way you can identify areas where action needs to be taken and where there is potential for optimisation. Section 4.4.2 provides specific guidelines for analysing the IT landscape.

Map out a target status for all IT assets:

- To-be application landscape framed by landscape planning (see Sect. 4.4.3)
- To-be blueprint framed by technical standardisation (see Sect. 5.4.3)
- Planning of operating infrastructure (see [Buc07] and [Foe08])
- Insourcing and outsourcing focus

Compare your as-is situation with the to-be landscape. Identify the gaps and use these as the basis for developing planning trajectories.[3] Map each of these planning trajectories to your timeline. Appraise each one in terms of how well it can cover the requirements IT is expected to fulfil, how closely it ties in with strategic objectives, plus cost, duration and implementation risk.

For guidelines on staking out the to-be IT landscape and the roadmap for implementation, please refer to Sects. 4 and 5.

Important:

Document the planning trajectories and decision-making criteria such that other readers will be able to follow the reasoning. Include a statement of the

---

[3] A set of options for action.

corporate goals, business requirements, and how these were progressed into a particular choice of planning trajectory.

In the IT strategy document, state the strategic IT planning and roadmap agreed upon for implementation. Intermediate versions of the IT strategy document can also be created to record alternative planning scenarios.

VII. Define Control Metrics and the Measurement and Control System

- Identify the relevant control objects, e.g. for all IT assets and project portfolios. More information is provided in Sect. 6.3.
- Define metrics for all strategic objectives as a way of measuring and verifying implementation of requirements, progress toward the target status and along its roadmap for implementation. Also ensure due consideration is given to aspects such as security, compliance and risk management. Guidelines on identifying appropriate metrics are provided in Sect. 6.3.

  Examples of areas to address:
  - Planning and monitoring goal attainment, early warning in the event of changes or deviation from goals
  - Securing and complying with strategic policy and directives
  - IT make-or-buy (management and control of compliance with insourcing/outsourcing concept)
  - Steering of project portfolio
  - Verifying execution of strategy and organisation projects
  - Verifying effectiveness of projects
- For all your strategic metrics, you should define indicators, verifiable targets and tolerances, and clear links with operational-level metrics (see Sect. 6.3).

VIII. Define Your IT Organisation and Processes

Document your IT organisation and any changes that occur over time, processes for planning and delivering services and for making decisions.

Be sure to highlight any changes, e.g. insourcing or outsourcing decisions, new responsibilities or roles, also personnel increases or enhanced skillsets of personnel. The following aspects are key:

- Current and planned headcount, and existing and required competency profile
- Responsibilities and roles, IT structure and management model for planning and control

- How the IT organisation is embedded in the organisation as a whole; decision processes such as project portfolio management and other decision-making bodies
- IT processes for strategic and operational-level planning and control of IT service delivery such as IT landscape management, technical standardisation, IT innovation management, strategic and operational IT controlling, project execution, service and supply management plus supporting processes such as HR, procurement, finance and controlling (see Sect. 6.3). For more information on operational-level IT processes and the supporting processes, please refer to relevant literature, e.g. [Vah05], [Win03], [War02], [Ber03-1] and [Ber03-2].

IX. Actions and Investment Planning

Define practical actions and the roadmap for implementation, including investment planning. This entails pulling together a range of individual items.

Determine what direct and indirect actions are required to implement strategic IT planning and goals, and enact the current business requirements.

Evaluate and prioritise these measures according to the criteria relevant for your enterprise, e.g. from project portfolio management. Where possible, you should already have put together projects of whatever nature (on strategy, infrastructure, standardisation, organisation or development), grouped them by priority in your medium-term planning, and integrated them into your project portfolio management.

This will also include actions of a more indirect nature, e.g. for building expertise (bearing in mind that there will always be a learning curve involved), realigning the corporate culture or changing established mindsets, the creation of a communication plan,[4] or defining goal agreements and SLAs to shore up implementation efforts.

You must have ongoing measurement and control in place to keep strategic re-engineering on track and ensure consistent progress toward goals (see Chapter 6).

Prerequisites for successful strategic IT planning:

- Be sure to make an accurate appraisal of the current performance potential of IT, and ensure the backing of senior management for deciding on its strategic positioning. If you do this, you will be better able to manage user expectations appropriately.

---

[4] Creation of a communication plan, including method and content, scheduling, target audiences, target group-specific content and processing of feedback.

- Be sure to use appropriate granularity at each planning level. Strategic planning of IT requires a big-picture view. If you amass too much detail, you won't be able to see the wood for the trees.
- Define appropriate strategic objectives, technical standards and the target landscape as an authoritative framework to guide and inform the actions of IT management. Document these definitions in your IT strategy document.

Chapter 3
Enterprise Architecture

The loftier the building, the deeper must the foundation be laid.
Thomas à Kempis (medieval monk and author of
the Imitation of Christ)

Embracing all the major business and IT structures, as well as the associations that
exist between them, an enterprise architecture creates a helicopter view of the entire
company. It serves as basis for describing both the business and IT, as well as the
connections between the two, and for rendering explicit mutual dependencies and
the impacts of changes in either camp. A common language is created, bridging the
gap between business and IT (Fig. 3.1):

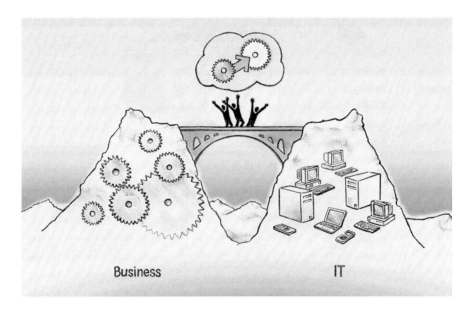

Fig. 3.1 Bridge between business and IT

I. Hanschke, *Strategic IT Management*, DOI 10.1007/978-3-642-05034-3_3,
© Springer-Verlag Berlin Heidelberg 2010

What an enterprise architecture does is to pull together the pockets of information scattered across the organisation's various business units and projects, creating a unified picture which highlights how the information is networked and what mutual dependencies exist. This big-picture view is of inestimable value for every enterprise in underpinning a range of IT management tasks. In particular, the enterprise architecture is the basis for strategic management of the IT landscape. Other IT management tasks may at first glance appear to have no direct connection with the enterprise architecture – such as the enforcement of compliance and security requirements, business continuity management and corporate risk management (see [Rom07]). However, only when the enterprise has a complete picture of the landscape – an awareness of its components and the links between them – can it hope to take appropriate action for business requirements.

Questions answered in this chapter:

- What is an enterprise architecture? What is it required for?
- What EA frameworks exist, and how do they differ?
- What characterises a good enterprise architecture?
- What components does an enterprise architecture consist of?
- What contribution does an enterprise architecture make to strategic evolution of the IT landscape?
- What views are there of the enterprise architecture? Which stakeholders need which information?
- Which roles and processes are required to manage the enterprise architecture?
- How do you arrive at your particular enterprise architecture?

3.1 Scope and Definition

Developed well, an enterprise architecture enables you to respond quickly and effectively to the challenges of ever-faster changing market and technology environments. Transparency in your IT landscape will enable you to see how business and IT interrelate, and where the mutual dependencies lie.

The significance of enterprise architectures grows with the company's size and the number of IT systems it operates. Every new application, every new interface or technology that joins the landscape adds to its complexity and increases the risk of data redundancy and inconsistency. It's rarely possible to "ring-fence" individual applications when making changes. Application engineering and operating costs spiral upwards. Without an enterprise architecture, the IT landscape can easily become unmanageable.

An enterprise architecture describes the structures in business and IT and the links that exist between them. The business side of the company is shaped by the business model (see Chapter 2), whose key structures are the products your company sells, its business processes and the organisation. To put your business model into practice successfully, you have to know your business capabilities (your business functions) and have high-quality business data (business objects) to work with. IT, in turn, is defined by the application landscape in the enterprise, its technical implementation and the operating infrastructure.

Adding transparency throughout the business and IT is in itself a valuable exercise: it gives you a basis for communicating with the business and inside IT. However, an enterprise architecture can do more. It enables you to codify the connections between business structures and IT structures. With these associations clearly laid out, you know which applications make which contribution to which business processes (to give just one example). In this way, an enterprise architecture creates an overall view of IT in your enterprise.

There are myriad questions to clarify while introducing an enterprise architecture. As experience shows, the more you look into an issue, the more questions arise. Here are just a few examples:

- What business structures and what IT structures do we need?
- What sort of granularity are we looking for in the structures? For instance, do we want to elaborate business processes down to the level of activities, checkpoints and sequences? Do we have to map application releases? Is the topology of the operating infrastructure decisive?
- What connections do we need between business and IT structures? Are the associations between applications and business processes important, or should we instead be looking at interdependencies with business functions or products?
- At what level of granularity do we want to map the connections between business and IT structures? Do we want to map applications to the activities of a business process, or preferably to the business process as a whole? Or do we even need to map application releases to activities?
- How can we establish and manage a base of data with information about business and IT structures? How can we ensure that the landscape model is always adequately up-to-date, complete and consistent?
- How much effort will it take to manage an enterprise architecture? What processes, roles and responsibilities are necessary? Who has to be involved, and when? Which entities take the decisions? Who will supply which data? What quality does the data have, how up-to-date is it? Who will oversee quality assurance?
- What benefit and value can we expect? Who are the beneficiaries and what are their interests? Is the cost-benefit ratio reasonable?

These questions can be organised into three categories: "why? – goals and benefits", "what? – structures of the enterprise architecture" and "how – management of the enterprise architecture":

- Why do you need an enterprise architecture in the first place? – Objectives and benefits

The objectives and benefits you have in mind should be assessed in terms of your particular company – however, you can expect benefits to be largely qualitative in nature. You may need transparency to make your IT manageable at all, or to fulfil compliance obligations such as SOX. The related mandatory documentation is also easier to assemble and produce if there is a working enterprise architecture in place.

Another important argument in favour of an enterprise architecture is that it enables decisions to be taken on the basis of facts and evidence, making it easier to pull together the data and information for informed decisions.

Important:

Which arguments work best for the case you are making will depend on your own enterprise scenario.
Other arguments you can use are provided in Chapters 4 and 5.

- What do we need for implementation? – Structures of the enterprise architecture
  Your goals and areas of concern will scope and inform your choice of structures. You have to establish who will benefit from the enterprise architecture, and what interests and concerns these stakeholders have. This will enable you to figure out what information the architecture will need to deliver. By evaluating the effort for storing data and providing it (e.g. with diagramming) to the people who need it, you can determine the enterprise architecture which works best for you.
- How you going to manage your enterprise architecture? – Management of the enterprise architecture
  What matters here are roles and responsibilities, processes and how they are embedded in the overall organisation. You have to define these specifically for your enterprise, ensuring that they are in alignment with your corporate organisation and its culture.

It is important to have guidelines to help you navigate the process of establishing and managing an enterprise architecture. A range of Enterprise Architecture Management (EAM) approaches are discussed in relevant literature (see Sect. 3.2). However, these approaches are not always practicable or ready for use "out of the box". Many require you to wade through reams of documentation and then make your own appraisal of which parts are relevant or applicable for you. Hands-on, specific guidelines for customising the architecture and getting it into operation are few and far between. Process management is the sole exception, where there is already a good body of experience and valuable guidelines to call on (see [All95], [Ses07] and [Ahl06]).

This was the background fuelling the development of a best-practice enterprise architecture and a method for strategic management of the IT landscape. The method described here, with its practice-tested approach, is designed to make your initial venture into this complex subject matter a whole lot easier. The best-practice enterprise architecture is an enterprise architecture framework from which you can derive your own specific architecture through simple configuration. The best-practice enterprise architecture is described in Sect. 3.3. Guidelines on deriving your own architecture are provided in Sect. 3.2.

The method for strategic management of the IT landscape is based on the best-practice enterprise architecture and embraces all the elements of Enterprise Architecture Management upon which IT can feasibly have an impact. Strategic management of the IT landscape comprises both the planning and steering aspects of IT management:

- **Strategic planning of IT landscape**: Strategic planning of the IT landscape defines the scope of evolutionary development of the IT landscape. The key elements are IT landscape management and technical standardisation.

  IT landscape management embraces all the processes for documenting and analysing the IT landscape and for the strategic evolution of the application landscape (see Chapter 4). The technical standardisation side of the planning stakes out the technical standards for the development trajectory of the IT landscape (see Chapter 5).
- **Strategic direction of further IT landscape development**: A strategic control toolkit helps the organisation implement strategic objectives, work toward the to-be landscape and enforce technical standards. A set of appropriate indicators are used which are associated with metrics taken from operational-level project management and the operating business (see Chapter 6).

Where IT does not have an impact is on the business aspects of Enterprise Architecture Management. This side of EAM, termed business landscape management, is described briefly in Sect. 3.4. Business landscape management defines the business structures with which the connections to IT structures are defined (in IT landscape management). For details on business landscape management, please refer to the relevant literature (see [All05], [Ses07] and [Ahl06]).

Fact file:

Define the enterprise architecture which is the best fit for the goals you are working toward. You can make good use of the best-practice enterprise architecture here (see Sect. 3.3).

3.2 Enterprise Architecture Frameworks

The subject of enterprise architecture is nothing new in information technology. The
foundation for later approaches and ideas was laid back in the 1980s by John A.
Zachman (see [Zac87] and [Zac08]). In his work, Zachman discusses the relevance
of taking a holistic view of architectures at enterprise level. The Zachman Enterprise
Architecture Framework ranks today as one of the best-known of all frameworks.
It has had substantial influence on modern understanding of enterprise architectures
and many of the frameworks which were subsequently developed.

John A. Zachman published the first version of his proposal for an EA framework
in 1987 (see [Zac87]). He later collaborated with John F. Sowa on an extended
version, published in 1992 (see [Sow92]), which led into the version of the Zachman
Enterprise Architecture Framework known today (see Fig. 3.2).

The framework is designed to provide a set of artefacts suitable for mapping the
variety of interfaces of an application's components and how they integrate into the
organisation.

	DATA What	FUNCTION How	NETWORK Where	PEOPLE Who	TIME When	MOTIVATION Why	
SCOPE **(CONTEXTUAL)** Planner	Things important to the Business	Processes Performs	Business Locations	Important Organisations	Events Significant of the Business	Business Goals and Strategies	**SCOPE** **(CONTEXTUAL)** Planner
ENTERPRISE **MODEL** **(CONCEPTUAL)** Owner	Semantic Model	Business Process Model	Business Logistics System	Workflow Model	Master Schedule	Business Plan	**ENTERPRISE** **MODEL** **(CONCEPTUAL)** Owner
SYSTEM MODEL **(LOGICAL)** Designer	Logical Data Model	Application Architecture	Distributed System Architecture	Human Interface Architecture	Process Structure	Business Rule Model	**SYSTEM MODEL** **(LOGICAL)** Designer
TECHNOLOGY **MODEL** **(PHYSICAL)** Builder	Physical Data Model	System Design	Technology Architecture	Presentation Architecture	Control Structure	Rule Design	**TECHNOLOGY** **MODEL** **(PHYSICAL)** Builder
DETAILED **REPRESENTATION** **(OUT-OF-** **CONTEXT)** Subcontractor	Data Definition	Program	Network Architecture	Security Architecture	Timing Definition	Rule Definition	**DETAILED** **REPRESENTATION** **(OUT-OF-** **CONTEXT)** Subcontractor
FUNCTIONING **ENTERPRISE**	Data	Function	Network	Organisation	Schedule	Strategy	**FUNCTIONING** **ENTERPRISE**
	DATA What	FUNCTION How	NETWORK Where	PEOPLE Who	TIME When	MOTIVATION Why	

Fig. 3.2 Zachman Enterprise Architecture Framework

The Zachman Enterprise Architecture Framework presents various views and
aspects of the enterprise architecture in a highly structured and clear-cut form. It
differentiates between the levels "Scope", "Enterprise Model", "System Model",
"Technology Model" and "Detailed Representations". Each of these views is presented as a row in the matrix. The lower the row, the greater the degree of detail

of the level represented. The model works with six aspects of the enterprise architecture: "Data", "Function", "Network", "People", "Time" and "Motivation". Each view (column) interrogates the architecture from a particular perspective. Taken together, the matrix cells create a complete picture of the enterprise.

> **Zachman's framework in summary:**
>
> The Zachman Enterprise Architecture Framework is a good introduction for an initial venture into the highly complex subject matter of enterprise architectures. However, it does not actually comprise any specific method, nor is there adequate tool support or guidelines for designing and rolling out an architecture customised for your enterprise.

There is little verified information available on the use of EA frameworks. According to a 2005 survey by the Institute for Enterprise Architecture Development (see [IFE05]), there is reasonably widespread occurrence in practice of the following frameworks (as well as the Zachman framework):

- **The Open Group Architecture Framework (TOGAF)**: TOGAF is based on the "Technical Architecture Framework for Information Management" (TAFIM) of the US Department of Defense (DoD). The first version of TOGAF was developed by the Open Group[1] in 1995. The current version is Version 9 (see [TOG01], [TOG03], [TOG07] and [TOG09]), published in early 2009.

  TOGAF is introduced in Version 8.1 as an EA framework, the term here being understood as a methodological framework for developing different enterprise architectures, with a focus on application landscapes. The most significant new feature compared to predecessor Version 8.1.1 is the modular structure; many aspects of the framework have also been extended. Version 9 provides guidelines for adapting the framework for particular enterprise contexts.
- **US Federal Enterprise Architecture Framework (FEAF)**: Developed for the US Government, FEAF was published in Version 1.1 in 1999 (see [Skk04]). It establishes a structure for the enterprise architecture in US government organisations, enabling the development of unified, standardised processes to simplify information exchange between governmental offices.
- **Department of Defense Architecture Framework (DoDAF)**: DoDAF, first published as Version 1.0 in 2003, is a further development of the C4ISR[2] (see [DOD04-1] and [DOD04-2]).

---

[1]http://www.opengroup.org. The Open Group is a consortium of companies with a common interest in establishing vendor-neutral standards in IT.
[2]Command, Control, Communications, Computers, Intelligence, Surveillance, and Reconnaissance.

DoDAF is used for enterprise architectures in the military context in the USA. It is particularly suitable for large systems with complex integration and communication challenges. Accordingly, DoDAF is also found in non-military contexts in large public and private-sector organisations, particularly enterprises which either do business with the DoD or which simply wish to adapt an EA framework.

- **Extended Enterprise Architecture Framework (E2AF)**: The first version of E2AF was published in 2003. E2AF is based on existing frameworks such as FEAF and TOGAF and on practical experience with the use of enterprise architecture frameworks (see [Skk04]).

One of the best-known EA frameworks, TOGAF, is described briefly below. For information on the other frameworks, please refer to the specified literature.

TOGAF

TOGAF essentially presents a methodological framework for developing diverse architectures. It provides building blocks (descriptions of predefined components) and a process model to help organisations define their particular enterprise architecture. The EA model described in TOGAF is organised into four sub-architectures.

- The **Business Architecture** describes the strategies, governance, organisation and business processes of the enterprise.
- The **Data Architecture** describes the data, the associations that exist between data, and principles for organising and managing resources in the context of the application landscape.
- The **Application Architecture** describes applications and the relationships that exist between them, and the relationships between applications and business processes.
- The **Technology Architecture** describes the current technical implementation and the future technical standards specific to the enterprise, such as runtime environments or application middleware and the operating infrastructure.

Together, the Data Architecture and Application Architecture form the Information System Architecture.

The framework which underpins the development of an enterprise architecture comprises the following components:

- **Architecture Development Method(ADM)**: ADM is a generic method for developing an enterprise architecture (see Fig. 3.3). All eight phases of the enterprise architecture lifecycle are addressed. The goals, approaches, required input, activities and deliverables are documented for each phase separately. The ADM method is enriched by specific ADM guidelines and techniques.
- **Architecture Content Framework**: The Architecture Content Framework provides a detailed model for deliverable types in the development and evolution of the enterprise architecture.

Fig. 3.3 TOGAF ADM (see [TOG09])

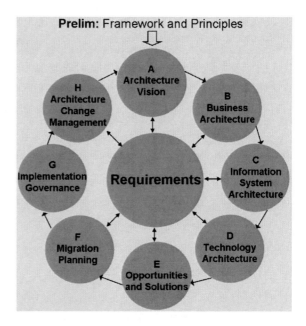

- **Enterprise Continuum**: The Enterprise Continuum is a collection of reference descriptions in the form of graphic models and text documents. It comprises the Architecture Continuum and Solutions Continuum.
- **Architecture Repository**: The Architecture Repository serves to store various types of architecture deliverables. Alongside the Architecture Metamodel and Architecture Capability, the key elements of the repository are the Architecture Landscape, the Standards Information Base (SIB), the Reference Library and the Governance Log.

  - **Architecture Metamodel**: The Architecture Metamodel provides the meta-model for the architecture content.
  - **Architecture Capability**: These store the instructions, structures and processes for managing the Architecture Repository.
  - **Architecture Landscape**: The Architecture Landscape serves to render the IT and business structures (building and solution blocks) transparent at various levels of abstraction.
  - **Standards Information Base (SIB)**: This comprises a taxonomy of the technical components which have been standardised for the enterprise.
  - **Reference Library**: The Reference Library provides guidelines, templates, patterns and other types of reference documents.
  - **Governance Log**: The Governance Log provides a record of governance activities in the enterprise.

- **Resource Base**: The TOGAF Resource Base comprises additional resources such as templates or supplementary notes for executing the activities in the TOGAF ADM process model.

- **Reference Models**: The main components of the reference models are the Technical Reference Model (see Fig. 3.4) and the Integration Information Infrastructure Reference Model (IIIRM). The Technical Reference Model (TRM) provides a taxonomy on which technical standards can be built. The IIIRM is a description of a reference architecture for integrating applications.

TOGAF is free of charge, provided it is used exclusively for internal purposes. However, it requires membership in "The Open Group's Architecture Forum". The Open Group also offers a certification programme for TOGAF.

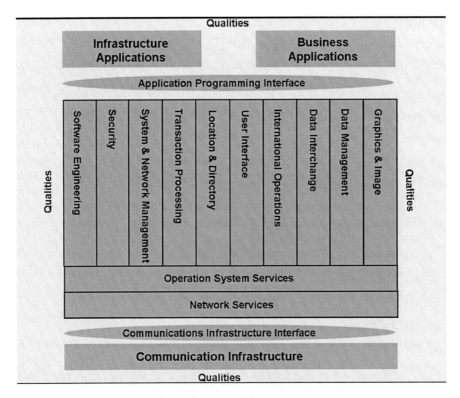

Fig. 3.4 TOGAF Technical Reference Model (see [TOG09]))

TOGAF – in summary:

TOGAF is an extensive Enterprise Architecture Framework with a highly generic structure. It addresses the entire enterprise architecture lifecycle. At the heart of the framework is the Architecture Development Method (ADM).

The enterprise architecture development process is very well documented, and is enriched by a collection of reference descriptions and a description of components (in Version 9, these provide various touchpoints for deriving specific enterprise architectures).

However, the level of abstraction of the framework is too high for ad-hoc use. Hruschka and Starke view it as "slightly remote from real-life practice" (see [Hru06]).

EA Frameworks in Summary

What all the EA frameworks introduced here have in common is that the enterprise architecture is described through various views and aspects (see [Der06]). Common views are the business architecture, data architecture, application architecture and technology architecture. The links between these various sub-architectures create a complete view of business and IT structures. The aspects addressed in the EA frameworks (what, how, where, who, when and why) are in many cases based on the aspects in the Zachman Enterprise Architecture Framework an (see Fig. 3.2).

Fact file:

Existing EA frameworks are highly abstract, somewhat remote from real-life practice and do not permit ad-hoc use.

3.3 Best-Practice Enterprise Architecture

The experience acquired in many consulting projects and in using the enterprise architecture frameworks described above has been channelled into developing a best-practice enterprise architecture which is ready for use straight "out of the box". You can derive your specific enterprise architecture quite simply from the model. Guidelines for adapting the best-practice enterprise architecture to your circumstances are provided in Sect. 3.6.

Figure 3.5 presents an overview of the best-practice enterprise architecture. It essentially comprises a range of sub-architectures, each of which examines IT in the enterprise from a different perspective. The business architecture describes the business structures for which IT support can be provided. The remaining architectures each describe the IT structures from various IT perspectives.

Each sub-architecture stakes out specific rules for how the constituent entities should be modelled. For instance, the business architecture defines rules for the

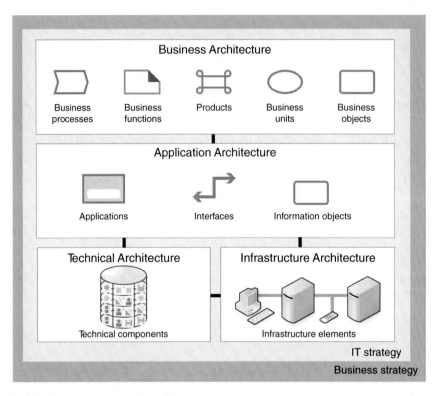

Fig. 3.5 Best-practice enterprise architecture

business landscape model: how business processes are to be described and which business process levels (see [All05]) are to be taken into consideration.

We differentiate between the following sub-architectures and their landscape models:

- **Business Architecture**: The business architecture describes the main business structures of an enterprise which drive the enterprise's activities. The main elements of the business architecture are business processes, business functions, products, business units and business objects. You can structure this architecture by defining suitable functional-type categories, known as business domains.
- **Application Architecture**: The application architecture provides the means for describing the enterprise's application landscape, i.e. for the applications, their data and interfaces or information flows. The application landscape model can be structured by defining application domains, also known as landscape clusters.

  The application architecture serves as the bridge linking the business architecture with the technology and infrastructure architectures. The links into the business architecture shed light on how and precisely where IT delivers support for the business. The technical implementation of applications and interfaces is documented by assigning elements from the technology architecture to each application. These assignments show which infrastructure the applications run on.

- **Technology Architecture**: The technology architecture is all about defining enterprise-specific technical standards for implementing applications, interfaces and infrastructure elements. Technology architecture can comprise reference architectures and templates, bought-in IT products, tools for software engineering and system management, as well as IT components such as frameworks. You can structure this architecture by organising it into architecture domains. For more information, please see Chapter 5.
- **Infrastructure Architecture**: The infrastructure architecture describes – at a coarse level of granularity – the infrastructure elements on which the applications run. This forges a connection with the infrastructure elements used in operational-level IT management (see [itS08] and [Joh07]).

Important:

- Unlike the EA frameworks introduced above, the best-practice enterprise architecture is ready to use as it is. By omitting building blocks and relationships you do not need, you can derive your own enterprise architecture quite simply. Guidelines are provided in Sects. 3.3.2 and 3.6.
- Unlike frameworks such as TOGAF, the best-practice enterprise architecture differentiates between the technology architecture and the infrastructure architecture. This enables you to present planned standards separately from the present-day reality in the enterprise.
- There are no provisions in the best-practice enterprise architecture for a separate data or information architecture. The aspects which are modelled in the data architecture in TOGAF are here part of the business or application architectures.

The **business architecture** defines the business objects and their relationships (in the form of a glossary or similar), and describes the use of these objects in business processes or functions.

The **application architecture** describes the data which is used by or exchanged between applications. This enables you to accommodate the different perspectives of the business landscape and application landscape models.

3.3.1 Information Timeliness and Granularity

Things should be made as simple as possible, but not any simpler.

Albert Einstein

To retain an overview of your enterprise IT landscape and identify interdependencies and the impact of changes in the business, the information which is mapped into the enterprise architecture must be reasonably complete, up-to-date, high-quality and have the right level of granularity. This is no easy matter – for a number of reasons:

Each of the different elements of the enterprise architecture uses different planning and control processes. A case in point: business processes are planned under the auspices of process management, and applications are planned as part of IT landscape management. With planning generally taking place at different times of year, the status of the resulting landscape models will inevitably not be the same.

Process documentation is as a rule updated at least annually, often linked to the review cycles which might be in place for other reasons (e.g. compliance requirements). As a rule, the documentation of the current and future application landscape is updated at least annually as part of IT strategy development. However, updates are in many cases more frequent, prompted by events in IT processes such as the commissioning of a new system. Whenever a new or changed application goes into operation, the documentation is revised.

The technical landscape model tends also to be updated annually. Like the application landscape model, this is framed by IT strategy development. However, changes can also be made between times, the driver here is the technical standardisation. The operating infrastructure is defined in operational-level IT management in alignment with these planning cycles.

The differences in these update times can easily lead to inconsistencies in the overall landscape model. For instance, the process documentation might reference applications which are no longer in productive operation. The tighter the links between the various landscape models is, the greater the danger of inconsistencies.

Useful hints:

- Consider the questions you wish to resolve with the enterprise architecture, and decide on this basis how up-to-date the various elements of the architecture will have to be.

  For example: if you want to be able to find out at any time which applications support which processes, you will have to take steps to ensure the relationships between business processes and applications are updated following every modification.
- Put appropriate organisational mechanisms in place to ensure information will be as up-to-date as you need. This means codifying roles and responsibilities, as well as maintenance and update processes which are integrated into IT and decision-making processes. Guidelines are provided in Chapter 4.
- When mapping out your enterprise architecture, ensure that landscape model elements which have lifecycles of different lengths are connected as loosely as possible. This is essential to keep the overall landscape model adequately consistent after each update and maintenance operation.

In deciding on the right level in a granularity, you should strike a balance between fine granularity and abstraction (see [Nie05]). IT landscape management does not require finely detailed information. Quite the opposite: if you amass excessive detail you will not be able to see the wood for the trees!

Examples of excessively granular information are the detailed activities of business processes, attributes and signatures of business objects, detailed network topologies, hardware elements such as routers and cluster configurations, detailed controlled flows or UML class diagrams.

The effort for keeping such information up-to-date and consistent far outweighs the benefits. If you just consider the effort for making a detailed process description or documenting an application, it is clear what time you would have to invest to record this information and – more to the point – complete the matching processes to ensure its consistency. Nor is this a one-off job. This information with all its relationships, typically maintained and updated by different individuals in different processes, has to be kept up-to-date and consistent all the time.

Hitting on the right level of abstraction and the appropriate strategic or operational direction is somewhat of a challenge. You should try to refine the information to a level where you are not just using empty phrases or container terms. However you should not drill down any deeper than this.

Useful hint: stick to what you need and what you know!

You should limit yourself to the information which is genuinely essential to answer specific areas of concern you have identified. Omit any other issues and concerns which have not yet been finalised – that means leaving out the "nice-to-have" information which you could possibly need at some point in the future! It is not until an area of concern has really been finalised that you will know precisely what information is required to clarify questions. For the time being, you can save yourself the non-essential effort, and most importantly limit the volume of data that you will need to keep up-to-date.

Finding the right strategic and operative orientation is essential for answering questions in your areas of concern in the context of managing the IT landscape. Guidelines on this are provided in Chapter 4.

You have to strike a balance between abstraction and detail. Modelling has to remain manageable, and at the same time be meaningful enough to deliver answers to the questions your enterprise is likely to want to ask. A key factor is the ease of maintenance of the information base. The more detail there is, the greater the need for ongoing maintenance and updates. Always weigh up the expected benefit in terms of the effort it will entail. Examples are provided in Sect. 2.1.

Fact file:

- In the best-practice architecture we differentiate between the business, application, technology and infrastructure architectures.
- The interaction between these architectures renders transparent the inter-dependencies and connections that exist between business and IT.
- It is key to have data which is as **complete** and **up-to-date** as necessary and has the **right level of granularity**. You need to retain a big-picture view of the landscape; on the other hand the landscape model must have enough detail to really deliver answers to the questions and issues which are of interest in your enterprise. Guidelines are provided in Chapter 4.

3.3.2 Constituents of Best-Practice Enterprise Architecture

We now examine the various constituents of the best-practice enterprise architecture in greater detail. Of course, it takes more than structures and datasets to accomplish the goals you have in mind with the rollout of an enterprise architecture. The real benefit derives from pulling the data together in an appropriate form – usually visualised in graphic presentations – for target audiences. The sections that follow therefore also recommend suitable diagrams as well as describing structures.

Important:

From the structures and diagrams recommended, choose those which are most appropriate for your areas of concern. Guidelines for making a selection are provided in the following sections.

3.3.2.1 Business Landscape Model

The business landscape model comprises all the structures and relationships which are essential for the business. You can use the business landscape model to address the following questions:

- Which business processes, products or business functions differentiate the company from its competitors? Which are critical for the company or for a particular environment in which it operates?

- Which organisational structures (e.g. sales structures, locations, plants or logical user groups) are relevant for the business? Which products, business processes or business functions are assigned to which business units?
- Which business process is responsible (in terms of business content) for which business objects?
- Which business objects are used in which manner (reading, creating, modifying, deleting or simply using) or as input or output by which business processes or business functions?
- Which relationships exist between the business objects? Are business objects part of others, or are they related in a different way? What do the life cycles[3] of business objects look like?
- Which business segment is the data owner, e.g. for customer or product data?
- What need for action and potential for optimisation exist at present?
- What are the business goals? How are they to be accomplished?
- How is the business changing in which business segment? Which products, business processes or functionality will be needed in future?

Building Blocks

The following building blocks – elements of landscape models – are required to answer such questions:

- **Business processes**: A business process is a sequence of logically connected activities or sub-processes that contributes in some way to the enterprise's value-added. Each process has a defined start and end, is as a rule recurring and is expressed in terms of performing some action for customers.
- **Business functions**: A business function is a distinct, cohesive set of business functionality such as "customer relationship management". The enterprise's capabilities are expressed in terms of the business functions it carries out. Business functions can be organised into sub-functions and have defined relationships with the other building blocks of the business landscape model.
- **Products**: A product is the outcome or deliverable of an enterprise's service process. Products can be either material (e.g. goods such as cars or computers) or immaterial (services) and can consist of sub-products.
- **Business units**: A business unit is either a logical or structural unit of the enterprise such as a plant or factory, or a logical user groups such as "field sales service" or "internal staff". Business units can be organised into sub-units, for instance the unit "location A" can have sub-units which include the field sales service attached to location A.

---

[3]States and their transitions.

- **Business objects**: A business object represents a real-world entity – abstract or concrete – which encapsulates some part of the business activity of an enterprise (customers, for example, products or orders). Business objects can be associated with one another by relationships. An "order" can be decomposed into sub-objects such as "order header" and "order content". A customer can have a "creates" relationship with an order and an order can have a "uses" relationship with products. The specific data, also termed information objects, of an application can have a logical reference to a business object. For example, an application can be the master for customer numbers and names and exchange this information with other applications via its interfaces.

  The management of business objects straddles both the business and IT territories. In business terms, information landscape modelling entails defining a shared language and associations in order to create a basis for communication between business and IT. Additionally, information modelling documents which business objects are used in what manner by which business processes and applications. This creates clear, transparent connections between the business and IT.

  These interrelationships are particularly relevant in master data management. By reducing and consolidating master data, the enterprise can achieve substantial cost savings.

Dependencies can exist between the business landscape elements. For example, a business unit might be responsible for the business object "customer" and maintain customer data as part of the "customer management" business process. Another business unit might enter "visitor reports" as part of the same "customer management" business process.

Useful hints for deriving your business architecture:

"Cherry-pick" the elements of the best-practice architecture you really need to answer the questions which are of interest to you. Here are a few pointers for making the selection:

- Use just products or just business processes.
  The choice will depend on the industry in which you operate. Industries such as banking and insurance will tend to be more product-oriented; manufacturing companies will be more process-oriented.
- Use business functions if your enterprise organisation changes frequently or is not yet decided, e.g. if you are in the midst of a restructuring or merger. The business functions can then be considered as being equivalent to the capabilities of the enterprise (see [Ost03]). Once the structure has firmed up, you can add other blocks such as business processes to describe the interdependencies in the business.

- Use business objects as a glossary, building a common understanding among stakeholders of what the objects mean. However, you should limit the number of business objects to approximately 20. When you are first venturing into Enterprise Architecture Management, do not document the relationships between the business objects, since each relationship will push up the complexity of the overall model.
- Do not use the organisational units in your enterprise as business units. Otherwise you will have to map each organisational change into the model later down the road. Use logical user groups instead. Examples are provided in Sect. 4.5.
- Where possible, avoid modelling dependencies between building blocks in terms of business content. Each block and each relationship pushes up the effort for maintaining the architecture and ensuring consistency.

Business-type (functional) building blocks are generally described with differing granularity. Business processes, for example, are described in business process modelling very generally, in terms of links in the value chain – for example, procurement, production and sales processes. Elsewhere, business processes can be broken down to the level of individual activities, which are often modelled as EPCs (see [Sch01]). The activities in the EPC may also use fine-grained business functions.

Which level of granularity is appropriate for each block will depend on the questions you need to address. Define the number of modelling levels, and the semantics at each level, for each building block in the business architecture.

Useful hints for defining granularity:

- Model all business building blocks with a granularity as coarse as possible. This enables you to maintain an overview, and the effort for maintaining the data and ensuring consistency remains manageable.
- From the viewpoint of Enterprise Architecture Management, business processes should be modelled on value-chain level. In practice, two or no more than three modelling levels have proven viable.

  In process management, it is customary to model down to the level of individual activities, since the sequences and particularly the checkpoints are of major significance for compliance requirements. Guidelines for process modelling can be found in [Sch01], [Ber03-1], [Ber03-2] and [Ost03].
- Like business processes, business units should be documented in two or no more than three modelling levels. A sales level, for example, can be refined by defining its logical user groups.

- When you first start working with EAM, you should not refine products, business functions or business objects at all. Start by modelling flat lists. You can then pick up experience without investing too much time and effort up front, and build more detail into your model later.

Graphical Presentation

The following types of diagrams are particularly appropriate for mapping information pertaining to your areas of concern:

- **Business conceptual model** for presenting the relationships between business objects (see [Sek05] and [Sch01]).
- **Business cluster diagrams** for presenting products (for the product map, see [Mat04-1] and [Mat04-2]), business processes (process map, see Fig. 3.6) or business functions (function map see Fig. 3.7).
- **Business landscape diagram** for presenting business/functional dependencies between three building blocks, such as assignments of business functions to business processes and business units (see Fig. 3.8).
- **Mapping table** for presenting the functional dependencies between two building blocks, such as the assignments of business objects to business processes (see Fig. 3.9).

These graphics are illustrated in the following by examples. A conceptual model describes the relationships between business objects, e.g. in UML. For examples of conceptual models please refer to the relevant literature (see [Sch01]).

Just two types of business landscape elements are used in **business cluster diagrams**. Figure 3.6 represents a process map as a cluster diagram. Business processes on the value-chain level create the "umbrella" clusters, each of which contains a set of sub-processes. For example, the sub-process "sales planning" is assigned to its parent process, "sales and marketing".

Important:

In general, a single business cluster diagram will do for the entire enterprise. The diagram shows an agreed summary of business functionality present in the enterprise. In many cases, business objectives or strategies are defined for the applications which support the items in each cluster. A case in point: it is possible to specify for each cluster whether it is a differentiator or is subject to stringent SLA requirements.

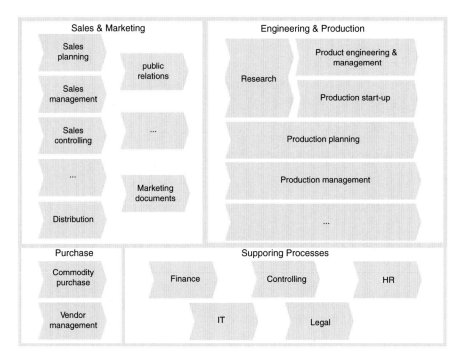

Fig. 3.6 Example of a process map

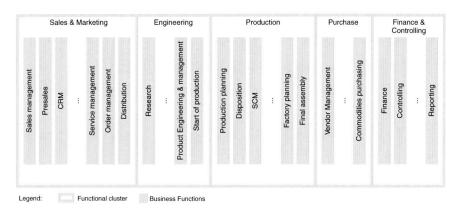

Fig. 3.7 Example of a business cluster diagram

In Fig. 3.7, as in the preceding figure, the business processes on value-chain level are used as cluster categories. Individual business functions are then organised into these clusters – e.g. the "sales management" business function is placed in the "sales and marketing" process cluster.

It is equally possible to use other business-type categorisations, termed business domains. The business landscape model can then be structured according to these domains (see Fig. 3.8).

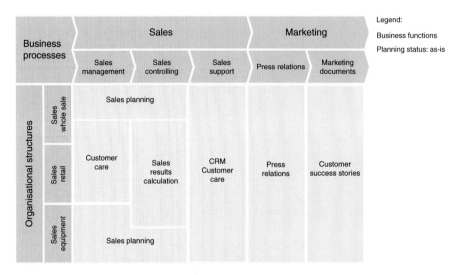

Fig. 3.8 Example of a business landscape diagram

A **business landscape diagram** is a tool for presenting the business dependencies between three types of building blocks. Two blocks are assigned to the two axes of the model, and a third block is assigned to the cells of the matrix. In Fig. 3.8, the business functions are assigned to business processes along the *x*-axis, and to business units along the *y*-axis.

To pick an example from the diagram, the business function "sales planning" is used by both the "sales wholesale" and "sales equipment" organisational structures. The business function "customer care", on the other hand is used only by "sales retail".

All the blocks in the business landscape model can be used in a business landscape diagram as axes of the diagram and as elements to populate the diagram. However, not all combinations will be of relevance or value for providing answers to your areas of concern. The following combinations are common:

- Business processes and business units as the axes, and business functions as the filler elements.

    This enables you to answer questions such as: which business functions are used by which business units in which business processes?
- Business processes and business units as axes, and business objects as filler elements.

    This enables you to answer questions such as: which business objects are used by which business units in which business processes?

- Products and business units as axes, and business functions as the filler elements.
  This enables you to answer questions such as: which business functions are used by which business units in which products?
- Business processes and business objects as the axes and business functions as the filler elements.
  This enables you to answer questions such as: which business functions use which business objects in which business processes?
- Business objects and business units and business functions as filler elements.
  This enables you to answer questions such as: which business objects are used by which business functions by which business units?

Mapping tables (see Fig. 3.9) are a useful tool for presenting functional-type dependencies between two building blocks. This mapping table serves to assign business objects to business processes. The mnemonic "CRUD" summarises the ways in which business objects are used in business processes. For example, the business object "sales order" in the "disposition" business process is "Read" only (R). The business object "production order", on the other hand, is either created (C), updated (U) or deleted (D) in the business process "disposition".

Fig. 3.9 Example of mapping table

Business objects		Business processes: BP1 Disposition	BP2 Production management	BP3 Factory planning	BP4 Resource planning	...
Sales order	BO1	R				
Production order	BO2	CUD	CUD	R		
Factory order	BO3			CUD	R	
Stock location	BO4	R	R	R		
Goods receipt doc.	BO5			R		
Storekeeper	BO6				R	
...	...					

CUD Create, Update, Delete
R Read

The assignments can also be made simply by check-marking the relevant cells of the matrix. It is also possible to differentiate between "inputs" and "outputs" of business processes.

All types of diagram and mapping table also permit you to use colour coding to highlight particular aspects, such as competitive differentiation, criticality or process maturity.

Important:

Choose the diagrams which are most appropriate to resolve your questions. Guidelines are provided in Sect. 3.6.

3.3.2.2 Application Landscape Model

The application landscape model describes the application landscape and acts as a link which ties together the business landscape model and the technical and infrastructure models. The application landscape model is documented and designed as part of IT landscape management (see Chapter 4). It enables you to answer questions such as:

- Which applications are there, and which are important for the core business?
- What strategy contribution and value contribution does each application make? Which business segments does it support? Which customer groups does it address?
- Which business processes, products or business functions are supported by which application? Which business units use which application for which business process or business function?
- Which applications depend on which other applications? What interfaces are there? What data is exchanged via these interfaces?
- What are the requirements in terms of business quality, e.g. fulfilment of function, degree of maturity, availability, reliability, performance, ergonomics, future sustainability and flexibility?
- What sort of technical quality do the applications have? What is the expected service life of the applications? At what phase in their life cycle are they? What about ease of maintenance, customisability and integration ability?
- Which data can be assigned to the applications? How is the data used by the applications – does the application read, create, modify, delete or simply use the data?
- How is the application or interface implemented in technical terms? Do the implementations comply with the enterprise's standards?
- What about the lifecycle of the applications, interfaces and data?
- What will an application landscape look like, in functional and technical terms, in year X?

Building Blocks

The following building blocks and their relationships with other landscape models are required to answer such questions:

- **Applications**: An application is a cohesive entity which users perceive as a technical and functional unit (see [Sie02]). In general it supports associated business functions which are logically and technically distinct from other functions.

- **Interfaces**: An interface defines a dependency between two applications. Some interfaces are one-way, others permit two-way communication. They can take the form of information flows or control flows. In the context of IT landscape management (see Chapter 4), the term "interface" is taken to mean an information flow between applications.
- **Information objects**: Information objects are artefacts specific to applications. They can be used by applications in different ways (e.g. "CRUD") and are transported via interfaces. They have relations with business objects which represent the overarching business artefacts agreed in conceptual design. Information objects can have relationships with other information objects. For example, an information object can be part of another information object, as is the case with address data, which is part of customer data.

Important:

In general, information objects differ from business objects in terms of their content. Ultimately, the business objects derive from the language of the business, whereas information objects are described in the language of the application manager or in the language of the bought-in software (e.g. SAP).

Maintaining information objects, particularly ensuring that their assignments to business objects are kept up-to-date, is a time-consuming process.

Useful hint:

When you first embark upon IT landscape management, do not make a differentiation between business objects and information objects. Instead use a common list of terms. For the time being, you can save yourself the effort, and build up your experience with information landscape management. You can add more detail later.

The relationships between application landscape model and the other models are key to rendering explicit the interdependencies and connections between business and IT and showing the knock-on effects of ideas and changes. The relationships forge a link between the business and IT structures, or rather between the logical and physical IT structures. The required relationships are described in detail in Sect. 4.3.2.

Like the building blocks in the business landscape model, the blocks in the application model can be described at varying levels of granularity. The most appropriate granularity for each will depend on the nature of the questions you are looking to answer. Define the number of modelling levels, and the semantics at each level, for each building block.

Useful hints for defining granularity:

- Applications can be modelled with various levels of granularity. As a rule, however, no more than two hierarchy levels should be used. With two levels, an application can consist of one or more other applications or services which, in turn, use other applications. Guidelines on choosing the right granularity are provided in Sect. 4.4.1.
- When you first start working with EAM, you should not refine interfaces or business objects at all. Start by modelling flat lists. You can then pick up experience without investing too much time and effort up front, and build more detail into your model later.
- When mapping relationships between the application landscape model and other models, you need to decide the level of granularity at which you will define the connections – for instance, whether you are going to assign applications to business processes at the value-chain level or drill deeper into the hierarchy and make the assignments at the level of individual activities (see Sect. 4.4.1).

Graphical Presentation

The following types of diagrams are particularly appropriate for mapping information pertaining to your areas of concern:

- **Landscape diagram** for presenting dependencies between three blocks of the model, e.g. assignments of applications to business processes and business units (see Figs. 3.10 and 3.11).
- **Information flow diagram** for presenting dependencies between applications and the business (logical) information flow (see Fig. 3.12).
- **Portfolio diagram** for an at-a-glance overview of the interdependencies (see Sect. 2.4.3).

Important:

Portfolios are an important tool for delivering an at-a-glance overview of relations. They can also be used for visualising application landscape models. Applications can be classified in the diagram by criteria such as potential benefit, cost, strategy contribution, value contribution and risk.

Portfolios can be used to map the as-is status of the landscape, its to-be or planned status or a combination, using criteria of your choice. They help organisations develop planning scenarios to roadmap development of the IT landscape.

Portfolios are now routinely used to provide input for decisions in strategic IT management and in project portfolio management. They have gained widespread acceptance among business managers, not least because they pull together salient information in concise form.

- **Master plan diagram** for presenting chronological dependencies of projects and also of applications and technical IT products (see Fig. 3.13).
- **Mapping table** for presenting dependencies between two building blocks of the model, such as the assignments of business objects to applications (as shown in Fig. 3.9).

These graphics are illustrated in the following by examples.

In the application landscape model, the **landscape diagram** is a valuable tool for presenting the dependencies that exist between three building blocks.

A landscape diagram is a snapshot presentation of part of the landscape model either for the entire enterprise or for some part of it, e.g. a business domain. The axes of the matrix represent items such as business processes or products and business units.

A landscape diagram can present the as-is status, or the to-be or planned status of the landscape. A to-be landscape diagram shows what the landscape will look like in the future. However, the diagram is equally valuable for documenting planning scenarios in readily comprehensible form. See Sect. 4.4.3 for more information.

The landscape diagram in Fig. 3.10 indicates which applications are assigned to which business processes and customer groups in the sales and marketing segment of the overall process flow. The x-axis shows the business processes and the y-axis the business units, expressed as customer groups.

The x-axis and y-axis create a frame into which you can organise the applications. The following frames are commonly used:

- Business processes and business units: This enables you to answer questions such as: which business unit uses which application for which business process?
- Products and business units: This enables you to answer questions such as: which business unit uses which application for which product?
- Business processes and business objects: This enables you to answer questions such as: which business object is used by which application for which business process?
- Business objects and business units: This enables you to answer questions such as: which business object is used by which application in which business unit?

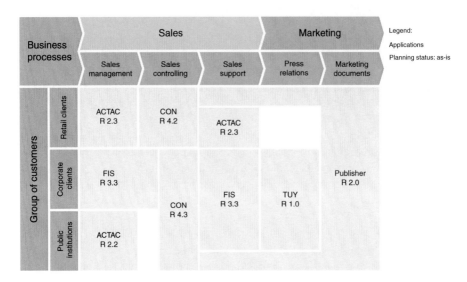

Fig. 3.10 Example landscape diagram

Important:

The associations between business structures and IT structures must be modelled with the appropriate level of granularity. To give an example, applications should only be assigned to business processes at a level above the EPC level. This maintains clarity in the documentation and keeps within manageable proportions the effort for keeping data up-to-date and consistent. Plus, given that documentation on EPC level is generally produced by function specialists without a direct IT focus, it is questionable whether assignments on this level will be of any practical value.

The associations between the application landscape model and technical and infrastructure landscape models make the technical interdependencies between these models transparent. All the diagrams already discussed can be used to present these relationships. However, the most common is the **technical landscape diagram**, as shown in Fig. 3.11.

A technical landscape diagram, as shown in Fig. 3.11, typically uses the x-axis as "drawer"-type holders for the technical components, also termed architectural domains, and the y-axis for the applications. The technical realisation of a given application is then described along a horizontal row by indicating which technical standards from the various "drawers" are used to implement it.

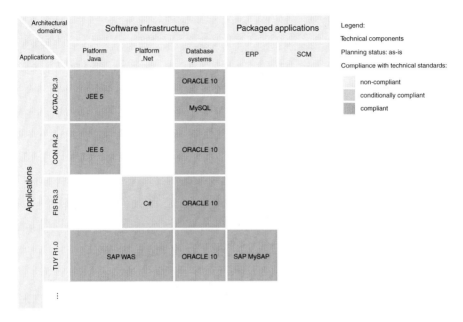

Fig. 3.11 Example of technical landscape diagram

An **information flow diagram** maps the dependencies between applications, their information objects and interfaces, and the functional (logical) information flow between (sub-) applications. The elements in an information flow diagram can also be organised into clusters reflecting the structuring. This type of diagram is then termed a cluster information flow diagram.

The information flow diagram in Fig. 3.12 shows applications, their information objects and interfaces, including the information flow for the business clusters "sales", "purchase", "dispatch" and "production".

The information flow between applications can be presented at varying levels of detail. In this example, applications APP1 and APP3 exchange the "delivery data" elements of the "customer" data via the interface from APP1 to APP3. It is also possible to denote the interface in greater detail. The type of edge used in the diagram, for example, denotes whether this is a manual or an automated interface.

The **master plan diagram** presents a concise overview of chronological dependencies between projects (or between applications or technical IT products). As well as the project runtime, the diagram also shows the status of each project.

It is possible to enrich the diagram with other information, possibly mapping the dependencies between projects and applications. The life cycle of the applications which are rolled out, modified or decommissioned over the course of the project can be presented as data associated with a particular project.

All types of diagram and mapping table also permit you to use colour coding to highlight particular aspects, such as strategy contribution or value contribution, state of health or life cycle status. Examples are provided in Sect. 4.4.2.

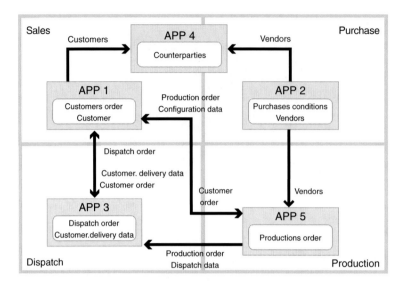

Fig. 3.12   Example of a cluster information flow diagram

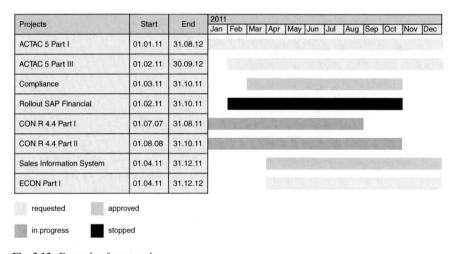

requested   approved

in progress   stopped

Fig. 3.13   Example of master plan

Important:

Choose the diagrams which are most appropriate to resolve your questions.
Guidelines are provided in Sect. 3.6.

3.3.2.3 Technical Landscape Model

The technical landscape model defines the technical standards specific to your enterprise for implementing applications, interfaces and parts of the operating infrastructure. A technical landscape model can comprise technologies, reference architectures and architecture templates, bought-in IT products, tools for software engineering and system management, and IT components such as frameworks. The building blocks in the model can be organised into architectural domains (see Chapter 5).

The technical landscape model helps you answer the following questions:

- Which IT products, middleware solutions and databases have been defined by IT as standards?
- Which release or standardisation status do the various technical standards have?
- What sort of lifecycle do the technical standards have?
- What tools are used in IT for software engineering and system management?
- What trends can be identified on the IT market regarding technical standards?

As well as mapping tables, cluster landscape diagrams and technical landscape diagrams are particularly suitable for presenting the technical landscape model (see Sect. 5.3).

All types of diagram and mapping table also permit you to use colour coding to highlight particular aspects, such as the degree of standardisation, future sustainability or state of health. Examples are provided in Section 5.3.

3.3.2.4 Infrastructure Landscape Model

The infrastructure landscape model describes the infrastructure elements on which the applications are run. The model has a coarse granularity. It forges the connections with the infrastructure elements in operational-level IT management. The links with the technical landscape model enable you to identify technical objectives and the degree of standardisation of the operating infrastructure.

Important:

The elements of the infrastructure landscape model must be consistent with the real-life operating infrastructure – in other words relationships must be refined down to the level of individual units of hardware, software, environment and services as stored in a Configuration Management Database (CMDB) (see [itS08] and [Joh07]).

Recommendation:

Define the associations between the high-level elements in the infrastructure
landscape model and the real-life operating infrastructure in service management by making definitions in a CMDB. Service management is the only
entity which has the requisite knowledge about these associations.

The infrastructure landscape model enables you to answer the following questions:

- Which infrastructure elements have which service levels?
- Which infrastructure elements are offered at which locations?
- Which infrastructure elements are implemented now or will be in the future by
  which technical components with which degree of standardisation?
- What consolidation opportunities are there regarding the shared use of infrastructure, taking into account aspects such as performance, security and maintenance
  windows?

   The key means for visualising infrastructure landscape models are topology diagrams and technical landscape diagrams (see [Haf04] and [Buc07]). In technical
landscape diagrams, the locations are frequently arranged along the y-axis. The
x-axis shows the infrastructure standards, where appropriate grouped according
to operating structures such as server platforms. Another way to present relationships with other elements, e.g. with technical standards, is to use mapping
tables.
   All types of diagram and mapping table also permit you to use colour coding to
highlight particular aspects, such as service level or cost.

Fact file:

- The main components of the best-practice enterprise architecture are the
  business, application, technical and infrastructure landscape models.
- Each model illuminates particular questions from a specific perspective.
- It is essential to choose the right level of granularity for documenting the
  various landscape models and the associations between them. For further
  information, please refer to Sect. 4.4.2.
- Each landscape model has its own particular types of diagram – e.g. cluster
  diagrams or landscape diagrams – which are of relevance for answering
  questions.
- Make use of the guidelines in Sect. 4.4.2 for deriving your specific
  enterprise architecture.

3.3.3 Landscape Planning Status

The landscape models can document both the as-is and to-be status of the landscape planning status, as well as interim stages along the trajectory. This enables you to describe the salient elements of the current or future business model and how they interrelate.

The level of detail in the landscape model diminishes along the trajectory from the as-is landscape, through planned, to the to-be landscape, i.e. from today through the foreseeable future and into the remote future. In each landscape model, we differentiate between the as-is, planned and to-be status (see Fig. 3.14).

- **As-is landscape model– the reality today**

  What does the current IT landscape look like, where is action needed, and where is there potential for improvement?

  The as-is model describes the current productive status of the landscape. For instance, it comprises all the applications which are in productive operation, or all current valid business processes and technical standards.

- **Planned landscape– the foreseeable and already planned future**

  What does the roadmap look like for progressing toward the to-be status, and how can it be implemented?

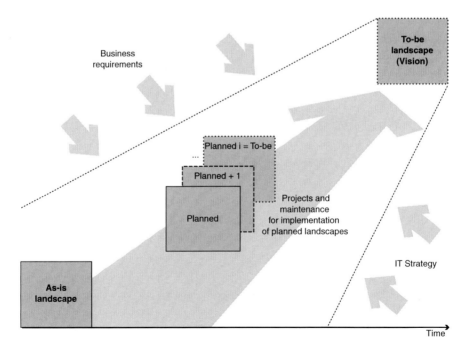

Fig. 3.14   As-is, planned and to be landscape

A planned landscape model documents the specific plans for the landscape at a particular point in the future. Frequently the plans are produced with annual time horizons. A planned landscape model describes one step on the trajectory from the as-is model to the to-be landscape model, or one step between two planned landscape models. In medium-term planning, you will typically map out the target landscape model for an extended period of time, but not too far into the future. A horizon of three to no more than 5 years is customary. Accordingly, medium-term planning is a milestone on the road to the to-be landscape model.

It is possible for multiple planning scenarios to exist simultaneously. Each of these scenarios will represent one possible route to the to-be status of the landscape, and serves as input for business decisions.

- **To-be landscape– a vision of the future landscape which stakes out the general trajectory for implementation**
What is the future vision of the IT landscape which you have derived from the business goals?

The to-be landscape is the vision for the future, the target status in which the business and its goals will be implemented. It is documented either without any statement on times and schedules, or, if times are included, they are in specific steps, e.g. 2012 and 2015.

The to-be landscape is the optimal landscape. Implementation is uncertain, because parameters, constraints and business requirements can easily change over time. What the to-be landscape does is stake out a general direction: it creates an authoritative scope – or "guiderails" – within which the enterprise moves towards implementing the landscape. The to-be landscape is where we find general strategic statements such as which technologies to use (e.g. .Net), which manufacturers (e.g. IBM) or IT products without version numbers, e.g. SAP for logistics processes.

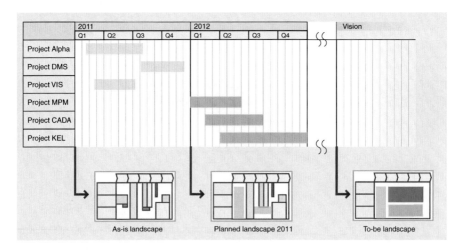

Fig. 3.15 Example of implementation planning

Alongside the strategic goals, the existing landscape model, including definitions on required action on strategic and operational levels, is a key input for deciding on the to-be landscape model. This model can be defined either for the entire enterprise, or individually for each business segment.

Implementation planning can be presented with the help of a master plan or a sequence of landscape diagrams. Figure 3.15 shows an implementation plan which maps the planned projects such as "project alpha". Using annual timeframes, the planning is presented on a master plan diagram, and the deliverables in each case are presented in a landscape diagram.

Useful hints:

- When documenting your landscape model, take care to consider the planning status. Take steps to ensure that the building blocks of the landscape model presented in a diagram are all valid concurrently.

A word of caution: when stocktaking the IT landscape, there is often a tendency to include planned projects in the as-is landscape.

- Document the as-is landscape model in detail, and describe the planned and to-be models at a rather higher level, since correspondingly less knowledge will be available on these two future states. When defining the planned and to-be landscapes, be sure to include only pre-agreed planning that has already been signed off. Otherwise you will find it difficult to maintain consistent and meaningful documentation over time.

3.4 Business Landscape Management

Business landscape management is a key part of Enterprise Architecture Management. The latter is concerned with documenting, analysing, planning and directing the evolutionary development of the landscape as a whole. Business landscape management, on the other hand, is concerned with managing the business-specific parts of the enterprise architecture. It also acts as an umbrella function for the management of the IT landscape, enabling it also to oversee the IT parts of the enterprise architecture. Managing the IT landscape, in turn, consists largely of IT landscape management and technical standardisation. Details on IT landscape management are provided in Chapter 4, and on technical standardisation in Chapter 5.

Business landscape management entails aligning the business processes, products and organisation of the company towards accomplishing the corporate goals.

Important:

The assignments of applications to business processes, products, business functions, business objects and business units create the visible associations between business requirements and corporate goals on the one side and the IT landscape on the other. Accordingly, the business landscape model creates the framework for managing and directing IT in terms of business goals.

Business landscape management is often mentioned in the same breath as process management. Often though, the process landscape in enterprises resembles more of a patchwork quilt, and documentation is inconsistent. Business process modelling tends to go no further than the current processes. The drivers for process modelling tend to be initiatives such as business process re-engineering, the need to fulfil compliance requirements, or obtain quality management certification such as TQM or ISO-900x. Companies might also use business process modelling as a way to identify which processes they can automate or have controlled by a workflow engine (see [Ost03], [Fis08] and [Fel08] for more information).

By way of contrast, business landscape management has a much broader scope. It frames the design of the current and future business landscape, consisting of business-type building blocks: business processes, business functions, products, business units and business objects.

The important aspects in business landscape management are:

- The structures of the business landscape model
- The roles and processes in business landscape management, and how these are integrated into the organisation.

We are now going to examine these in greater detail.

Structures of Business Landscape Management

Figure 3.16 shows the relationships of the building blocks in the best-practice enterprise architecture discussed in Sect. 3.3. For details on the notation, please refer to Sect. 4.3.1.

All the building blocks in the business landscape model can be linked by means of relationships. For example, each business object can be assigned to the business processes which handle it. The assignments can be elaborated, as indicated by the asterisk * for "extension" in the business assignment. One example of such an extension is information on how a business object is used in the business process, e.g. as input or output. An "order", for example, can be an "output" of the business process "order processing".

It is also possible to place further constraints on the business-type association which exists between building blocks. This is illustrated by the business landscape diagrams (see Fig. 3.8).

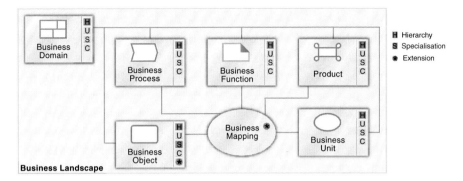

Fig. 3.16   Example metal model of the business landscape

The business-type building blocks can be clustered by organising them into business domains. Business processes, products, business functions, business units and business objects can all serve as categories for clustering. Accordingly, all business building blocks are associated with the "business domain" in Fig.3.16.

The letters at the edge of the building block symbols indicate the relationships between instances of blocks in this particular class. "Is part of" relationships are labelled "H" for hierarchy, and "specialisation" relationships have "S". Business processes can consist of sub-processes (a hierarchy relationship). Products, business functions and business units can be refined along similar lines.

Business objects can consist of sub-objects and may also be in a specialisation relationship with other business objects. To give an example, an order can consist of delivery information and payment information (hierarchy relationship). However, we might also need to differentiate between "domestic orders" and "international orders". This is a specialisation relationship. In addition, business objects can be associated by a wide variety of other relationships such as "is used by". This is indicated by an asterisk and is often described by means of a business object model (see [Sek05] and [Sch01]).

Important for business object model:

- There must be unique and comprehensible descriptions of the semantics of each type of relationship.
- Take care to restrict the number of relationship types. The more types you use, the greater the update effort and the greater the risk of inconsistency. Before introducing each type of relationship, you should carefully weigh up the effort and benefits.

Roles and Processes in Business Landscape Management

The key role is that of the business enterprise architect, who is responsible for documenting, analysing and designing the business processes, business functions, products, business units and business objects and the interactions between them.

> **Important:**
>
> You can split the business enterprise architect role into a number of sub-roles to match the scenario in your company, and have several individuals occupying the role. However, take care not to have so many people that coordination becomes a problem. Many enterprises find it works to split the role into a process architect and information architect.

A key process in business landscape management is process management. This commonly involves documenting business processes and their interactions with organisational structures, applications and business objects as EPCs using tools such as ARIS. The focus is on documenting workflows and highlighting risks and checkpoints.

For information on subsequent processes, refer to Sect. 4.4 and the relevant literature already mentioned.

> **Important:**
>
> Be sure to embed the business landscape management processes in your organisation. Their effectiveness hinges on having clearly delineated responsibilities, with integration into IT organisation and decision-making processes. This is the only way to ensure landscape data is adequately up-to-date, complete and of high enough quality.

Also key for managing the IT landscape are business reference models which serve as touchpoints for defining associations with IT structures. This aspect is discussed in the following, illustrated by various examples.

Business Reference Models

Reference models provide an enterprise – or a class of enterprises such as an entire industry – with a recommendation for structuring. The telecommunications industry has eTOM, for example. TOGAF is also a reference model, as are ITIL and Cobit (see [Ber03-1] or [Joh07]).

A business reference model gives recommendations for structuring business processes or business functions along appropriate business-based lines. Before being introduced, a reference model generally has to be adapted to the company's specific business requirements and environmental parameters. In general cluster diagrams are used to present the model (see Fig. 3.7).

How does one define an enterprise-specific business reference model if there is no standard model to apply?

Structuring can follow a range of criteria. What has been shown to work in practice is the use of elements of the business landscape model as a basis. Often, products or core business processes are used as the overarching structural criteria. In banking and insurance, organisations will typically choose product-oriented structuring; manufacturing companies will tend to use process-oriented or functional structuring. However it is equally possible to choose other elements of the business landscape model.

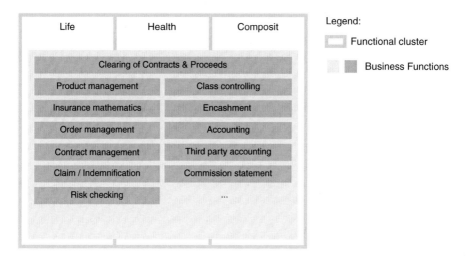

Fig. 3.17 Part of a business reference model from the insurance industry

Figure 3.17 shows part of the business reference model from the insurance industry. This industry structures its business along product lines. The products "life", "health" and "composite" each comprise the same business functions, so these are shown overlaying the diagram.

Accordingly, the top level of the structure and also substructure levels chiefly contain business processes, products, business functions and business objects, but also business units such as user groups, locations or plans.

Business functions, business objects or general corporate functions are often included in the root structuring levels alongside business processes and products. Business objects which can feasibly be included at this level are partner management or contact management. Supporting processes, business functions such as HR

or management-level processes such as risk management are all overarching functions in the enterprise and can thus merit inclusion as structural criteria. Figures 3.18
and 3.19 give a few examples.

In Fig. 3.18, the top-level structuring comprises products and the business data
processes that cut right across the company, including partner management, general

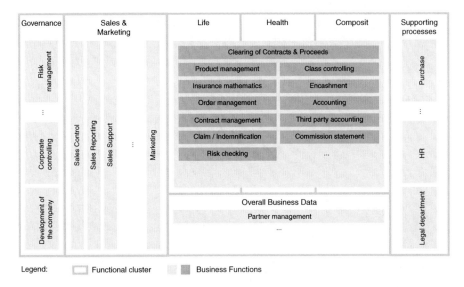

Fig. 3.18 Example of reference model from the insurance industry

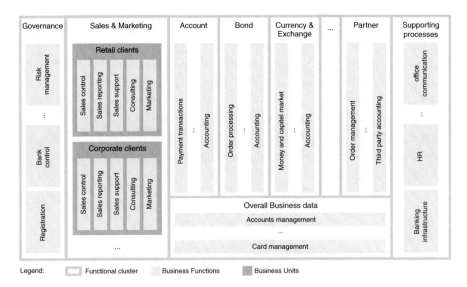

Fig. 3.19 Example of reference model from the banking industry

functions in sales and marketing, management and supporting processes such as risk management or HR.

The reference model from the banking industry in Fig. 3.19 is structured along similar lines.

Figure 3.20 presents a reference model used in the automotive industry. This is organised largely around the core business processes on value-chain level. Other examples illustrating these models can be found in literature such as [Die06].

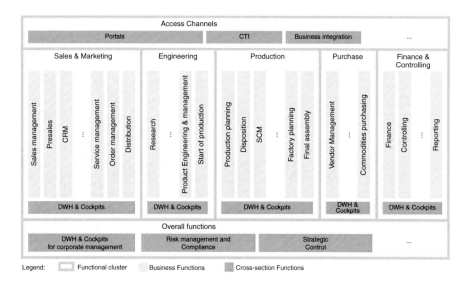

Fig. 3.20 Example of reference model from the automotive industry

When it comes to refining the details, you can use other aspects of these business building blocks, such as customer groups (private customers, corporate customers, private investors and institutions), access channels (self-service, call centre, sales and branches) or locations and plants. The resulting categories can themselves then be refined according to criteria of your choice. For instance, account products can be refined by access channels as shown above into self-service, call-centre service, or branch account products. It might also be feasible to use these aspects for the main structuring.

Figure 3.20 shows the sales and marketing activities organised by relevant customer groups. This structure largely corresponds to the organisational structure.

Here are the steps for defining the business reference model in summary:

1. Define your main structural criterion.
   Choose either business processes or products, or other elements of the business landscape model.

Important:

Take care to arrange building blocks correctly in the matrix. The business blocks should only be organised into one "drawer"!

2. Enrich this structure with functions and business objects which cut across the business.
3. Refine the business reference model using the business aspects which are of importance for you – for example, you can model customer groups, access channels, locations or plants.
4. Now you have assembled a set of potential criteria for the main level of business structuring and substructure, choose the criteria which are most appropriate for you. You may need to group some of the criteria or subdivide them further.
5. Arrange the selected structural elements into an overall structure which makes sense for your purpose. Aesthetic considerations also play a role. However the arrangement must primarily be designed with a view to responding to the relevant areas of concern your enterprise is likely to be enquiring into.

You can also define a business reference model for planning and controlling the development trajectory of the IT landscape. Applications and other IT building blocks can be assigned to appropriate business building blocks such as business processes or business functions in the cluster.

Such assignments enable you to create visible associations between the business objectives and the corresponding IT elements. It is also possible to define a different IT landscape development strategy for each of the clusters. Clustering also stakes out the general structural frame for the IT landscape. In many cases, this structure will be mapped to roles and responsibilities within the organisation. For instance, the building blocks of a particular cluster can be distributed between a number of enterprise architects. Each of these architects can then concentrate on the subject matter of their particular cluster.

For further information about business landscape management, please refer to [All05], [Ses07] and [Ahl06].

Useful hint:

If you do not have the requisite information to design business building blocks such as business processes, make an attempt to draft out the blocks and then refer your ideas to relevant entities in the company for discussion and approval. The basic setup can serve as a reference point for steering IT in alignment with the business. This is also an opportunity to produce landscape diagrams – you can demonstrate the power of the toolkit and help embed it in your organisation's resource sets.

Generally the basic setup is extended or restructured by business enterprise architects, the CEO, or the CEO's direct reports. The links with the applications then have to be revised by the IT enterprise architects in cooperation with the business enterprise architects. The result is an agreed reference model that stakes out the terms of the business. There are also benefits in communication: greater mutual understanding between stakeholders!

3.5 Views of the Enterprise Architecture

An enterprise architecture and EAM are not ends in themselves. But what benefit does EAM deliver to your enterprise? The benefit is largely qualitative. There are enormous savings opportunities, for example, achievable through improved business support, since it is easier to identify workflows which can be automated. EAM can also help pick out the points where there is potential for improvement. However such benefits are tricky to quantify, which hardly makes it easier to put forward a sound case for EAM in the company. To gather enough arguments to back your case for EAM, you have to work out which stakeholders will potentially benefit, and what their interests are.

Beneficiaries

Important:

Figure out which stakeholder groups in your enterprise can derive which benefits from EAM.

The beneficiaries might be individuals and entities tasked with implementing compliance and security requirements, business continuity management and/or enterprise risk management. Other examples of key stakeholder groups and the benefits they could expect through EAM are:

- Senior corporate management: Define corporate goals. Obtain information on the status of business operations and progress toward corporate goals.
- CIO and IT managers: Plan and direct IT in its interaction with the business, and monitor compliance with development trajectories. Identify need for action and potential for optimisation in the IT landscape.

- Project portfolio controllers: Render transparent the interdependencies and impacts of business and technical aspects in projects.
- IT strategists: Use analysis and planning toolkit for strategic evolution of the IT landscape.
- Project managers: Obtain easily identifiable drilldown points.
- Business managers: Put forward business requirements and monitor implementation. Identify need for action and potential for optimisation in the IT support of the business. Render transparent the impact and mutual dependencies of changes in the business and IT.
- Application managers: Simplify production of mandatory documentation and obtain valuable input for maintaining applications, e.g. interface information.
- Infrastructure architects: Render transparent the impact of changes in the business and application landscape. Use objectives and requirements from the business such as SLA requirements to frame and direct infrastructure planning.

Useful hint:

- You can identify the potential beneficiaries by conducting a stakeholder analysis. Good guidelines on this are provided in [Ker08].

Having identified the beneficiaries, the next step is to win some of them over to champion the EAM undertaking. You will need to conduct an intensive dialogue with the individuals concerned (see Sect. 4.5.4).

You then have to produce a cost-benefit analysis, which weighs your benefits and those of the other potential beneficiaries against the costs that would result. This is key to obtaining the go-ahead for EAM, championed by your sponsors, from your enterprise management. You can estimate the costs by analysing data procurement and EAM processes, and how they will be integrated into your organisation. Guidelines on this step of the process are provided in Sects. 4.4 and 4.5.

Useful hints:

- Illustrate benefits by presenting negative examples.
Negative examples from the past without EAM lend credence to your case – e.g. "How can we find out the answer to this particular question with the documentation we have right now?"
- Guidelines on identifying your benefit arguments are provided in Chapter 4.

When deriving your specific enterprise architecture, it is important to identify the objectives of all potentially relevant stakeholders, and find out what specific questions they are looking to have answered.

> **Important:**
>
> - EAM can only be rolled out successfully if you have champions with a securely embedded role in the company.
> - All the areas of concern of potentially relevant beneficiaries must be addressed by structures in the enterprise architecture and its diagrams.
> - It must be possible to obtain the information for answering these questions without undue effort – seen in terms of the resulting benefit.

Data procurement should be co-ordinated and overseen by enterprise architects. These individuals ensure that beneficiaries' questions can be answered. The architects pull together the requisite information from the various data sources along the process chains, check the data, and consolidate and enrich it as necessary.

As well as the beneficiaries, there are two other important stakeholder groups: the enterprise architects and the data providers (see Fig. 3.21). These individuals also each have their own perspective on the enterprise architecture. Let's look at this in more detail.

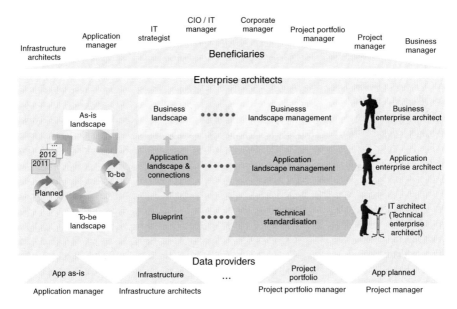

Fig. 3.21 Perspectives on the enterprise architecture

Enterprise Architects

Enterprise architects are tasked with documentation and analysis, strategic planning and control of one section of the current and future landscape model.

They have overall stewardship of one part of the landscape model. When detailed data is collected from sources right across the enterprise, it will inevitably vary in terms of quality, granularity and how up-to-date it is. It is the task of the enterprise architects to pull this data together, quality-assure and consolidate it.

All data must be available in adequate quality and granularity, and be adequately up-to-date (see Sect. 3.3.1). Building on this high-quality base of data, the enterprise architects can deliver answers to the various questions which the beneficiaries have, and scope out the future landscape model.

> **Important:**
>
> To take decisions based on solid evidence, the enterprise needs data which is up-to-date, complete and meaningful enough for the job. Consequently, architects need to be proactive in pulling in this data – which means prompting sources to deliver if necessary – and conducting ongoing quality assurance for the data supplied.

How many enterprise architects you appoint, and which roles you create, depends on the circumstances in your enterprise. Figure 3.21 differentiates between three types of architect:

- The IT architect or technical enterprise architect is responsible for technical landscape modelling (see Chapter 5).
- The application enterprise architect is responsible for application landscape modelling, and for the links between this and other landscape models (see Chapter 4).
- The business enterprise architect is responsible for the business landscape model, and liaises closely with other architects, in particular the application enterprise architect (see Sect. 3.4). The business enterprise architect often belongs to another part of the organisation, not IT.

In practice, though, medium-size companies will tend to have a single architect responsible for overall landscape modelling. Some companies might have an additional role, that of the information landscape architect. This individual is responsible for information landscape modelling, i.e. for the business objects and information objects from the business and application landscape models, the interaction between these building blocks and with the business and application landscape models. Enterprises with an information architect will often also have an information architecture or information landscape model as a separate sub-architecture or model.

Data Providers

This stakeholder group includes individuals such is application managers. Unlike the enterprise architects, who take an overall view of the business, application or technical landscapes, the data providers provide detailed data on individual building blocks such as applications. They deliver the detailed descriptions of applications and interfaces, including information such as manufacturer data or responsibilities. How your company schedules such data deliveries will depend very much on what sort of processes it operates, e.g. in project management, service management or project portfolio management. To give an example, interface information will not be available until the functional design phase of a project is complete, so you can link the delivery of this information with a milestone such as "function design handover".

Figure 3.21 shows common data providers and the data they provide. This is not an exhaustive list – there may also be other suppliers. Information such as SLA data, data on information security, IT products or services used in IT charging, or corresponding purchase lists might also have to be considered.

Important:

Everyone who provides data must if possible derive some benefit from this. Data delivery should also be made simple or even be automated.

- Data providers must deliver data which is adequately up-to-date and of sufficient quality to provide an adequate base of information for robust decision-making.
- Delivery of data must be made as simple as possible to minimise effort for the people who supply it. Good tool support is important here, to automate routine operations and provide import functionality.
- If you integrate data delivery into processes, notably in project management, commissioning and project portfolio processes, it is in your power to ensure data will be adequately up-to-date. You can define update checkpoints by means of milestones such as project initialisation and commissioning.
- Maintenance should follow the principles "as easy as possible", "as little as necessary" and "maintenance by the people who have the knowledge". This is the only way you can genuinely create a base of data for informed decision-making. If maintenance is well supported and restricted to genuinely essential data, the data providers can fulfil their documentation obligations with relatively little effort.
- At the same time, the data providers must themselves also have some benefit – such as simplified processes for documentation, or also the provision of information such as sections of the landscape model as input for projects or

maintenance measures. By providing information that demarcates a problem area, enabling people to more easily drill down into specific issues,
perceptible benefit can be created.

3.6 Guidelines for Personalisation of Best-Practice Enterprise Architecture in Practice

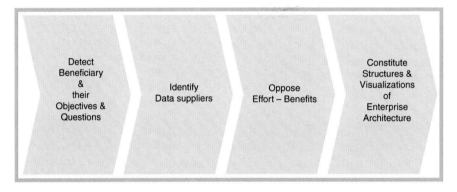

Fig. 3.22 Deriving your enterprise architecture

You have to describe structures in your enterprise architecture and select appropriate
diagrams for the goals and areas of concern you wish to address. On the basis of
the best-practice architecture, you can quickly derive an architecture appropriate
for your needs in a step-by-step process (see Fig. 3.22). The following steps are
required:

1. **Identify the relevant beneficiaries, and determine what their goals and areas
   of concern are**: Find out who your potential beneficiaries are. Often this will
   be the CIO or head of IT, senior management, IT strategists, project portfolio controllers, project managers, business managers, application managers,
   infrastructure architects, security representatives or risk managers.

   Find out what objectives these stakeholders have, what questions they are
   looking to answer, and reach a common conclusion on these findings with the
   stakeholders you have identified.

> **Useful hint:**
>
> Use the diagram examples to show how questions can be answered. This gives the various stakeholders a better idea of the possibilities and makes it easier to bring them on board for the EAM undertaking.

Guidelines for determining objectives and questions, and selecting suitable diagrams are provided in the download in Appendix D of [Han09].

2. **Identify the data providers for the information that will be required**: Determine what information will be required to find answers to the questions your stakeholders have. Identify the providers of this data and assess the effort for data procurement. Guidelines on appraising the effort, and examples of data providers in terms of IT landscape management, are provided in Sect. 4.1.1.

3. **Weigh effort for data procurement against the benefits**: Weigh up the effort for procuring the information required to answer questions against the expected benefit.

> **Useful hint:**
>
> It is often difficult to quantify the benefit. Often, just working out the effort will be enough to estimate whether a question is really important. For this reason you should confront the beneficiaries with the efforts that will be necessary to answer their questions. As a rule, following this, a certain number of the questions will vanish.

4. **Define your specific enterprise architecture**: For each landscape model, specify which building blocks and which relationships are relevant to you. For the remaining areas of concern, decide together with beneficiaries which diagrams will be appropriate for the questions. The best-practice enterprise architecture can provide guidelines (see Sect. 3.3).

Provided the data can be procured without undue effort, you must ensure that the resulting enterprise architecture will be able to address the goals and areas of concern of all relevant beneficiaries, particularly of your sponsors.

Important: stick to what really matters!

Every item of information, every building block and every relationship will push up the effort to ensure landscape models are kept adequately up-to-date, complete and consistent.

Section 4.6 provides guidelines for enterprise-specific design of business landscape management. It comprises guidelines for elaborating the required processes and embedding them in the organisation.

Requirements for a successful rollout of an enterprise architecture:

- Design an enterprise architecture which specifically matches your goals and the areas of concern you wish to address. It is of primary importance to identify the beneficiaries and analyse the questions they wish to have answered.
- Make sure that the data required to answer these questions can be provided on an ongoing basis with an appropriate effort-to-benefit ratio.
- Make sure that the overall landscape model can be kept complete, of a high enough quality, up-to-date and in the right granularity at all times.
- Establish clearly defined roles and EAM processes and embed them in your organisation. Their effectiveness hinges on having clearly delineated responsibilities, with integration into IT organisation and decision-making processes. This is the only way to ensure landscape data is adequately up-to-date, complete and of high enough quality.

Chapter 4
IT Landscape Management

> *One cannot look into the future – but one can lay the*
> *groundwork for what is to come – one can build the future.*
>
> Antoine de Saint-Exupéry

IT landscape management builds transparency into the IT landscape and forges links between business and IT structures, bridging the gap between the two camps. What an enterprise architecture does is pull together disparate information from business and IT and create associations between elements such as business processes (from the business) and applications (from IT). It creates a unified picture of IT in the enterprise, and renders explicit the interdependencies and impacts of changes in business and IT. IT landscape management creates a transparent picture of the as-is and to-be status, and of the implementation roadmap.

Fig. 4.1 Landscape management in practice

It also enables the IT landscape to evolve in close association with the business requirements. IT landscape management provides a robust, up-to-date base of data which enables informed decisions to be taken speedily. It evaluates business processes, information and applications both in their entirety and in terms of how they interact, using information and enterprise architecture views which are of relevance for steering the company and its IT (see Chapter 3 and Fig. 4.1).

I. Hanschke, *Strategic IT Management*, DOI 10.1007/978-3-642-05034-3_4,
© Springer-Verlag Berlin Heidelberg 2010

Questions answered in this chapter:

- What part of the enterprise architecture does IT landscape management address?
- How do I proceed with linking strategic IT planning, business landscape management and operating-level IT planning?
- What goals are being pursued with IT landscape management? What qualitative and quantitative benefits are we expecting?
- How can the IT landscape be documented and diagrammed?
- What processes are required to establish IT landscape management, and how should these processes be embedded in the organisation?
- What degrees of maturity can be distinguished in IT landscape management?
- In what steps can we introduce IT landscape management?

4.1 Scope and Definition

IT landscape management provides a toolkit for managing the complexity of the IT landscape and gearing the application landscape to the strategic goals of the enterprise. The process entails documenting and analysing the application landscape, its business support, technical implementation and infrastructure – all of which together make up the IT landscape. Once you have this base of information in place, you can proceed with shaping the future application landscape to fit your enterprise goals and business requirements.

The practical interventions that move the landscape toward the to-be status take place in projects and maintenance measures. Each project or measure changes one section of the IT landscape (sometimes overlapping sections). With IT systems being so tightly meshed, changes to one application can send shockwaves across the entire application landscape. Another point to consider is that activities, particularly projects, can sometimes take on a life of their own. The outcomes of projects and maintenance are not always consistent with the original planning, and therefore have to be brought back into line.

By promptly integrating the planned changes arising out of individual measures into the integrated documentation of the IT landscape (a task which is part of IT landscape management), you can highlight any departure from plans at an early stage, also revealing any points of dependency and impact of changes.

However, the changes and their impacts are not always immediately obvious in the reams of project & maintenance documentation to describe individual systems. The salient aspects, and a picture of how everything fits together, have to be distilled out of this information – the only way to obtain the essential helicopter view of the IT landscape. Creating this overall view is the task of IT landscape management.

Interaction with Enterprise Architecture

The enterprise architecture (see Chapter 3) stakes out the basic structures of the business and IT, and the links which exist between them. As such, it provides key input for strategic management of the IT landscape.

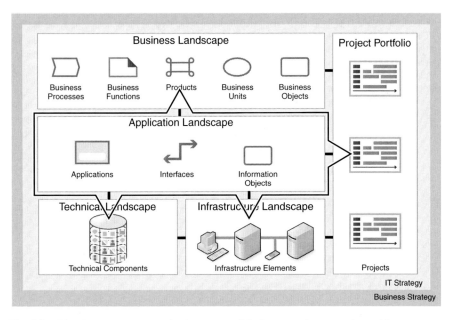

Fig. 4.2 IT landscape management in the context of the best-practice enterprise architecture

Figure 4.2 shows the parts of the best-practice enterprise architecture which are addressed by IT landscape management. IT landscape management documents and shapes the application landscape in interaction with the business, technical and infrastructure landscapes and with the project portfolio. The application landscape largely comprises applications, their data and interfaces.

By assigning the business landscape elements to the elements present in the application landscape model, you can make apparent the points at which IT delivers support to the business. For every business process and every product of the enterprise, the model makes clear which IT system makes which contribution. The mutual dependencies and connections in and between the business and IT sides of the enterprise become transparent. With a landscape model such as this, you can more easily identify the business and technical points where there is a need to take action or make improvements in order to raise the level of business support. It also enables you to make an informed statement on what impact business decisions will have on the IT landscape: this is valuable input for project portfolio management and multi-project management.

You describe how applications and interfaces are implemented in technical terms by defining links into the technical landscape model, the "blueprint". Like the other

connections, these links create clarity, enabling the enterprise to identify technical
dependencies and points where there is a need for action or potential for improvement. To give an example, the blueprint can help answer questions such as: "which
applications are affected by the release upgrade of the existing ORACLE database
system?"

Links from the application landscape to infrastructure elements map the connections with real-life operating infrastructure. These connections can be used to map
operational objectives such as SLA requirements to infrastructure. Information can
also be mapped back from the real-life infrastructure into IT landscape management: for instance, to find out which applications are genuinely used in productive
operation and which SLA requirements are really being enacted.

The interplay of the various elements – particularly also in conjunction with the
project portfolio – renders explicit what mutual impacts there will be in the event
of changes in the business or IT. To analyse the interdependencies and impacts of
projects, all the various landscape models have to be linked into the project portfolio.

Bear in mind that managing the portfolio also means changing it: each time a
new project is approved, or an existing project suspended, continued, postponed or
stopped, the portfolio changes – as do the mutual dependencies with the overall
landscape model.

Integration into Enterprise Architecture Planning Levels

Figure 4.3 shows the various planning levels in the enterprise architecture, and what
type of planning is done at each level.

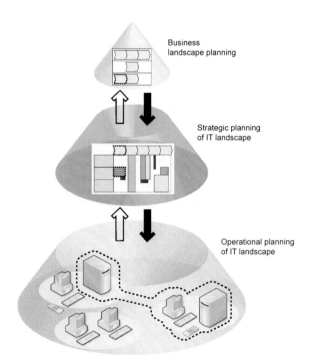

Fig. 4.3 Planning levels in
the enterprise architecture

The task in business landscape planning (see Section 3.4) is to document the current and future business. This entails describing the business processes, business functions and products, and also the business units and objects in terms of the interactions between them. This is a key input for strategic planning of the IT landscape, which largely comprises IT landscape management and technical standardisation (see Chapter 5).

Figure 4.3 presents a symbolic process map, with business landscape planning at the top of the tree. At the strategic IT landscape planning level, the application landscape model is presented by a landscape diagram. This diagram references the processes in business landscape planning and thus acts as a bridge between business landscape planning and IT. The business processes in the landscape diagram forge the links between business planning and IT planning.

The operating IT planning level is represented by real-life IT units such as software, hardware and network components. Planning becomes more detailed as it progresses from strategic to operating level. The dotted lines surrounding components at each level highlight the associations between each of the levels and show how they become more detailed from one level to the next.

Strategic Objectives as a Guide and Frame of Reference

The strategic objectives frame and guide the choice of practical interventions to move the enterprise in its chosen direction. Guided by the strategic positioning of IT, these IT objectives are developed on the basis of the corporate strategy and business requirements (see Chapter 2).

The strategic objectives are binding for strategic management of the IT landscape and act as a measure of progress on implementation. IT goals, principles and strategies are all channelled into the strategic objectives. The application strategies, in particular, provide guidelines for the decisions that will impact on the future development of the IT landscape. See also Section 2.4.3.

Fact file:

- IT landscape management, along with technical standardisation, is a core part of strategic management of the IT landscape.
- The enterprise architecture prescribes the structures for IT landscape management.
- IT landscape management documents and shapes the application landscape in interaction with the business, technical and infrastructure landscape models and project portfolio.
- The strategic objectives frame the scope of design and development in IT landscape management.

4.2 Objectives and Benefits

This section investigates the goals and benefits of introducing IT landscape management. In summary, you can:

- Create transparency across the current IT landscape
- Provide relevant information promptly, filtered and composed according to the needs of each stakeholder group
- Create a basis for communicating and aligning with business
- Effectively plan and control evolutionary development of the IT landscape

These goals and the attendant benefits are discussed in detail below.

Create Transparency Across the Current IT Landscape

A systematic, clear-cut presentation of the IT landscape in terms of how it interacts with business structures renders explicit the associations and mutual dependencies between the two. In fact, in some cases it is only when the landscape is actually mapped out in this way that the interdependencies can be fully understood. As such, IT landscape management helps substitute guesswork through knowledge.

> **Important:**
>
> Diagrams are an essential aid to understanding. A picture does indeed say more than a thousand words. Examples of the diagrams you can use are provided in Sect. 4.4.1.

An overview documentation creates the following benefits:

- In many companies, there are only ever a few individuals with overall "context knowledge", i.e. an overall grasp of how things fit together. Knowledge monopolies can easily arise as a result. Overview documentation and a strong base of landscape data make this implicit knowledge explicit and generally accessible.
- Making the key interactions and mutual dependencies transparent is critical to managing and directing IT appropriately. Without an adequate basis for control – information that shows IT where it should be heading – it becomes difficult to enact risk management, security and compliance requirements properly, or to manage operations and external service providers. Without a robust base of data to work with, the IT changes that follow in the wake of major restructuring or mergers & acquisitions cannot be enacted quickly enough. The same goes for make-or-buy decisions: when the enterprise is deciding whether to outsource parts of the IT landscape.

- A good base of landscape planning data will make it far easier to fulfil documentary obligations as mandated by law, or security and compliance requirements. When a question arises, the data to answer it is already there. There is no need to stock-take or sift through information to locate what is required.

Provide Relevant Information Promptly, Filtered and Composed According to the Needs of Each Stakeholder Group

Each stakeholder group will in general need to investigate different areas of concern. Business managers, for instance, will want to know about the degree and quality of business support. A project manager, on the other hand, will be primarily interested in project-related aspects.

A good base of landscape planning data can help you respond promptly to the questions posed by each stakeholder group (see Sect. 3.5). People generally wish to investigate the following:

- Show up the associations and mutual dependencies in business and IT.
- Identify need for action and potential for optimisation.
- Locate drill-down points for further analysis.
- Render transparent the feasibility and impact of changes in business and IT.
- Prompt provision of the relevant information, custom-assembled to suit the needs of stakeholder groups, delivers the following benefit:
- If stakeholders have the information they need to address their areas of concern, project portfolio management, projects and maintenance measures will all be based on informed input, and decisions can be taken on the basis of hard fact rather than assumptions. Business elements and IT elements can be appraised in their entirety, and also in terms of how they interact, applying appropriate criteria for project portfolio management. Diagrams are also used to add visual clarity to the information. Interdependencies and impacts in business and IT are rendered transparent, as are dependencies between projects. Decisions can be taken quickly and securely based on up-to-date information which is genuinely reliable. This builds greater security into planning processes, and heads off the risk of unwise investment decisions which may have serious consequences far into the future. And, last but not least, it takes far less time and effort to pull together the information required for decisions.

Important:

Decisions are only ever as good as the information on which they are based!

- Considerable help is afforded to projects and maintenance measures. By analysing the landscape model, you can easily single out the sections which are relevant for the project in question. Mutual dependencies, overlaps and risks are more easily identifiable, as are the likely drill-down points to leverage potential or take action. Accordingly, IT landscape management provides valuable input for deciding on the content of projects and maintenance and for defining clear demarcation lines between initiatives. Projects and the dependencies between them become easier to manage and control.

- Members of the project team can find out more quickly what's happening and easily pick up the gist of their part of the project. Projects are a lot quicker to prepare and get on track. Content can be defined more precisely and preproject planning quality is better. The project team is less likely to have to retrace its steps and spend valuable time redoing preparation once the project is underway.
- Other cost savings and efficiency gains derive from identifying and addressing points where there is need for action or potential for optimisation. Even when you first take stock of your application landscape, i.e. document the existing and future applications, you can be identifying likely-looking points for optimisation. Merely by consolidating redundant information or by simplifying routine tasks, you can deliver quick wins in the form of measurable cost savings.

Create a Basis for Communicating and Aligning with Business

> It's important to speak to people in their own language.
>
> Lee Iacocca (*1924), US top manager, 1979–92
> CEO of the Chrysler Corp.

A common language – in which everyone agrees on the meaning of terms and expressions – between business and IT is paramount for the two camps to understand each other and achieve a consensus, particularly regarding investment decisions and for strategically managing the evolution of the IT landscape. A common language prevents misunderstandings. The people working in the business understand why IT decisions have been taken as they are, and what impact these decisions will have.

Key to driving forward this common understanding are the elements of the business landscape model, i.e. the business processes, business functions, products, business units and business objects. These elements must be defined succinctly and without excessive detail (see Sect. 3.4). It must be clear what precisely people mean when they talk about "sales processes", for instance, or "orders".

By linking the business landscape elements with IT landscape elements, the enterprise can derive IT-related goals and objectives from the overarching business goals and objectives. As outlined in Sect. 3.4, a business reference model creates the basis and frame for business-oriented planning and control of IT.

The shared communication base with the business can deliver the following benefits:

- A common language helps speed and streamline coordination processes and prevent misunderstandings.
- The business reference model creates a basis for business-oriented planning and control of IT and for aligning IT with the business.

Effectively Plan and Control Evolutionary Development of the IT Landscape

One job of IT landscape management is to stake out the parameters of the to-be landscape, and to plan how this is to be implemented. This sets objectives particularly for project portfolio management and for operating-level IT management. It is also possible to compare planned and actual data to obtain an up-to-date picture of the implementation status. This is a key input for strategic management and control of the IT landscape.

Over the course of strategic IT landscape planning, you can develop various different planning scenarios, analyse and evaluate the impacts and interdependencies of these alternatives, and thus create an informed basis for strategic and operating-level investment decisions.

In summary, the benefits of strategically planning and controlling the development of the IT landscape are as follows:

- The to-be landscape and implementation roadmap exist as documented objectives for operating-level IT management and project portfolio management.
- The implementation status – the extent to which planning has already been enacted – is more transparent.
- The planning toolkit enables you to analyse and appraise alternative planning scenarios.

Benefits of IT Landscape Management

Table 4.1 summarises the benefits from the perspective of business managers, and from the perspective of strategic and operating-level IT managers.

Table 4.1   Benefit of IT landscape management

Business alignment of IT (business manager perspective)
Common business language Transparency of business impacts/dependencies Linkage between business and IT Optimising of business through IT Business-oriented control and direction of IT (objectives for IT, control of project portfolio)
Strategic planning and control of IT (strategic IT management perspective)
Overview of IT landscape Strategic objectives Optimisation of application landscape Supporting technical standardisation Supporting infrastructure planning IT landscape planning (define target landscape and implementation roadmap) Governing further development of IT landscape
Operational planning and control of IT (operating-level management perspective)
Simplified documentation requirements Reduced effort in initiation of projects and input for project management Supporting operational planning and control of IT Supporting internal service delivery and vendor management

Can the Qualitative Benefit Also be Quantified?

IT landscape management is particularly strong on qualitative benefits, with the greatest potential usually being on the business level. By automating workflows and interfaces or standardising business processes, the enterprise gains huge opportunities for savings.

However, the qualitative benefit – particularly the significantly greater security when taking investment decisions – cannot be evaluated properly, if at all, without a thoroughgoing knowledge of the enterprise in question. Quantifying the benefit entails finding out precisely what value IT landscape management delivers to each of the various stakeholders, such as the owners or managers of the company or its departments. Aspects such as reputation, trust or image should also be considered in any evaluation.

It is essentially up to you which aspects you investigate and measure – but do be sure to consider the following quantitative benefits:

- Savings can be achieved in the production of statutory reports (e.g. application lists for compliance). Regular reports can be produced without doing a complete situational review each time.
- It is far easier to pull together the information on which management teams and boards will base decisions.
- With less upfront research and more options available for analysis, project preparation becomes substantially easier. To give an example, there is no need to complete a fresh survey of business or application managers with each new project you start.
- You can reduce business costs by leveraging opportunities for optimisation, e.g. by consolidating redundant information, simplifying routine tasks, eliminating multiple data entry or automating workflows.

Useful hint:

Find out how many reports, decision papers or project preparations your enterprise conducts, and estimate the average savings.

You can also estimate what effort you will be saving on maintenance of master records, once you have eliminated those which are redundant. Remember to factor in the effort you will save on each transaction. Then extrapolate the savings to quantify the benefit.

The short-term quantitative benefit you can achieve represents a relevant saving. If you focus on the key essentials when you first roll out IT landscape management (see Section 4.6), the quantitative benefit will in practice often already outweigh the extra effort to introduce IT landscape management and to get the processes into operation. And given the variety of qualitative benefits you can expect, the overall benefits will be substantially higher [Klue06] and [Krü03].

Fact file:

- IT landscape management creates transparency across the IT landscape, ensures relevant information is provided promptly to the people who need it (with information filtered and composed to meet the needs of the various stakeholder groups), creates a common base for communicating with the business, and provides a complete toolkit to effectively control development of the IT landscape.
- To accomplish the goals of IT landscape management, the landscape database must be adequately up-to-date, complete and of high enough quality.

4.3   Constituents of IT Landscape Management

IT landscape management documents and shapes the application landscape model in terms of its interplay with the business, technical and infrastructure landscape models and the project portfolio. All this is underpinned by your specific enterprise architecture (see Sect. 3.6). The core constituents of IT landscape management are the application landscape model itself, and the relationships to the other landscape models, and with the project portfolio. These relationships are described in detail in the following on the basis of the best-practice enterprise architecture (see Chapter 3).

You can use the following explanations to elaborate your own enterprise architecture.

4.3.1 Elements of Application Landscapes

Figure 4.4 shows the elements of the application landscape and how these elements interrelate. The notation has rather less detail than for example UML class diagrams, enabling the diagram to show an overall picture of the salient information. The notation presents the main landscape modelling elements such as applications or interfaces, and also the relationships that exist between them. To keep things simple, one key item of information which is deliberately omitted is the cardinality of relationships. The relationships within one type of element are presented as a list of letters on the right-hand side of the element type. An asterisk (∗) indicates that attributes of relationships can be varied depending on the instance.

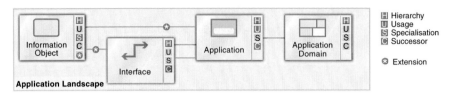

Fig. 4.4 Logical data modelling in the application landscape model

The application landscape model largely comprises applications, their data and interfaces (see Fig. 4.4). The data is termed "information objects" in the following. The application landscape model can be organised into application domains, also termed landscape clusters. This enables related information to be grouped together – for example, you can arrange the application landscape model to reflect the organisational units within your enterprise.

Applications are connected with one another by interfaces. The two lines (connections) between an interface and application describe which applications are connected via a particular interface. Interfaces are the channels of communication for information objects. This communication is termed "information flow" in the following. The information flow can have a specific direction. The flow direction is one possible attribute value on the connection between the interface and the information object in Fig. 4.4.

Applications use information objects. The nature of this use is often summarised by the "CRUD" model – in other words, an application can create, read, update and/or delete information objects. These possible characterisations of the usage are indicated in the model by means of the attribute on the connection between the application and information object.

An application can be the successor of another application – particularly relevant when new releases of an application are introduced. Interfaces can also have successors and predecessors. The successor landscape elements are then denoted by "C" ("successor").

Like interfaces, information objects and application domains, applications can be organised into a hierarchy. This is denoted by the label "H". In practice, this means an application can consist of one or more sub-applications. The sub-applications can be components of third-party software such as SAP FI, or be services which are grouped by means of a parent application. Interfaces can also have a sub-structure, and consist of technical sub-interfaces which implement a specific protocol.

The calling relationship between applications is denoted by "U" – "Usage". Each application can use a variety of different services (sub-applications). By modelling these relationships, you can map the shared use of the service by several different applications.

The information objects – the data itself – can be organised in a variety of ways. An information object can be part of another information object (a hierarchical connection). To give an example, the information objects identifier, address, classification, and account status are all part of the customer data. This is a vertical division (if we imagine the table with real instances of the information object along a row and the attributes in the columns). Each instance of an information object is divided into its logical components.

The horizontal divisions are termed "specialisations" in the following, and are denoted in the figure by "S". The instances of an information object are organised into different groups depending on the specialisation criterion. To stay with the customer data example for a moment, grouping the information according to geographic region would result in a series of objects named "customers_Europe", "customers_Asia", etc. What the specialisations ultimately do is create the dimensions, or criteria, for analysing the information landscape model from various perspectives, e.g. in master data management.

Information objects can also be connected by relationships such as "is used by", "is dependent on", or "merges into". This is indicated by the attribute "*" in the information object in Fig. 4.4, shown in the right-hand key. These relationships are often described using a business object model (see [Sek05] and [Sch01]).

If you are using a business object model, take care that the semantics of all the relationships such as "part of" are clearly defined. Keep the number of relationship types to a minimum. In many cases, the only relationships you will need are "is part of" and "is associated with".

Useful hint:

Avoid – at least when you are first embarking into IT landscape management – mapping relationships between interfaces and relationships between information objects. These drive up the complexity of the overall model and the effort required to keep it up-to-date. In many cases, the effort far outweighs the benefit of the extra detail.

Applications

The following information is required to document an application. Optional elements are enclosed in square brackets []. Implementation aspects such as identifiers for applications are not addressed in the following.

• **Name**: Name of the application, e.g. "ACTAC" or "TUY"
• **[Release no[1]]**: Release number of the application, e.g. "ACTAC 2.3"

Together, the name and release number serve as the unique identifier of an application.

---

[1] Also termed version number.

- **Description**: Description of the application, e.g. "sales management and support for private clients"
- **[Instance ID]**: You may need to instantiate applications, e.g. when applications are used in different ways at different locations. As well as locations, information such as plants, user groups and sales structures can be combined with the name and release number to create a unique identifier for a particular instance of an application.
- **Position in application domains**: The domains into which this application has been placed.
- **Planning status**: The planning status of the application: this can be "as-is", "planned" or "to-be".

  - **"as-is"** denotes productive applications.
  - **"planned"** is the status attributed to applications which are being planned or whose development is already underway, or third-party IT products for which purchase negotiations are in progress.
  - **"to-be"** describes the target vision of the application landscape. Applications with "TO-BE" status are part of the future landscape and serve as end objectives toward which the IT landscape is to be steered.

- **[Status in lifecycle]**: This allows conclusions to be drawn on questions such as the stability of the application. Settings can include: "prototype", "pilot", "in production", "legacy"[2] and "decommissioned".
- **[Utilisation period]**: The period over which the application is used. For applications with "as-is" status, this will be the period of time over which the application is in productive use. For "planned" or "to-be" applications, this is a statement on the planned period of use.
- **[Hierarchy]**: An indication of what the application consists of.
- **[Successor]**: A link with the chronological predecessor or successor of the application in question, e.g. successor release.
- **Assignment of interfaces**: An indication of which interfaces the application has.
- **Assignment of information objects**: Which information objects are used, and the nature of this usage, e.g. "CRUD" or "data master application"?

Important:

- The planning status is required to draw a clear demarcation between the current landscape model (as-is), the landscape as it will be in the near future (planned), and in the more distant future (to-be). When documenting an application landscape, you must also specify the planning horizon. This

---

[2]Also termed "phase-out".

enables a line to be drawn between what actually exists now, and what is still at the planning stage.

- It is only by documenting the utilisation period that you will be able to answer the question: "what will the IT landscape look like at a particular point in time in the future?"
- There are mutual dependencies between the planning status and the utilisation period. The utilisation period of as-is (current) applications should include "today", and that of planned or to-be applications should lie in the future.

You must make suitable practical interventions to ensure consistency (see Sect. 4.4).

This core data can be enriched by additional information specific to your enterprise. Here are a few examples:

- **Application category**: You can differentiate between third-party or individual software, and also the nature of the use: "OLTP", "OLAP", "infrastructure system[3]" and "COTS", or the nature of the operation interface: "web-based", "rich client" and "host client".
- **Responsibilities**: can be assigned to individuals, to groups or to entire organisations. Individual responsibilities are business and technical responsibilities (such as the application manager, business manager, or business contact person). Groups and organisations can be entities such as the support organisation or business organisation. It is also possible to include specific details here, e.g. you can indicate who is responsible for assigning authorisations.
- **Manufacturer information**: The manufacturer, such as "SAP", "Oracle" or "internal".
- **Strategic classifications**: You can enter the strategy contribution as a numeric value, or classify applications into categories such as "high potential", "strategic", "core business" and "support". Further examples and explanations of these examples are provided in Sect. 2.4.3.

  Another common classification is to specify business criticality, SOX relevance, or estimate the state of health of the application. You can channel both business and technical criteria into the appraisal of an application's state of health, and include an estimate of the quality of business support as well as technical aspects (see Chapter 5). For details on indicators, please refer to Chapter 6.
- **Required security level**: For example: low, medium and high.
- **SLA requirements and references to SLAs**: SLA requirements such as availability, performance or downtime, details on SLA agreements such as contract numbers and periods of validity.

---

[3]For example portal or identity management.

- **Technical information on applications**: This category can include the size of the application (using measures such as Lines of Code – LOC), special properties such as the ability to integrate into portals, GUI classification, the number of users, how permissions are managed, or special requirements e.g. for clients.

Important:

The more optional or enterprise-specific attributes you use, the more this will drive up overall complexity.

What also increases is the danger of inconsistency. There tends not to be one-to-one correspondence between the planning status and the status in the lifecycle. There can be status overlaps between "to-be", "planned", "in development", "prototype", "pilot", "introduction", "legacy", and "replaced". To answer questions such as "how will the IT landscape change between today and a certain point in the future", a particular lifecycle status must be assigned to a particular planning status.

Useful hints:

- Use the status in the lifecycle only as an additional information field: making it mandatory will unnecessarily drive up complexity when you come to use and update the information.
- If you genuinely need the status in the lifecycle as a central attribute for the areas of concern you wish to investigate, you can use this status instead of the planning status. Do not use both in combination, because it makes it considerably more complicated to ensure consistency. You then have to define the utilisation period for each status in the lifecycle. This increases the complexity exponentially, because the utilisation period can have a different meaning for each status, and moreover these periods can overlap. This makes the model difficult to use and to update.
- If possible, assign each application to no more than one landscape cluster. There is then less likelihood of coordination problems owing to unclear division of responsibilities.

When you are starting work with IT landscape management, choose the attributes which are most appropriate to describe the applications in your enterprise. The following summary provides valuable ground rules for your first venture into IT landscape management.

Getting started: ground rules for IT landscape management

- Do not use all the optional information from the above list.
- To start with, just document the as-is and the planned applications. Documenting the to-be applications is part of introducing and establishing landscape planning (see Sect. 4.4.3). Before you get this far, you need to stake out a clear concept determining how the landscape will be maintained and updated, who is responsible for updating information, and how visible the to-be landscape model will be.
- The **release number** is essential to highlight any dependencies between versions.

  The release number is not required for to-be applications, since these are often described in very general terms such as "new sales application".

  You should only document releases when the IT landscape changes. As a rule this will only happen when a major release is introduced.
- You can use the **hierarchical relationships** to create a clear picture of what main components an application consists of. However, stick to just one hierarchy level. Drilling any deeper will substantially increase the effort for updates and maintenance, and your presentations can easily lose their visual clarity.
- Only use the concept of application instances when you genuinely need it. If you do use the concept, bear in mind you will have to keep all the application instances up-to-date.

Interfaces

There are two types of interfaces: "from-to" and "offers-uses", the semantics of which differ. A "from-to" interface describes the direct, logical connection between applications. A "from-to" interface is defined by stating the applications which are connected by means of this interface. An "offers-uses" interface is nothing other than an interface in UML (see [Rup07]). The interfaces are offered by an application and are used by other applications. An application offers other applications a service such as "provision of customer contact data".

Important:

Decide on one of these two types of interfaces: using both would be totally redundant!

Useful hint:

Model just "from-to" interfaces. Modelling explicit interfaces and how these interfaces are used is highly time-consuming and delivers little added value, because most of the key areas of concern in strategic management of the IT landscape can also be addressed through the "from-to" interfaces.

The following information is required to document interfaces. Optional elements are enclosed in square brackets []. Implementation aspects such as identifiers for interfaces are not addressed in the following.

- **[Name]**: Name of the interface, e.g. "Interface 1"
  It might also be possible to identify the interface by specifying which applications it connects.
- **[Release no]**: The release number of the interface, e.g. "Interface 1 Release 2.3"
  Together, the name and release number serve as the unique identifier of an interface release.
- **[Description]**: Description of the interface, e.g. "manual interface between application ACTAC and application TUY".
- **[Planning status]**: The planning status of the interface; as for applications this can be "as-is", "planned" and "to-be".
- **[Status in lifecycle]**: This allows conclusions to be drawn on questions such as the stability of the interface.
- **[Utilisation period]**: Period over which the interface is used in productive operation ("from-to" specification).
- **[Hierarchy]**: Hierarchical composition of the interface.
- **[Successor]**: A link with the chronological predecessor or successor of the interface, e.g. successor release.
- **Assignment to applications**: Which applications are linked by this interface.
- **Assignment of information objects**: Which information objects are used, and the direction of the flow (information flow)?

Important:

The more optional attributes you use, the more this will drive up overall complexity and the danger of inconsistency.

There is a particular danger of inconsistency when the planning status and utilisation period are specified both with interfaces and with applications. It is not rare to find documentation in which interfaces have a different utilisation period than the applications they connect. Do not underestimate the effort to keep this information consistent.

This core data can be enriched by additional information specific to your enterprise. The following attributes are commonly used to characterise interfaces:

- **Degree of automation**: Categorisation in terms of automation – e.g. manual, semi-automated and automated.
- **Update period**: Categorisation in terms of when interfaces are updated, e.g. online and batch or instantly, daily, weekly, monthly and annually.

When you are first getting started with IT landscape management, choose the most appropriate information to describe the interfaces in your company. However, certain information is essential to direct the evolution of the application landscape effectively. These essentials include the technical implementation of the interface (see Sect. 4.3.2), which you should definitely include.

Getting started: ground rules for IT landscape management:

- Do not use all the optional information from the above list.
- Use only "from-to" interfaces, and document the information flow.
- Do **not** use the release number, planning status, utilisation period, hierarchy and successor relationship. This will keep the effort for documenting the interfaces to manageable proportions, and you will still be able to address virtually every area of concern which will arise in the context of managing the IT landscape.

Information Objects

The following information is required to document information objects. Optional elements are enclosed in square brackets []. Implementation aspects such as identifiers for information objects are not addressed in the following.

- **Name**: Unique name of the information object, e.g. "ActacCustomer".
- **Description**: Description of the information object, e.g. "customer data from the application ACTAC".
- **[Status in lifecycle]**: This allows conclusions to be drawn on questions such as the maturity of the information object. For example: a product can mature over its lifecycle from research through to general release.
- **[Hierarchy]**: The hierarchical composition of the information object.

- **[Specialisation]**: Specialisation relationship of the information object.
- **[Relationships with other information objects]**: Enterprise-specific relationships between information objects, e.g. "is used by", "is dependent on", or "merges into" in the context of a business object model (see [Sek05] and [Sch01]).
- **Assignment to applications**: The applications to which the information object is assigned, including how the applications use the object.
- **Assignment to interfaces**: The interfaces to which the information object is assigned, and the flow direction (information flow).

Important:

As with applications and interfaces, the more optional attributes you use, the more this will drive up overall complexity and the danger of inconsistency.

This core data can be enriched by additional information specific to your enterprise. One common addition for information objects is to differentiate between master data and transaction data.

When you are first venturing into IT landscape management, choose the most appropriate information to describe the information objects in your enterprise.

Getting started: ground rules for IT landscape management:

- Do not use the optional components.
- Just use **flat information objects**, i.e. when you are first documenting landscape data, do not include relationships such as hierarchies or specialisations. Otherwise, the coordination effort to agree on a shared business object model will turn the rollout of IT landscape management into a long-drawn-out process, and drive up the effort for ongoing maintenance and updates.

Fact file:

- Make sure you have core data which is sufficiently up-to-date, complete and of sufficient quality!

- When you are first embarking into IT landscape management, pare down the overall complexity by using as "light" a data model as possible for establishing your landscape data. You can use the entry-level configurations for this purpose.

4.3.2 Relationships in Application Landscapes

The information in the application landscape model is in itself adequate to provide a general overview of the mutual dependencies between applications. The associations between the applicaiton landscape model, other landscape models and the project portfolio also shed light on impacts and interdependencies between business and IT ideas, from business processes through to infrastructure.

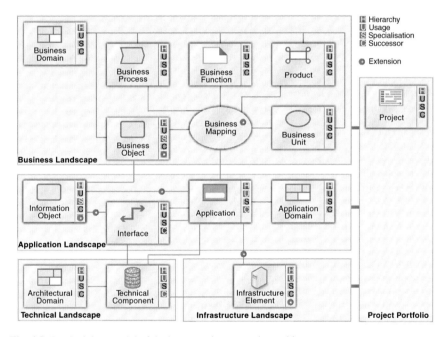

Fig. 4.5 Logical data model of the best-practice enterprise architecture

Using the best-practice enterprise architecture from Chapter 3, we now go on to describe the relationships which connect the application landscape model with the other landscape models and with the project portfolio. Figure 4.5 presents a skeleton view of the logical data model of the best-practice enterprise architecture. The application landscape model, particularly the applications themselves, is essentially the centrepiece of the overall landscape and connects outwards to the other land-scape models and the project portfolio. For details on the notation, please refer to Sect. 4.3.1.

Relationships of the Application Landscape Model to the Business Landscape Model

It is by assigning applications to specific business landscape elements that you describe what support each of these applications delivers to the business. Applications can be assigned to business processes, business functions, products, business units or business objects. You can also restrict the scope of these business assignments, for instance by indicating that an application is used by a particular group of people to execute a particular business task. Other user groups might use a different application for the same purpose.

The assignments between the elements in the business landscape model and the applications can be made at varying levels of granularity. Process modelling on the basis of EPCs (see [Sche01]) will generally assign applications at the level of individual activities – the finest level of detail. However, for presentation in the form of a landscape diagram – which is the main view in IT landscape management (see Sect. 4.4.1) – applications have to be seen in terms of where they fit into the value chain. It is at this coarse level of granularity that you have the essential big-picture view.

Process modellers will in many cases not assign applications in terms of specific application releases, preferring instead to specify applications without a release number. However, this information is not really enough, because the release number is a key item of information in IT landscape management. Normally there will be differences in functionality from one application release to the next, and this will also change the nature of the assignments to other elements of the landscape, e.g. business processes.

Useful hints:

- As with business units, products and business objects, you should make your assignments of business processes at a coarse-grained level. This will help keep the work for managing data and ensuring consistency to manageable proportions.
- If your enterprise has already modelled its processes, and made reli-able, up-to-date assignments of applications to processes, you may be able to aggregate up from this finely-grained assignment back to a more generalised view, possibly using an appropriate tool.
    Caution: the quality of the application assignments in the process model must be good enough for use in IT landscape management: make sure there

> is a common list of application releases used in IT landscape management
> and in process modelling.

Table 4.2 shows the required degree of granularity of the business landscape
elements for assigning to applications.

Table 4.2   Granularity of business landscape elements for assignment to applications

Business landscape elements	Granularity of assignment
Business processes	Value chain level; refined no deeper than business process level down to the level of individual activities
Business functions	Capabilities level (see [Ost03]) without refinement
Products	IT products or the products which the company sells, on the highest level or with no more than one refinement level
Business units	Campuses
	Plants
	Corporate units
	Locations
	Logical user groups and roles
	Sales structures such as sales levels
	No more than one refinement level

Business objects can also be assigned directly to applications. There are no constraints regarding granularity here – or rather none are required. Business objects,
by their very nature, are coarse enough in granularity.

It is equally possible to assign business objects to applications indirectly, by
means of the relationship with the information objects (see Sect. 3.3.1).

Recommendation for information landscape modelling:

- When you are first getting started in IT landscape management, use just a
  flat list of business objects which you can use unchanged as information
  objects.
- It takes considerable perseverance to design and establish information landscape modelling, including management of the business objects in the
  business landscape and the information objects in the application landscape model. You're taking too much on if you start it all at the same
  time!
- Once you feel you have IT landscape management successfully underway,
  you can expand the information landscape model step by step.

Relationships of the Application Landscape Model with the Blueprint

You document the technical implementation of applications and interfaces by assigning technical components to them. Technical components can be technologies, reference architectures and architectural patterns, IT products, IT components and tools for software development or system management (see Chapter 5). Architectural domains serve to organise the technical components into "drawers" and "trays" such as "database systems", "middleware", or "SCM applications". This makes it easier for developers to locate the right components when they are including technical building blocks in the blueprint.

You can specify the standardisation status of each technical component. This enables you to determine the degree of standardisation of the IT landscape as a whole, information which is key input for strategic IT management and moving your landscape closer toward prescribed technical standards

Important:

You can only implement technical standardisation by defining connections with IT landscape management. This is what provides a picture of the degree to which the IT landscape is standardised, and highlights necessary action points.

Relationships of Application Landscape Model to Infrastructure Landscape Model

The relationships between the application landscape and the infrastructure landscape enable you to perform cross-checks with your IT reality. The infrastructure landscape model must contain coarse-grained infrastructure elements such as "portal infrastructure". These building blocks must be consistent with the real-life operating infrastructure, and be connected with these real-life entities by means of refinement relationships. The assignments between the more detailed elements and higher-level elements of the infrastructure must be made by operating-level IT management (e.g. in a CMDB). This is after all the level with the knowledge on which associations exist.

Given that IT management has to embrace a wide scope of issues, it is also essential to define the assignments between applications and software units. These can be deployment units which run the web server, application server and database elements of the application. It is these assignments which enable you later to communicate SLA requirements for applications to operating teams and verify that requirements are being met.

Important:

- The CMDB and the EAM database must share a meta-model in order for you to automate the synchronisation and matching processes between the two. You must define the associations which exist between the high-level elements in EAM and the operating-level elements in the CMDB. These assignments – between high-level infrastructure elements and more detailed infrastructure elements – must be part of the shared meta-model, as must the assignments between applications and the software units of which the applications consist.
- It must be clear who precisely is in charge of keeping landscape elements and relationships up-to-date. IT landscape management should have stewardship of the applications, since this is where strategic planning takes place. Service management, more exactly the CMDB, should have stewardship of the relationships between high-level and lower-level elements, and of the infrastructure, since it is only here that the requisite knowledge on the associations exists.

Relationships to the Project Portfolio

The relationships to the project portfolio map the migration steps which take the landscape from its as-is status to the to-be status. These steps are implemented in individual projects. By analysing the landscape data, you can review dependencies, mutual impacts, synergies and redundancies between projects (see Sect. 4.4.2).

Fact file:

Elaborate the detail of your enterprise architecture by defining core data, enterprise-specific attributes and relationships.

- Work out which core data you need to document your application landscape. The "getting started" guidelines in Sect. 4.3.1 provide some useful pointers.
- Define your enterprise-specific data and the relationships to the other landscape models in accordance with your objectives and the areas of concern you wish to address. Guidelines are provided in Sect. 4.6. To obtain a few quick-win benefits, stick to the data and relationships which are genuinely necessary to address your areas of concern, and where the data will be easy

to obtain. For each attribute and relationship you include, you will have to
invest considerable time to collect and maintain data.

4.4 IT Landscape Management Processes

IT landscape management comprises all the processes for documenting, analysing
and modelling the to-be landscape and the practical interventions to usher your
present landscape toward this status. It also comprises all the supporting measures to
help direct the evolution of the IT landscape. We differentiate between the following
processes:

- **Documenting the IT landscape** (as-is, to-be and planned): By documenting the
  IT landscape, you ensure the elements of the application landscape model and
  the relationships to the other landscape models and to the project portfolio are all
  up-to-date, complete and consistent (see Sect. 4.4.1).
- **Analysing the IT landscape model**: The analysis of the overall IT landscape
  model serves to address the various questions which stakeholders are looking
  to answer (see Sect. 4.4.2). It also helps reveal interdependencies and knock-on
  impacts of changes in business and IT, shows up evidence of areas warranting
  further analysis, and identifies points where there is need for action or potential
  for improvement (see Sect. 4.4.2).
- **IT landscape planning** (to-be and planned): This entails designing the target
  landscape and its implementation roadmap in line with business requirements,
  strategic objectives and internal and external constraints (see Sect. 4.4.3).
- **Governing the further development of the IT landscape**: With its clear snapshots of progress towards goals, IT landscape management provides effective
  support to strategic IT management (see Sect. 4.4.4).

When you first venture into IT landscape management, you will generally begin
by documenting and analysing the IT landscape. The documentation and analysis processes are what gives you an adequately up-to-date and consistent base
of data to work with. It is this data on which you build when you come to
plan the IT landscape and direct its evolution. Guidelines on how to break down
the introductory process into manageable steps are provided in Sects. 4.5.3 and
4.6. Let's now investigate the IT landscape management processes in greater
detail.

4.4.1 Documenting the IT Landscape

The process of documenting the IT landscape creates an overview of the applications, the associations that exist between them, and between applications and

the business, technical and infrastructure landscape models and the project portfolio. This data is the foundation for answering the specific questions of your stakeholders and for keeping development of the IT landscape aligned with objectives.

Important:

When documenting the IT landscape, keep in mind the areas of concern you are looking to address. Include the information required to address these questions – and make sure the information can actually be obtained.

Section 4.6 provides guidelines for identifying relevant areas of concern.

Lifecycle of Documentation

Like other elements of IT landscape models, the documentation has a lifecycle:

- Documentation first has to be created. You begin by taking stock of what exists. It might be possible, for example, to use existing collections of data and pull together information from projects, business process analysis, process documentation, purchase lists, the product and service portfolio and service management lists (CMDB). The drawback is that information like this tends not to be fully up-to-date. Quality and granularity also vary, and sometimes data will be incomplete.

Important:

Verify the completeness and quality of existing data resources and check they are up-to-date before including them in your landscape data!

- Any changes to the IT landscape must be integrated into landscape models and diagrams promptly.
- Be sure to delete outdated aspects of the documentation. You might also elect to archive older versions.

Creating this first version of the documentation is a relatively simple process, despite involving so many points in the organisation, since once the basic parameters of IT landscape management have been staked out, the work can be completed by a few people within a relatively short time (usually no more than a few months). However, ongoing maintenance (including general tidying) requires close coordination with a wide number of stakeholders. Also, such processes must be embedded into the organisation (see Sect. 4.4.4) to make them effective. To ensure the documentation is maintained permanently, with adequate quality and granularity, you have to develop a maintenance concept.

Maintenance Concept

A maintenance concept lays out the guidelines and processes for documenting the IT landscape – essential if you want your documentation to be up-to-date, complete and consistent at all times.

The concept focuses on two aspects: modelling guidelines and data provision. Modelling guidelines enusres documentation is standardised and has appropriate granularity.

Data provision is a multifaceted process. Aspects to consider are the origins of the data, the processes and responsibilities for providing and communicating it, and quality assurance. For each landscape element and relationship, and for all their attributes, it has to be clear via which processes the data is provided, who the providers are, and what exactly triggers the provision of the data. As well as defining these parameters, the maintenance concept must define the measures will be applied to keep data sufficiently up-to-date, complete and of sufficient quality for the intended purpose.

The term "sufficient" is of course relative. One must distinguish here between core data, extended data, control quantities (indicators) and relationships. These categories can be characterised as follows:

- The core data is the data which describes the application landscape model as such. It includes the names of applications, information objects or other elements (see Sect. 4.3.1).
- Extended data comprises the optional information which can be used to enrich the definitions of landscape elements. This data is part of the enterprise-specific data described in Sect. 4.3.1. To give an example, you might decide to specify the size of an application in lines of code, or include manufacturer information.
- Control quantities and indicators are key for managing and directing IT (see Sect. 6.2). Control quantities make up the second part of enterprise-specific data (see Sect. 4.3.1). They include data such as the strategy contribution or state of health of an application. It is possible to restrict the visibility of such data – for example, if you want to prevent an application manager from finding out that "his" application is soon due for retirement!

Core data, extended data, control quantities and relationship data being delivered by various stakeholders along different IT process chains. There will inevitably be disparity in terms of quality, age and completeness. The planning status can also give rise to differences:

- Over the course of projects and maintenance measures, the core and extended data of as-is and sometimes planned landscape elements will undergo change. The task of updating this data must therefore be integrated into IT processes, and information should be up-to-date before a system goes live.
- The target landscape and implementation roadmap are progressively revised as IT landscape planning proceeds, with adjustments being made to planned and to-be landscape elements across all data categories. Such plans may initially be scenarios which have to be approved by a decision-making board before becoming official.
- The core data and control quantities of planned landscape elements change owing to decisions taken in project portfolio management.
- Business processes and business objects change over the course of process management. Business functions, products and business units change during business planning. The relationships of business objects with applications can undergo changes owing to updates during IT landscape planning.

Important:

For all the landscape elements, relationships and attributes you will be using, find out who makes changes to the data, and in which processes. You can channel this information into the data provision guidelines in your maintenance concept.

You might find the following checklist useful for defining data provision guidelines:

1. Over the course of which IT processes or decision-making processes does the application landscape change (applications with their interfaces and data)?

   - Project management
   - Maintenance measures
   - Project portfolio management
   - IT strategy development
   - Landscape planning

2. Over which processes do the other landscape models change (business processes, business functions, products, business units, business objects, technical components and infrastructure elements)?

   - Enterprise strategy development
   - Process management
   - Business planning
   - Organisation projects

- Infrastructure planning
- Service management
- Standardisation measures
- Blueprint maintenance
- Project portfolio management
- Other processes (which?)

3. Who are the providers, in which context, of core data, extended data, control quantities and relationship data?

- Application managers
- Project managers or special project roles
- Process architects
- Business analysts
- Organisation consultants
- Infrastructure architects
- Project portfolio controllers
- IT architects
- Strategists
- IT managers ("plan", "build" and/or "run")
- Business managers
- Security representatives
- Risk managers
- IT controllers
- Other data providers (which?)

4. Where are changes documented?

- Project documentation such as business concepts
- Project portfolio management, decision records
- Go-live documents
- Process models
- Business strategy
- IT strategy
- Infrastructure planning
- Specific lists or systems (which?) Under whose stewardship?

5. How is each change made known? Who informs about the change, or triggers its documentation?

- By chance
- Data provider informs personally, proactively
- Data provider is asked regularly where the changes have occurred
- Information from review or handover & signoff logs
- Direct involvement, e.g. participation in reviews or handover & signoff
- Other sources (which?)

6. How complete, consistent and up-to-date is the data? How can adequate quality be assured?
7. Which data in defined structures and relationships is not yet covered? Where can this data be obtained? Through which processes can continuous updates be assured? Or is it enough to collect an initial set of data even though the quality level may be low?

Useful hint:

If you are going to need certain structures and relationships to address specific areas of concern, but know they are not yet available in adequate quality, you can begin with a low quality level and see how well this basic data can resolve relevant questions. You can then gradually enhance the data by introducing and embedding appropriate quality assurance.

To give an example, let's assume your enterprise does not have a defined, agreed list of business functions or business processes. However, you need these structures to get talking with business segments about IT support. By pulling together a basic set of information – even though you know full well the list of business functions has not been approved – you can map relationships between applications and business functions to a landscape diagram or similar (see Sect. 4.4.2). This gives you something tangible to take to discussions with people from the business camp, helping achieve a consensus on structures and possibly also begin consolidating them.

Important:

- Define clear roles and responsibilities for data provision.
- For all core and extended data, control quantities and relationships, work out which processes provide the data, who provides it, when, and what events trigger the provision of fresh data.
- Be sure to have someone who will see things get done: someone who will press the relevant stakeholders if they fail to deliver the information they should have, and quality-assure this data. Guidelines are provided in Sect. 4.4.4.
- Quality-assuring the data also entails investigating all the important consistency conditions – including Interdependencies of status and utilisation periodsutilisation period (see Sect. 4.3.1). You will also need to review all the relationships for which the meta-model provides alternative routes. One example is the assignment of business objects to applications. These assignments can be made directly, or via information objects.

Table 4.3 illustrates one possible structure for a maintenance concept; Table 4.4 provides a template for documenting a update process.

Table 4.3 How a maintenance concept document might be put together

I. *Assumptions*
This section provides a brief introduction and sets out core principles for maintenance such as "stick to what is absolutely necessary" or "everyone maintains the information under their stewardship".

II. *Enterprise architecture*
This section includes the documentation of landscape elements, their relationships, core data, extended data and control quantities.

III. *Data providers*
This section documents the sources and origin of data for all elements, relationships and attributes of the enterprise architecture, stating which data is sourced from which provider (providers can also be IT systems) at what point in time along which process. You also determine for which data the landscape model database is to serve as the data master system.

IV. *Update processes*
This section describes data maintenance, imports from other systems and quality assurance of third-party data. The template in Table 4.4 can be used to document an update process.

V. *Modelling guidelines*
The modelling guidelines define how granularity, structuring and other aspects are to be treated in the documentation.

V. *Pending issues*

Table 4.4 Template for an update process

<Name of update process>		
Objective	Description	Landscape elements and their relationships
A statement of the objectives being pursued with this update process	A brief description of the update process	The landscape elements and their relationships, and the attributes to be maintained. Constraints can also be specified here, e.g. "only standard-compliant elements".
Person responsible for update		
Designation of the role		
Time of update Event-driven	Regular	
What event (e.g. when a new system goes live) is the trigger for the update?	Do updates take place regularly, independent of integration into processes? At what time, e.g. monthly or quarterly?	
Input	*Output*	
What information is required to complete the update process?	What is the deliverable of the update process?	

Modelling Guidelines

Modelling guidelines define the granularity and structural layout of the IT landscape documentation.

> **Important:**
>
> Define modelling guidelines as objectives for your IT landscape documentation and also to serve as a basis for quality assurance of the documentation. Without guidelines, it will be difficult to obtain consistent, standardised modelling.

The modelling guidelines discussed below have been derived from practical experience. You can choose the ones which best fit your needs.

- **(MI) Structure and granularity of an application**: An application is a software or software package for associated functionalities which are logically and technically distinct from other areas of functionality, and which are supported entirely or to a large extent by IT.

  - (MI.1) An application can comprise various sections: presentation, the business logic and database sections. These are not each modelled separately but subsumed in the application. Not all sections must be present.
  - (MI.2) Which data is associated with an application is described by assigning information objects to the application. Enter only the business-relevant data which is required for an understanding of what the application does and how it interacts with other elements. The nature of the assignment can be detailed by defining a data master application – i.e. which application has overall "ownership" of the data in question. There should be no further detail at this point, e.g. do not include CRUD.
  - (MI.3) Model no more than one hierarchy level. If you are describing third-party software, you can use components named by the manufacturer; these are then the sub-applications of the third party-software application. If you are describing custom-build software, model services or the logical functional components as the sub-applications; here, you should break down the application along the lines of the business enterprise architecture. Alternatively you can also apply technology-oriented subdivisions, if this is more relevant for addressing the questions your stakeholders have. For instance, technology-oriented sub-applications might be more appropriate if there is complex middleware between the software units of the application, or if software units are each based on different technologies or has different operating periods.

- (MI.4) Also model external applications if these are connected with your own applications. Differentiate between internal and external applications using the attribute "external/internal".
- (MI.5) Specify the application manager for each application.
- (MI.6) Model additional information as extended data (possibly also as technical components) and assign this data to your applications. For instance you can model information on client types ("thin client" or "fat client") as extended data.
- (MI.7) Specify the release number for each as-is or planned application.

- **(MII) To-be applications**: When modelling to-be applications, do not enter a release number unless you genuinely know what it will be. When entering the utilisation period, enter "1.1." for "from" and "31.12." for "to", both dates being in the year for which the to-be landscape model is to be valid.
- **(MIII) Data dependencies between software units**: Data dependencies can exist between software units. The modelling should differentiate between dependencies of different types:

  - (MIII.1) Shared databases can be mapped using a parent application, with software units as the sub-applications. The data is assigned as information objects to the parent application.
  - (MIII.2) A software unit needs data which is provided by another software unit, but the units in question are not directly linked via an interface. You can represent this by modelling the software units as applications and by assigning the same information objects to the two applications. If data is transferred from one unit to the other in a manual workflow, you need to model this by an interface which is characterised as being manual.
  - (MIII.3) A software unit exchanges data with another software unit via a data hub. You can represent this by modelling the software units as applications and by assigning the same information objects to the two applications. Model an information flow between the two applications, where possible complete with the flow direction.

    The data hub should be modelled as an application if it provides functions for maintaining, consolidating or distributing data. Model interfaces with the flow direction hub-to-application, and specify which information objects the interfaces transfer.

- **(MIV) Structure and attributes of interfaces**

  - (MIV.1) Model manual as well as IT-based interfaces. Characterise interfaces by their degree of automation and the interval between updates.
  - (MIV.2) Model interfaces without a hierarchy.
  - (MIV.3) When multiple information objects are exchanged between interfaces coincidental, model just one interface which subsumes the various objects (even when the flow directions are different).

- (MIV.4) Do not model control flows.
- (MIV.5) Interfaces between parent and sub-applications are prohibited.

- **(MV) Modelling infrastructure software units**: An infrastructure software unit has a reference to other business applications. Examples: portal, data warehouse, identity management solution or Enterprise Service Bus.

  - (MV.1) Model infrastructure software units as applications if the objective is to make the flow of information to the software unit transparent, to assign data to the software unit itself or to diagram the unit as an aggregation of sub-applications such as portal applications. The application should be denoted as an instance of the application category with an attribute to designate it as "infrastructure". You also have to create a technical component comprising the technical and standardisation data of the infrastructure software unit.
  - (MV.2) For all other cases, model infrastructure software units as technical components and assign them to the relevant applications.

- **(MVI) Modelling a service oriented architecture (SOA)**

  - (MVI.1) Model services as sub-applications if you need to show information exchange or interfaces between services or with otherd applications.
    If you cannot identify an obvious parent application, create one in accordance with the assigned business functions or business domains. If communication is via an Enterprise Service Bus, introduce an ESB as per (MV.1) and model interfaces from the services to the ESB. If you are not going to be using or modelling an ESB, model the "uses" relationship in the form of an interface. Where possible, also specify the information flow.
  - (MVI.2) In other cases, model services as business functions – also if you are using the model to identify business redundancies. Assign the business functions to the supporting applications. If appropriate, create a new application parent as per (MVI.1).
  - (MVI.3) Combine (MVI.1) and (MVI.2) if you want to identify both interfaces and redundancies.

Fact file:

- Landscape data must be sufficiently up-to-date, complete and of sufficient quality at all times.
- Put together a maintenance concept which determines how this is to be accomplished. The concept comprises two main parts: modelling guidelines and data provision.

• It is crucial to establish data provision in your IT and decision-making processes. Also vital is to introduce explicit roles and responsibilities for data provision and check all third-party-sourced data in terms of quality, granularity and consistency (see Sect. 4.5.2).

4.4.2 Analysing the IT Landscape

The analysis of the IT landscape model serves to address and answer the areas of concern of the various stakeholders. Section 3.5 surveys the various beneficiaries of EAM. These include the CIO or IT managers, senior enterprise management, IT strategists, project portfolio controllers, project managers, business managers, application managers, infrastructure architects, safety representatives and risk managers.

The areas of concern of these stakeholders can be organised into three main categories:

• **Context: Business alignment (business view)**: The evolution of the IT landscape has be in alignment with corporate objectives and business requirements. The current business landscape model documents the current business requirements. Likewise, the to-be business landscape model documents the requirements which are to be met by the future landscape, or rather by the interim steps of the implementation roadmap.

The focus of questions in this category is to:

– Create a transparent view of business correlations such as the criticality of business processes.
– Show up the interconnections that exist between business and IT, such as the degree and quality of business process support.
– Identify points where there is a need for action or potential for improving how IT supports the business – for example in business continuity management or by eradicating business redundancies.
– Obtain factual evidence promptly on the feasibility and impact of business ideas, such as the knock-on impact of changes when a particular project is implemented.
– Drive IT in terms of business needs, using business-oriented metrics such as benefit, contribution to strategy and to the value proposition as criteria for managing project portfolios.

• **Context: Strategic management of the IT landscape (IT view)**: Technical standards, the target landscape, and the implementation roadmap must be staked out in alignment with business requirements and the IT strategy. Another issue here is to oversee that objectives and plans are enacted as and when intended.

The focus of questions in this category is to:

– Obtain an overview of the IT landscape together with all its interactions, including identifying all technical implementations of interfaces.
– Define technical standards for applications and infrastructure, such as technologies or server platforms.
– Identify points where there is need for action or potential for improvement on technical standardisation: for example, inadequate standardisation across database systems.
– Identify need for action and potential for improvement concerning infrastructure, such as the degree to which economies of scale have been applied.
– Identify need for action and potential for optimisation in the application landscape.
– Deliver factual evidence promptly on the feasibility and impact of IT ideas, such as "can particular applications be integrated into a portal?"
– Design, analyse and appraise planning scenarios for the target landscape and its implementation roadmap.
– Effectively drive the strategic evolution of the IT landscape by actions such as checking progress and verifying consistency of implementation with the to-be and planned landscape models.

- **Context: Operating-level management of the IT landscape (IT view)**: IT service delivery has to be as efficient and goal-oriented as possible. IT landscape management can help operating-level management with fact and evidence-based input for projects, maintenance and service management and for vendor management.

  The focus of questions in this category is to:

  – Simplify documentation requirements (e.g. for auditing, regulatory frameworks).
  – Assist project preparation and management through sound input – for instance, identifying the right focus at the start of a project, locating areas that warrant more detailed analysis, or analysing project-specific areas of concern using IT landscape data which has already been collected – without having to take stock of the situation again.
  – Contribute to operating planning and control of IT, for instance, to break top-level strategic objectives and business requirements (e.g. SLAs) into specific targets for projects.
  – Identify need for action and potential for optimisation in operations.
  – Improve internal service and vendor management by introducing greater transparency into these areas.

Examples of specific questions:

- Which business units use which applications, and for what?
- Which applications support which business processes?
- Which IT elements are affected by a change in a business process?
- What impact would the outage of an application have on the core business?
- Which applications and interfaces are particularly critical in terms of security or compliance requirements or business continuity management? What is required in terms of availability, reliability and performance?
- What impact does a project-related change in the business have on the IT landscape? Which applications and which interfaces are affected?
- Which business objects are input or deliverables of which business processes? Which business process is the master? Which business segment is the data owner?
- What is the impact of changes to customer data? Which business processes, applications or interfaces have to be brought into line? Is the customer data kept redundantly in other applications? Does any need for action result from this?
- Which application is the data master application, e.g. for customer or product data?
- What redundancies are there in functions, processes, applications, business objects or infrastructure? Are there any cycles that can lead to inconsistencies?
- Which "sick" applications support business processes that contribute to competitive differentiation? What impact will the failure of such an application have on core business?
- Which applications rely on host technology for their technical implementation?
- Which IT systems are affected by a release upgrade, e.g. of database "ORACLE 9.2"?
- What impact does a technical change such as a release upgrade have on an application? Does this require adjustments in the infrastructure? Which interfaces are concerned? Which processes, products, business functions and business units are affected by the change?
- How is an application or interface implemented technically? Which applications and interfaces do not comply with technical standards or enterprise objectives such as reference architectures?
- Which applications or interfaces run on which infrastructure? At which campus is the infrastructure located? What costs are incurred for maintenance and further development of systems at these locations?
- What will the application landscape look like – in business and technical terms – in year X?

Your landscape data must include the relevant core and extended data, control quantities and/or relationships for the questions you wish to address. If the data has not already been collected, you have to assemble and enter it before you can begin to address stakeholders' question. For each question, you must also determine which diagrams (visualisations) will be most appropriate to present the findings.

> **Important:**
>
> It is the diagrams which turn raw data into business intelligence. The findings for a particular area of concern must be assembled into a format that delivers all the salient information for the target audience in question with at-a-glance visual clarity. A picture does indeed say more than a thousand words.

Diagrams

The following diagram types have proven valuable in practice for addressing stakeholders' questions:

- Landscape diagram
- Information flow and cluster information flow diagram
- Portfolio diagram
- Master plan
- Business cluster diagram (can also be superimposed by applications)
- Blueprint diagram
- Mapping tables

For a detailed discussion of each of these diagram types, please refer to Sect. 3.3.2. Examples of the main presentations in each of the above categories of questions are provided below.

As well as diagrams, simple lists are routinely also used to respond to stakeholders' questions. Depending on what stakeholders are trying to find out, the analysis might take in only one specific section of the overall landscape. By analysing the data with relevant criteria, you can uncover points where there is need for action or potential for optimisation, and isolate deltas by comparing to-be and as-is data.

Figure 4.6 illustrates a landscape diagram. This diagram presents the applications and the support they provide for two business processes (sales and marketing) and for three groups of customers (retail clients, corporate clients and institutions). Also presented is the technical implementation of these applications, showing at a glance which technologies can be deployed to support which business processes.

Landscape diagrams are a suitable tool to present correlations between three different landscape elements. The filler elements, in this example the applications, are plotted against the X and Y axes, each of which represent particular types of IT landscape element. Any constraints that exist (see Sect. 4.3.2) are immediately shown up in the diagram. Additional information can be coded into the filler elements: you can represent up to three different aspects by means of the colour, the fill pattern and edge type.

Important:

Decide which elements to plot along the two axes of the landscape diagram, which elements are to be the "filler" elements, and the nature of the relationship between these filler elements and the elements on the axes.

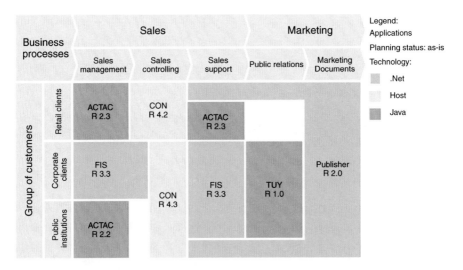

Fig. 4.6 Landscape diagram highlighting technical implementation

An information flow diagram presents the interplay between applications, their data and information flow. Figure 4.7 illustrates how one section of the application landscape can be plotted using an information flow diagram. Application ACTAC 2.3 is at the planning status "as-is", comprises the two sub-applications "Service Alpha" and "Service Beta" and uses "customer" data. The sub-applications also use specific data. Application ACTAC 2.3 is connected with application FIDO via an automated interface, over which the applications exchange "order configuration" data. Application ACTAC 2.3 is also connected with the planned and to-be applications VAS 1.7 and "Payment Transactions" via planned interfaces. This and other information can be taken from the information flow diagram. The aspects presented in Fig. 4.7 (see diagram key) are just examples: you are equally free to map other information such as the state of health of an application.

Important:

Do not include too much – single out just a few salient points. This ensures the key aspects stand out.

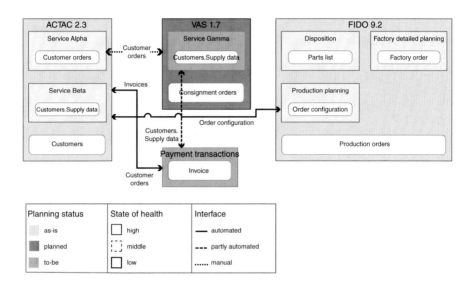

Fig. 4.7   Example of an information flow diagram

Figure 4.8 illustrates a cluster information flow diagram with as-is applications. The applications are organised here according to a single criterion, in this example business processes. This diagram is a good way to present organisational or technical groupings or separations.

A portfolio diagram is a good tool to provide management with an at-a-glance overview of multiple aspects of the landscape. For example, you can present the state of health of the applications in a portfolio by showing each application with a traffic light colour (see Fig. 4.9). The applications are classified here by their contribution to strategy and to value, and further characterised according to their state of health and cost. Applications which contribute to core business must be adequately reliable, in other words healthy. A diagram of this nature immediately identifies any points where there is a need for action.

Figure 4.10 shows a master plan diagram. These diagrams generally present lifecycles of or chronological dependencies between projects, applications or technical components, or combinations of these elements. The project master plan is a key tool for roadmapping the IT strategy (see Sect. 2.5.2).

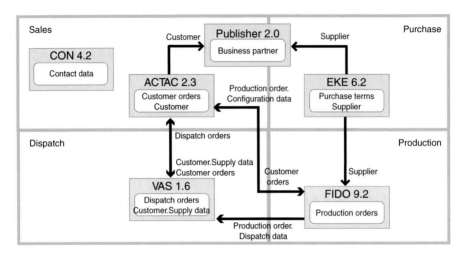

Fig. 4.8 Example of a cluster information flow diagram

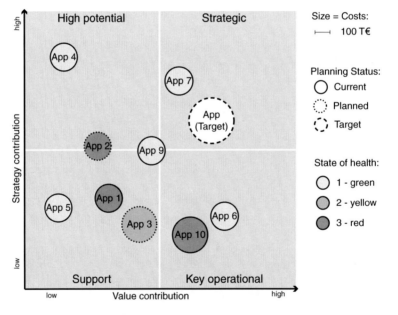

Fig. 4.9 Application portfolio based on McFarlan (see [War03])

Figure 4.11 illustrates a business cluster diagram; Fig. 4.12 illustrates the diagram superimposed by applications. A business cluster diagram creates the business reference model into which you place applications. For details on business cluster diagrams, see Sect. 3.4.

By mapping applications to the diagram, you can create a graphic presentation of the business support.

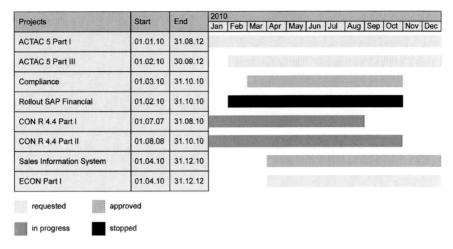

Projects	Start	End	2010 Jan	Feb	Mar	Apr	May	Jun	Jul	Aug	Sep	Oct	Nov	Dec
ACTAC 5 Part I	01.01.10	31.08.12												
ACTAC 5 Part III	01.02.10	30.09.12												
Compliance	01.03.10	31.10.10												
Rollout SAP Financial	01.02.10	31.10.10												
CON R 4.4 Part I	01.07.07	31.08.10												
CON R 4.4 Part II	01.08.08	31.10.10												
Sales Information System	01.04.10	31.12.10												
ECON Part I	01.04.10	31.12.12												

requested   approved

in progress   stopped

Fig. 4.10 Example of a master plan diagram

Business Domain I	Business Domain II	Business Domain III	...	Business Domain n	Supporting Functions
F I 1 ⋮ F I n	F II 1 ⋮ F II n	F III 1 ⋮ F III n		F n 1 ⋮ F n n	SF 1 ⋮ SF 2 ⋮

Overall Functions

OF 1

...

OF n

Fig. 4.11 Example of business cluster diagram

A blueprint diagram is essentially the technical version of a cluster diagram. The grid of cells formed by the clusters creates a general structural frame into which you place technical components (see Sect. 5.3.2).

Figure 4.13 shows an example of a mapping table between applications and business objects. The entries "CUD" and "R" indicate how the applications use the business objects. This type of presentation is a suitable aid for cluster analysis.

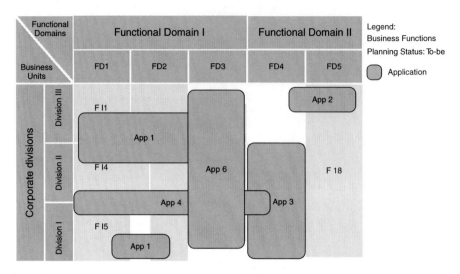

Fig. 4.12 Example of business cluster diagram, superimposed by applications

Mapping tables can be used for all landscape elements which are directly or indirectly related. You do not have to determine the nature of these relationships in the mapping table. In many cases, it is quite enough simply to enter "X", indicating that a relationship exists at all.

Fig. 4.13 Example of a mapping table between applications and business objects

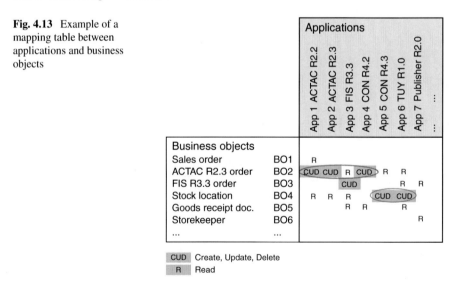

Figure 4.14 shows a list of applications with their main attributes. Such lists – which can also include highlighting for emphasis – are often used for documentation purposes in security and compliance.

Application	Description	as-is, planned, to-be	Utilisation period	Related Business processes	Extensibility	Adaptability	Modularity	Service orientation	...	Licence Costs	Operation & Maintenance Costs	Benefit	Security demand	Security level
ACTAC R2.2	Central logistics system	as-is	1.1.2006 - 31.12.2010	Sales management Sales support	X	X	X	X		200 T/year	40 T/year	500 T/year	high	high
ACTAC R2.3	Central logistics system	as-is	1.1.2008 -	Sales management	X	X	X	X		150 T/year	30 T/year	500 T/year	high	high
FIS R3.3	Sales management	as-is	1.4.2008 -	Sales management Sales controlling		X	X			-	150 T/year	300 T/year	high	high
CON R4.2	Controlling system	as-is	1.1.1999 - 31.12.2010	Sales controlling						-	250 T/year	100 T/year	high	high
CON R4.3	Controlling system	as-is	1.8.2008 -	Sales controlling						-	300 T/year	150 T/year	high	middle
TUY R1.0	Marketing system PR	as-is	1.1.2008 -	Press relations		X	X	X		-	100 T/year	90 T/year	low	low
Publisher R2.0	Marketing system WF	as-is	1.7.2008 -	Press relations Marketing documents			X	X		100 T/year	20 T/year	200 T/year	low	low
Publisher R3.0	Marketing system WF und PR	planned	1.1.2010 -	Press relations Marketing documents	X	X	X	X		100 T/year	20 T/year	200 T/year	low	low

Fig. 4.14 Example of a list of applications

Indications of a need for action or potential for improvement are identified by analysing the IT landscape model from a particular perspective using particular criteria. The findings of the analysis, which takes in both business and IT information, must be presented in the type of diagram best suited for the information and the target audience in question.

Often, though, the analysis will do no more than unearth likely-looking points warranting more detailed analysis – i.e. it is initially unclear whether there is genuinely a need for action or potential for optimisation. You have to drill deeper at these points, perhaps consulting specialists to obtain more information. As a rule, such drill-down analysis is carried out using specialised tools on detailed data, for example tools for project portfolio management and process management, also UML tools.

The landscape diagram in Fig. 4.15 highlights points where there is need for action, potential for improvement, or evidence that more detailed analysis is required (the "drill-down" points).

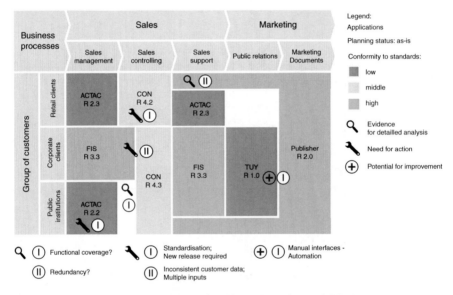

Fig. 4.15 Landscape diagram zeroing in on need for action and potential for improvement

To work out where there is potentially a need for action or improvement, it is a good idea to investigate the touchpoints between landscape elements – such as data shared by applications. You can also use business, technical or financial aspects. For example, you can appraise the landscape model by cost, contribution to strategy and to the value proposition, degree of coverage of business requirements and risks such as the technical state of health.

How do you find these investigation parameters, or criteria?

When there is an obvious and pressing need for action, it is often self-evident what needs to be investigated. For example, if one of your applications is often out of commission for troubleshooting or maintenance, this is a clear sign that its state of health is less than optimal. Other criteria emerge when you break down the landscape by different elements, for example, an analysis of individual business functions or business processes (see Sect. 2.4.1) can show up a need for action or potential for improvement. The whole process can also be simplified by applying analysis patterns.

Analysis Patterns

These are generalised, tried-and-tested templates of analysis to help you identify and present indications in your IT landscape where there is a need for action and potential for optimisation.

You can mix and match the patterns as you think fit, using a selection or the full set, in individual projects or throughout your landscape planning. The following patterns consolidate a range of common questions which stakeholders have posed in the course of introducing and optimising the best-practice architecture (see Chapters 3, 4 and 5) in their organisation. The detailed patterns are provided in [Han09].

- **R**: Redundancies – Redundancies push up costs because the organisation ends up paying for maintenance several times over, or investing extra effort in updating and consolidating information. Redundancies can also lead to inconsistencies with potentially wide-reaching impact. "Need-for-action" points on redundancy must be identified as early as possible. The following patterns have been identified:
  - Redundancies in business functions in the business landscape model.
  - Redundancies in business objects in the business landscape model.
  - Redundancies in support of business functions in the application landscape model.
  - Redundancies in business process support in the application landscape model.
  - Organisational redundancies in the business landscape model.
  - Organisational redundancies in the application landscape model.
  - Redundancies in business objects in the application landscape model.
  - Redundant interfaces.
  - Redundancies in the technical landscape model (blueprint).

- **I**: Inconsistencies – An inconsistency is a state in which two elements, both of which can be considered valid, cannot be combined with one another. Consolidating the data – to correct the inconsistency – tends to be a major undertaking. Inconsistent data can have a negative impact both in business terms and on image equity (for example, if price data in the order management system is inconsistent with data on the systems of local dealers). "Need-for-action" points on inconsistency must be identified as early as possible. The following patterns have been identified:
  - Inconsistencies in functional assignments.
  - Data inconsistency owing to redundancies, cycles or status.

- **O**: Organisational shortfalls: Missing or incorrect business responsibilities for domains, business objects, business processes, products, business functions and applications, technical components or infrastructure elements can all ultimately make data inconsistent. The following patterns have been identified:

  - Missing or inconsistent responsibilities – for instance, it is not clear who is overseeing business or technical issues, or who is tasked with operations and support.
  - Anomalies in how and where responsibilities are assigned in organisational terms.

- **B**: Implementing business requirements: Using the patterns in this category can help you identify possible points for optimising IT support of the current and future business. The following patterns have been identified:

  - Business coverage analysis to highlight areas where there is inadequate business support.
  - Determine where more integration is required to raise the level of IT support. For example, you can investigate manual interfaces, inadequate interface automation or integration gaps.
  - "Junk" analysis to expose elements which are superfluous to requirements, such as applications which are not required at all. Huge savings can be achieved by culling the junk.
  - Cluster analysis to identify closely associated functions, business processes, business objects and business units, also applications, infrastructure units and projects. This is a form of dependency analysis.
  - Data dependency analysis to identify applications which have a high degree of data dependency with other applications.
  - Compliance analysis to identify the extent to which the organisation has implemented statutory and voluntary codes of practice such as Solvency II, Basel II or the Sarbanes-Oxley Act.
  - Criticality analysis to identify business-critical business processes, products, business functions, business objects, applications, technical components and infrastructure units.
  - Business status analysis to identify inadequate IT support for business processes, business functions, business objects and products.
  - Analysis to identify potential security gaps.
  - Efficiency analysis to pinpoint areas where economic efficiency is suboptimal.

- **T**: Technical action and optimisation points: One key way to achieve and sustain better quality in the IT landscape is to simplify the landscape through greater standardisation, homogenisation and flexibility. By identifying the points where there is a likely need for technical action, you have a better idea of what sort of improvement is required.

The following patterns have been identified to underpin technical standardisation efforts and improve the technical quality:

– Blueprint cluster analysis to identify closely associated technical components – termed blueprint elements.
– Analysis of technical status in terms of risk management.
– Analysis of standardisation and heterogeneity to identify potential for improvement in these respects.
– Analysis to identify degree of integration of applications with regard to simplifying and standardising the integration of IT systems.
– Analysis to identify evidence of substantial dependency between applications, technical components, infrastructure elements and projects.
– Appraisal of technical integration ability and flexibility of applications (with a view to how well they will adapt to evolving business requirements).

Important:

The analysis patterns can do no more than provide pointers to areas where you are likely to find some need for action or potential for improvement. It is up to you to appraise the findings – e.g. whether a redundancy identified in landscape data genuinely reflects a redundancy in the real IT landscape, and what impact this has in the context. In many cases, you will have to dig deeper to make a definitive statement.

To give an example, the impact of permitting multiple applications to update the same customer or price data can be multifaceted: quite apart from the cost of duplicate entry and data consolidation, there might be the more serious consequence of making a negative impact on customers.

Example Analysis Pattern

Below is an example of an analysis pattern. The pattern is documented in the template, see Table 4.5.

The grey shading in the first line of the table indicates the landscape model from which the deliverables derive. Patterns may also include grey shading to indicate which of the landscape models are required to apply the pattern. In the example highlighting in Table 4.5, the findings of the analysis will apply to the application landscape, and elements of the business landscape model are required to apply the pattern.

One example of an analysis pattern is provided in Table 4.6. Pattern "R-A-BO" analyses potential redundancies in the application landscape model with reference to business objects in the business landscape model.

Table 4.5 Template for documenting an analysis pattern.

Business landscape model (B)	Application landscape model (A)	Technical landscape model (T)	Infrastructure landscape model (I)	Project portfolio (P)
< ID>	<Name of pattern >			<Version>

Description
<Description of the pattern: particularly of how the potential need for action or optimisation is determined>

Context	<What is required in order to use the pattern: e.g. which landscape elements and relationships, extended data and control quantities>
Dependencies	<Mutual dependencies with other patterns>
Deliverables	<A description of the outcomes of applying the pattern: Definition of landscape element type, instantiation, recommended diagram type for presenting the outcomes>
Example	<Description of the outcomes of applying the pattern, illustrated by a typical example>

Table 4.6 Example of an analysis pattern

Business landscape model	Application landscape model	Technical landscape model	Infrastructure landscape model	Project portfolio
R-A-BO	Redundancies in relation to business objects in the application landscape model		Version 1.0	

Purpose: to identify potential redundancies in terms of business objects in the application landscape model

A potential redundancy is considered to exist when one of the following conditions is met:

(1) Business objects are created, modified, read, deleted or simply used in multiple applications.
(2) Business objects are "delivered" to the same application via various routes. Each route is defined in terms of a sequence of interfaces via which all or part of the business object is transported.
(3) More than one application is the data master system for the same business object.

Application releases which are not in productive operation simultaneously are not investigated, nor are applications connected by a hierarchical relationship.

Apply the conditions relevant to the components used in your enterprise.

Context or	Landscape elements: applications, business objects and information objects
requirements	Relationships
for applying	For all conditions: functional assignment of business objects to applications
the pattern	(alternative I) or assignment of information objects to applications and assignment of information objects to business objects (alternative II)
	Interfaces between applications for condition 2

Table 4.6 (continued)

Business landscape model	Application landscape model	Technical landscape model	Infrastructure landscape model	Project portfolio

Where relevant, further characterisation of the nature of business object assignments (alternative I) or information object assignments (II) through "CRUD" for condition 1

Characterisation of the nature of business object assignments (alternative I) or information object assignments (II) by indicating which is the data master application for condition 3

Dependencies –

Outcome of applying the pattern   List of applications and interfaces, also business objects or information objects, for which the specified conditions apply. Potential redundancies are highlighted

Preferred diagram type:

Condition (1) and condition (3): mapping table (see Fig. 4.16)

For condition (2): information flow diagram or information flow cluster diagram (see Fig. 4.17)

Outcome of applying the pattern, illustrated by typical examples   Mapping table to highlight redundancies in business objects for applications as per condition 1 (condition 2 likewise):

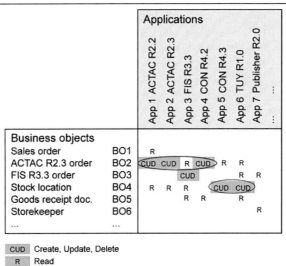

CUD   Create, Update, Delete
R   Read

Fig. 4.16 Example of R-A-BO (condition 1 and condition 3)

When the same business objects are modified by different applications, this is often a sign that some action needs to be taken. Also indicative of need for action is when there are multiple releases of the same application in productive operation simultaneously.

Table 4.6 (continued)

Business landscape model	Application landscape model	Technical landscape model	Infrastructure landscape model	Project portfolio
R-A-BO	Redundancies in relation to business objects in the application landscape model		Version 1.0	

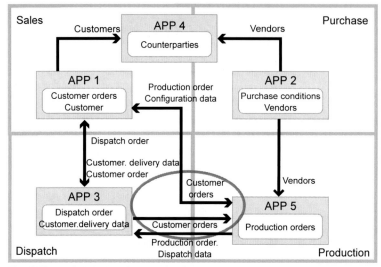

Fig. 4.17 Example R-A-BO (condition 2)

Information flow cluster diagram to illustrate potential redundancies in data delivery (see Fig. 4.17).

There is a potential need for action here, because customer orders are delivered to APP 5 by both APP 3 and APP 1.

The download attachment of [Han09] provides other patterns which you can use as input for analysing the overall landscape model.

Analysing the overall landscape model: ground rules:

- Robust analysis results are dependent on having the application landscape documented properly in the landscape database: the information must be adequately up-to-date, complete and consistent.
- Analysis is performed to resolve stakeholders' questions. The structures framing the analysis – and the types of diagram used to present outcomes – are determined by the questions which stakeholders are looking to answer. Deciding what questions and areas of concern to address is therefore the first step toward deciding the shape you will give to IT landscape management in your enterprise (see Sect. 4.6).

- Stick to the salient areas of concern which already constitute "burning platform" issues. Each new area you introduce will increase the efforts for ongoing data provision.
- Make sure you pick areas of concern which people will genuinely need to revisit on an ongoing basis. If you add attributes or relationships to the landscape database which you are only going to need sporadically, you will still have to keep the data up-to-date all the time. The effort has to be in proportion to the benefit.
- Make clear choices on which types of diagram you intend to use to address which areas of concern. Describe the content of these diagrams and their relationships precisely. This is a key part of designing the concept for IT landscape management.
- Another key success factor is to have quick, easy-to-use tools for maintaining information and for presenting diagrams.

  The quality of the data – and the extent to which it is genuinely kept up-to-date – is dependent on whether update and maintenance tasks are easy to execute. PowerPoint graphics become outdated relatively quickly.
- Use the analysis patterns to identify points where there is need for action and potential for optimisation.

4.4.3 IT Landscape Planning

Planning means replacing trial by error.

Peter Ustinov

IT landscape planning entails establishing the target landscape – the entire landscape or just sections of it – and defining the implementation roadmap. It takes place both in IT strategy development and in projects and maintenance. Particularly when there are major changes afoot in the enterprise such as mergers or major restructuring, IT landscape planning serves as a tool for drafting out the new design and planning the practical interventions to put it into practice.

Evolution of the application landscape is a continuous, goal-focused process of analysing the as-is landscape model, modelling the to-be landscape, and determining the planned landscape model (see Fig. 4.18). The to-be and planned landscape models are rolled forward either on an ongoing basis, or reviewed and updated at regular intervals.

The starting point for development is the current landscape model: the landscape as it is right now, plus project planning. The organisation proceeds through an analysis phase to identify points where there is need for action or potential for improvement in the current model. These "need-for-action" points, along with the business requirements, contribute to shaping and defining the to-be landscape model. Planners then develop and appraise alternative scenarios for the to-be

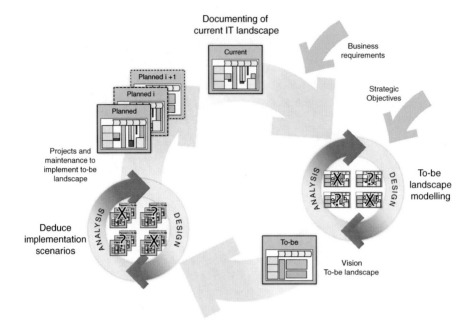

Fig. 4.18 IT landscape planning as ongoing process

landscape model, perhaps proceeding through multiple iterations, and present the alternatives to the decision-making board. The board then chooses the IT landscape model which the organisation will work toward.

In general, the gap between the current and to-be landscape models is so wide it cannot be bridged in a single step (see Fig. 4.19), meaning the challenge has to be broken down into manageable sub-steps. Each of these sub-steps may also entail iterative development of several planning scenarios, again with the board appraising the options and selecting the most appropriate implementation roadmap.

Each step in the implementation roadmap might comprise a series of interventions which are enacted in one or more projects or maintenance measures. Through incremental implementation of the roadmap, the current landscape model gradually progresses toward the to-be status. However, what makes this a challenge is that sometimes you have a moving target: after all, business goals and external constraints can easily change within planning horizons. And then the entire cycle starts all over again: the to-be and planned landscape models both have to be brought into line with the new requirements.

"Local" Landscape Planning

Alongside the "master plan" – continuous landscape planning framed by IT strategy development – some situations, notably major projects, maintenance and business

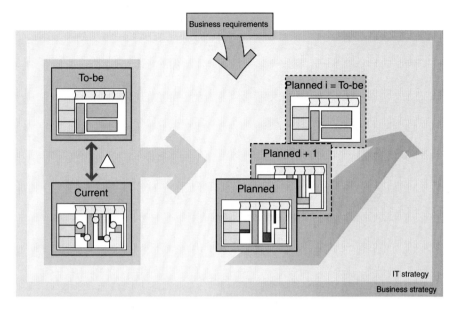

Fig. 4.19 Implementation of to-be landscape model through projects and maintenance

transformations, will also require "local planning". The outcomes of these local landscape plans must be consolidated with the overarching strategic planning; in some cases, however, the local planning will replace the high-level planning altogether.

Figure 4.20 presents two projects which have a different focus yet whose contents overlap. It is the task of IT landscape planning in such a case to produce a consolidated, synchronised plan which accommodates the content overlaps and chronological dependencies between projects. Mapping the chronological dependencies is particularly important when different end dates are scheduled for projects.

Even with a multitude of projects underway simultaneously, it must be possible to obtain a snapshot at any time of the overall situation. If projects are not going to be completed at the same time, it may be necessary to bring in interim solutions such as temporary interfaces. Aspects such as this must be considered when appraising alternative planning scenarios and must also be documented in the overall implementation planning.

Each alternative planning scenario must be appraised in terms of its fit with the to-be landscape model. Picking scenarios with a good fit will help usher your application landscape closer to the vision of the landscape model as it will be in the future.

Landscape modelling in the context of business transformations, projects or maintenance generally focuses on a single section of the landscape model, and shapes and designs this section to fit local objectives (see Fig. 4.21).

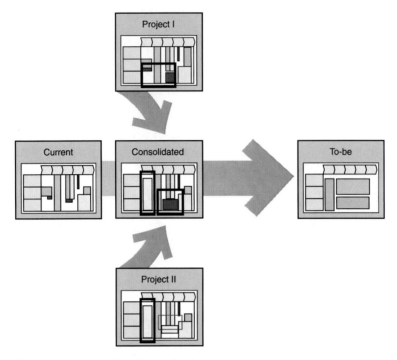

Fig. 4.20 Consolidating local landscape planning

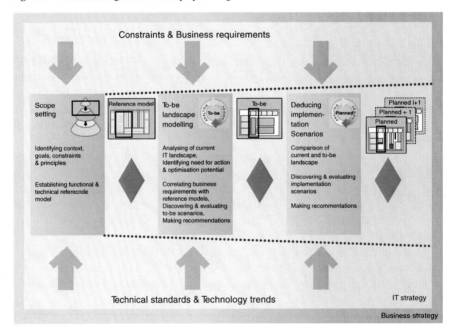

Fig. 4.21 Landscape modelling in projects or business transformations

Local landscape modelling helps speed and simplify the preliminary phases of business transformations and projects – essentially defining what the project is all about. This phase comprises three major steps:

- **Scope setting**: Define the area of interest you will be investigating, parameters and constraints for the to-be landscape model and implementation roadmap.
- **To-be landscape modelling**: Design the to-be landscape model for the section under consideration – take into account business requirements and the points where the status-quo analysis shows there is a need for action or potential for improvement.
- **Deducing implementation scenarios**: Plan your implementation roadmap for the to-be landscape model.

The context for projects and maintenance is largely set by the project mandate and strategic objectives. In smaller projects and maintenance measures, the "identifying context and goals" phase will therefore just be a check of whether constraints and requirements have changed. Landscape modelling in projects and maintenance tends to be about refining and detailing the to-be and planned landscape models which have already been drafted out.

Business Transformations

Business transformations affect the organisation and its business processes, products, business functions and business objects. They therefore impact on IT in its entirety. A business transformation is not considered complete until the organisation, business processes, IT and business objects, particularly the master data, have all been transformed.

A variety of events can be behind business transformations. Some examples are:

- Major restructuring in the enterprise owing to a change in business direction. A new "global strategy", for example, can bring in a raft of changes: a global sourcing policy to bundle purchasing volumes for resources, relocation of production sites, or less vertical integration by sourcing semi-finished goods from suppliers instead of making them in-house. Changes can also be more straightforward – for instance organisational changes in the wake of introducing new products, processes or regional structures.
- Corporate mergers and acquisitions.
- New or changed cooperation models with partners or vendors, e.g. supply chain initiatives.
- Process standardisation (e.g. Europe-wide or worldwide efforts), which goes hand in hand with a harmonisation of systems.

The type of landscape modelling which is instigated by business transformations has wide-reaching impact, often resulting in a radical overhaul of all or part of the enterprise and also its strategic IT planning. There are many risks inherent in such a major overhaul. To give just one example, if an enterprise is looking to globalise its sales and service structures, it will also need to globalise its customer data. In practice, this means harmonising all its customer-related structures and data worldwide, and ensuring consistent, high quality transaction data everywhere.

Landscape modelling in business transformations such as corporate mergers will also fundamentally change the to-be landscape, at least the relevant area of it, and the business transformation landscape models will replace the to-be and planned landscape models in the area under consideration. This of course has a huge impact on the current project portfolio. Each project has to be reviewed in terms of its fit with the direction in which the IT landscape is now heading. Some projects may have to be halted altogether, others brought into line with the new requirements.

In business transformations, it is paramount to define an overarching reference model for business and technical issues. As well as the strategic objectives for the business and IT, it is this reference model which scopes out the new business model and the future business and/or technical structures in the "new" organisation. For example, the business reference model – the model which defines what business functionality the IT landscape will have – is composed of various "to-be" elements: the to-be business landscape model, together with the future visions of business functions and business processes.

If this reference model has not already been defined, this step has to be completed with a matter of urgency in a strategy "mini-project". This is a prerequisite for modelling the IT landscape, because it is this reference model which determines the cornerstones and objectives which frame the entire planning process.

Useful hint:

Use the to-be business functions as your business reference model if the organisation and its business processes are going to be completely redesigned, rather than just modified, in the course of the business transformation. The business functions and the high-level corporate organisation are often marked out early on: the to-be business functions describe the future capabilities of the new organisation. These functions then serve as a basis for redesigning the business processes and organisation.

The current application landscape model is mapped to the new business reference model (see Fig. 4.22). As well as a one-dimensional presentation, you can use landscape diagrams to present two-dimensional reference models. Figure 4.22 shows a two-dimensional business reference model, with the new corporate divisions and functional domains along the axes, and the future business functions populating the diagram.

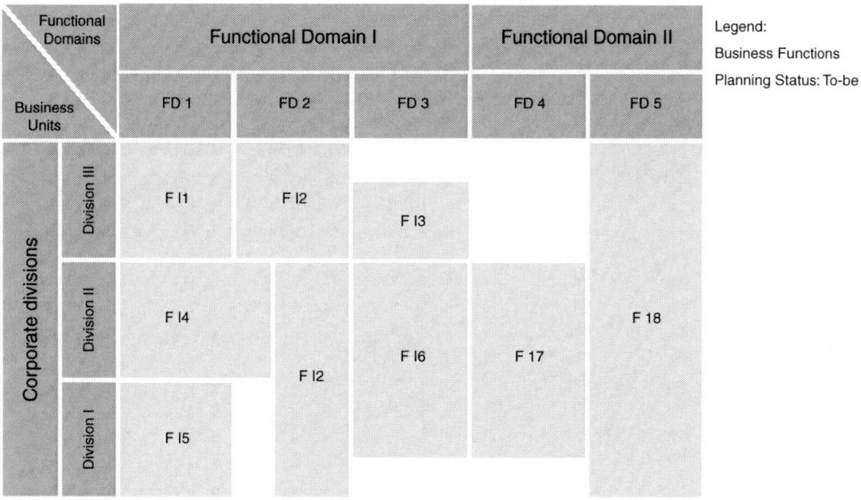

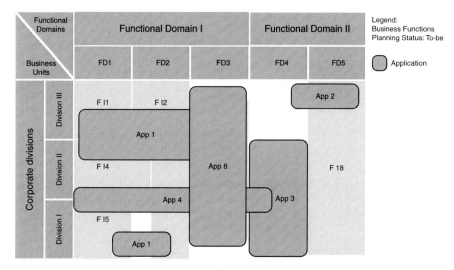

Fig. 4.22 Example of a business reference model (two-dimensional)

By assigning elements such as applications, information flows or business objects to the units in the business reference model and overlaying them onto diagrams, it becomes easier to identify evidence of gaps and/or inconsistencies warranting further investigation. Figure 4.23 shows the business reference model superimposed by the applications assigned to the model. This shows up the points where there is

Fig. 4.23 Example of a two-dimensional business reference model with applications a need for action or potential for optimisation in terms of implementing the new structure.

These "need-for-action" or optimisation points provide valuable input when it comes to redesigning the landscape. To return to Fig. 4.23, the overlaps at the interfaces between the new corporate divisions show up one definite "to-do" point: to redefine responsibilities for the applications.

However, at many points it will be necessary to go into greater detail both on business and technical levels, and dig deeper into structures to investigate elements such as information flows or interfaces.

Deliverable Document: Landscape Modelling

The outcome of landscape modelling can be summarised in a document. Table 4.7 shows the sort of information the document will contain.

Table 4.7   Example of how the landscape modelling document can be structured

---

I. *Management summary*

II. Contex: This section defines the goals, parameters and constraints, principles to apply, and business and technical reference models.

III. *Current landscape model*: The current business, application, technical and infrastructure landscape model, the current project portfolio, plus identified need for action and potential for optimisation

IV. *To-be landscape model*: A summary of all the planning scenarios plus an evaluation of each, including cost-benefit considerations and a recommendation on which scenario to go with.

V. *Implementation planning*: All required tasks in a chronological roadmap. If appropriate, alternative implementation scenarios can be compared and appraised on key criteria such as cost, benefit, risk and duration of implementation, strategic fit and consistency with the landscape plan.

VI. *Pending issues*

The following section describes the processes for modelling the to-be landscape and for deriving the planned landscape model.

4.4.3.1   To-be Landscape Modelling

To-be landscape modelling is a key part of the landscape planning process. The current landscape is gradually progressed toward the to-be landscape model through practical measures such as projects and maintenance. The to-be model serves as an authoritative framework to guide how projects and maintenance measures are managed at operating level (Fig. 4.24).

A to-be landscape model must meet the following criteria:

- Align IT to the business: The to-be landscape model is geared to enterprise strategy and business requirements and to the principles laid down in the IT strategy such as "make or buy" or "best of breed".

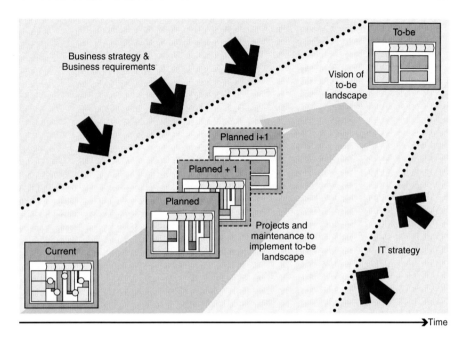

Fig. 4.24 To-be landscape model: roadmap for evolution of the application landscape

- Address and resolve points where there is a need for action; leverage optimisation potential
    Achieve effectiveness and efficiency gains, e.g. by reducing redundancy and delivering better business support.
- Create a reliable, future-proof IT landscape
    Ensure sustained reliability of business operation based on a robust application landscape which can take the business forward into the future.

Through the connections between the application and business landscape models, IT is linked with the corporate goals and business requirements which are the basis for deciding what form the IT landscape should take in the future. These corporate goals and business requirements are then broken down until they are detailed enough to define tangible activities for IT landscape planning (see Sect. 2.4.1). Let's look at an example of how this might work in practice.

Let's assume we have a general business goal of reducing new-product development times. One way into this issue would be to take a look at the business landscape model and investigate the business processes concerned with product development so as to locate the aspects which are relevant to IT. We might then decide that product development, product testing and series production all merit further analysis. These business processes can then be explored in terms of their impact on development times, so we'd probably investigate aspects such as how product data is managed, how well processes integrate with development partners or also with production systems.

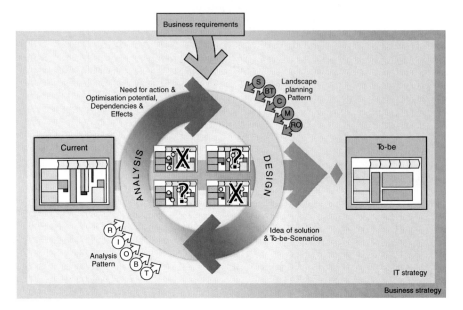

Fig. 4.25   Process of modelling the to-be landscape

Breaking business requirements down to IT-relevant aspects and analysing the existing landscape model from the perspective of these aspects are tasks which require a good grasp of the overall business issues and also method skills in IT landscape management. The outcome of this process is the basis for modelling the to-be landscape.

The to-be landscape model takes shape in an iterative process comprising **analysis** and **design** of the application landscape model and its relationships (see Fig. 4.25). Building on what each individual area – individual projects, for example – are actually about, the current landscape model is analysed from the perspective of the IT-relevant aspects which have been identified. IT-relevant aspects can include the ability of an application to integrate into a portal, support for product data management or how well IT systems can integrate into the environment.

Analysis

The **analysis** helps you zero in on points where it is likely there will be some need for action or potential for improvement. These findings serve as input for the design of the to-be landscape scenarios. It may also be necessary to enrich or update the landscape database by adding aspects particularly relevant for the analysis.

As well IT-relevant aspects, you will usually also analyse and appraise at least the following aspects:

- Business alignment: What contribution to strategy and the value proposition do the landscape elements make?
- Cost-benefit analysis: What overall costs can be allocated to the landscape element? How does this compare to the benefit the element delivers?

- Technical status: Is reliable, secure business operation assured?
- Risk: What risk is there at present, what risk will ensue if the enterprise goes ahead with the solution?

You might like to use the analysis patterns in Sect. 4.4.2. Figure 4.25 indicates that patterns "R", "I", "O", "B" and "T" have been applied in the analysis.

Design

The **design** part of the process is where you devise approaches and solutions to enact business requirements. These ideas are bundled into to-be scenarios, analysed and then appraised in terms of suitability as complete visions for the future landscape in the area under investigation. You can use design patterns (such as "locate coverage gaps" as an aid to creative processes.

Figure 4.25 shows the categories of landscape planning patterns which have been applied: "S", "BT", "C", "M" and "R". These categories are described later in this section.

Design work begins by defining the business and technical to-be landscape models (if not already done), the future business and technical reference models against to which you assign the current application landscape model. By forging links between the current application landscape model and the future frame of reference, you create common reference points for comparing the current and future landscape models.

The reference model also creates the starting point for analysing and designing the IT implementation roadmap. The technical to-be landscape model defines the scope within which ideas for solutions must remain. This has usually already been defined by this point, e.g. as the to-be blueprint in technical standardisation (see Chapter 5).

The creative design activity involves brainstorming ideas on IT-related aspects identified as pertinent for implementing business requirements. The ideas which emerge are roughly appraised to throw out those which are obviously inappropriate. Criteria for evaluating ideas can include the degree to which they address business requirements, strategic fit, implementation risk, cost and benefit, as well as other criteria of your choice (e.g. taken from project portfolio appraisal).

Useful hint:

This should be a genuine appraisal of ideas – don't just go through the motions!

If you are exploring a to-be scenario and cannot make any specific statement on its coverage of business requirements, omit the appraisal altogether so as not to falsify results.

In an iterative analysis and design process, the initial ideas are elaborated, refined and bundled into a set of alternative scenarios which cover all aspects of IT support for the area under investigation. These alternative to-be scenarios are each appraised according to predefined criteria, and those which do not fit are rejected. The remaining scenarios undergo further analysis to identify any mutual dependency and impact and explore other relevant issues.

These alternative scenarios are then presented to the decision-making board (e.g. IT landscape management board, see Chapter 6) with a recommendation on the preferred choice. The recommendation will usually include a draft implementation roadmap, enabling decision-makers to appraise the feasibility, duration, risk and cost of the scenarios. It is often sufficient at this stage make a generalised risk estimate (high or low risk). Table 4.8 gives an example of a scenario appraisal. As well as the table, portfolio diagrams are also a good way to present appraisals of alternative to-be scenarios.

Important:

Make a direct comparison between the alternative to-be scenarios and the current situation. Any scenario you envisage for the future must represent an improvement over the situation right now.

Following the decision, the new to-be model must be documented and communicated throughout the company in order to explicitly codify the policy and direction for the application landscape.

Overview of the Process

Your route to modelling the to-be landscape:

1. **Decide which area you are going to model**: Focus on the section of the landscape under investigation, document and consolidate the business requirements, and break these down into aspects which are relevant for IT.
2. **Design alternative to-be scenarios in iterations**

   - **Define the business and technical to-be landscape models**: If you have not already done so, model the business and technical to-be landscapes to serve as reference models for analysing and designing the IT implementation roadmap. The to-be models serve as reference points for linking the present application landscape model with the business and technical to-be landscape models.
   - **Analyse the current landscape model and the alternative to-be scenarios**: Analyse the current model by the IT-relevant aspects you have identified. It

Table 4.8 Example of appraisal of alternative to-be scenarios

	To-be scenario I	To-be scenario II ...
Business requirement 1		
IT-relevant aspect 1.1	8 (out of 10)	Not met
IT-relevant aspect 1.2	7 (out of 12)	9 (out of 12)
...		
Business requirement 2		
IT-relevant aspect 2.1	10 (out of 14)	10 (out of 14)
IT-relevant aspect 2.2	Not met	10 (out of 12)
...		
...		
Coverage of business requirements (weighted rating)	82%	88%
Fit with strategy		
Principle 1	high	low
Principle 2	medium	high
...		
Technical requirement 1	medium	high
...		
Fit with strategy	medium	medium
Risk appraisal	Low risk	High risk
Cost	300T – 500T	200T – 300T
Benefit	**200T/year**	**150T/year**

is useful to apply the standard analysis patterns. Document any points where there is need for action or potential for improvement.

If you find information is missing or that data is of insufficient quality or not up-to-date enough, work out what information you need and take steps to obtain it.

Analyse proposals for solutions and to-be scenarios which are already available, and determine their interdependencies and impacts.

   – **Identify and appraise proposals for solutions and alternative to-be scenarios.**

     (a) Pull together ideas on implementing business requirements in the section of the landscape model under investigation; apply the standard design patterns.

     (b) Appraise the ideas you have collected and reject those which are obviously unsuitable.

     (c) Bundle the remaining ideas into to-be scenarios which provide the complete IT support for the section of the model under investigation. Be sure to take into account the technical blueprint which might already have been defined at this stage.

     (d) Draft out an implementation roadmap, enabling decision-makers to appraise the feasibility, duration, risk and cost of each of the to-be scenarios.

     (e) Appraise the alternative to-be scenarios against appropriate criteria (e.g. from project portfolio management) for the issues your enterprise is seeking to address, such as cost, benefit, contribution to strategy and value proposition, strategic fit and implementation risk.

     (f) Formulate your recommendation.

3. **A decision on the authoritative to-be landscape model is taken by the relevant board e.g. IT landscape management board**
4. **Document and communicate the to-be landscape model**: Landscape planning patterns can help you model the to-be landscape. See the next Section and [Han09] for further information.

Planning Patterns for to-be Landscape Modelling

How do you find the ideas and to-be scenarios which implement business and IT requirements in the best possible way?

To-be landscape modelling is a creative process which requires in-depth understanding of the corporate strategy and business requirements, as well as how these requirements are mapped into IT. Modelling is made considerably easier by codifying this knowledge and experience. This is exactly what the following landscape planning patterns do: they distil experience and insights from a raft of projects and make this implicit knowledge explicit.

Landscape planning patterns are tried-and-tested, generalised templates for defining and diagramming a section of the to-be application landscape in a particular context. One example for a design template is a guideline for merging the various IT landscapes in the wake of a corporate merger.

You can use all or some of the patterns in to-be landscape modelling. They help produce proposals for planning scenarios in to-be landscape modelling quickly and easily. And, since they distil so much knowledge and experience, they are of considerable value to the creative design process.

Below is a summary of the various categories of landscape planning patterns, consolidated from experience across many projects. Detailed descriptions of these patterns are provided in the download attachment to [Han09].

- **S**: Identify isolated design components (the proposals for solutions). You need to brainstorm ideas for all IT-relevant aspects identified in the analysis. These are the ideas which are later merged to create the to-be landscape model.

    The following patterns were identified in this category:

    - Eradicate functional redundancy in business support and standardise competing applications.
    - Stop any gaps identified in the coverage of business support
        Improve business support by increasing the coverage of IT support with the help of new applications, or by extending the reach of adjacent applications to cover the gap.
    - Demerging: divide up applications by grouping them according to business criteria, e.g. for business clusters of applications.
    - Group applications with closely associated business functionality or strong mutual dependencies into a new to-be application (visionary modelling). Looser dependencies can be presented in the form of interfaces between applications.
    - Homogenise interfaces, thus reducing complexity by eliminating redundant interfaces or simplifying those which remain (e.g. m:n interfaces via a broker).
    - Apply a renewal strategy for applications or application clusters, with a range of action options or approaches such as introducing third-party software or open development depending on the outcome of analysis of criticality, technical state of health, etc.
    - Consolidate master data into central hubs to ensure consistency of business data.

- **BT**: Changes to the entire application landscape or large parts of it owing to business transformations such as corporate mergers.

    Business transformations such as mergers and acquisitions tend to bring a radical overhaul of the entire business model, changing the organisation, its business landscape model and by association its entire IT. Business transformations cannot be considered complete until the organisation, its processes, IT and particularly also the master data have all been transformed.

    In a business transformation, the business structure – the to-be business landscape model – is partly or completely overhauled, at least for the business units and enterprises involved. The new business structure forms the business reference model within which the new to-be application landscape will take shape. The current IT landscape model of the various business units then has to be investigated in terms of its fit with the new business reference model. This enables you to pinpoint areas where there is need for action or potential for optimisation to align the landscape with the new structure. Having identified these action points and potentials, you can develop and appraise ideas.

The following design patterns were identified for landscape modelling in the context of business transformations:

– Merge various IT landscapes: In mergers or acquisitions, the disparate IT landscapes have to grow and blend into a common landscape.
– Demerge an IT landscape: When an enterprise spins off parts of its operation, the IT landscape has to be modified accordingly, and non-essential parts have to be removed.

• C: Cost savings through consolidating the technical basis of applications and the infrastructure.

Technical consolidation carves out an opportunity for enormous cost savings. By standardising and homogenising applications, the technical basis and infrastructure, organisations can reduce their hardware, licence and maintenance costs and also cut their payroll. There also economies of scale obtainable by merging systems onto a single operating platform. Less technical diversity makes systems easier to integrate and reduces personnel costs: there are fewer systems to look after, and nor does the enterprise have to maintain a knowledge base (and integration capabilities) across a range of different technologies.

The following design patterns were identified in this category:

– Consolidate infrastructure (including data centres, hardware and networks) e.g. by merging various applications onto the same infrastructure units and also by merging locations
– Harmonise the technical basis of applications, e.g. databases or ERP base.

Important:

Each pattern can do no more than provide pointers for a particular section of the to-be landscape model. It is up to you to decide which ideas to use.

Landscape Planning Pattern: Example

Table 4.9 provides an example of a landscape planning pattern. The pattern "L-A-Red" enables you to produce a to-be landscape model without business redundancies. The general rules for documenting patterns are described in Table 4.4.

Table 4.9 Example of landscape planning pattern

Business landscape model	Application landscape model	Technical landscape model	Infrastructure landscape model	Project portfolio
L-A-Red	Eradicate functional redundancies in business support			Version 1.0

To eradicate functional redundancies and unify competing applications by consolidating business support

Procedure:

1. Identify functional redundancies in business support by applying analysis patterns R-A-Fct and R-A-BP

2. Define the to-be applications which will resolve these functional redundancies. The approach can be different depending on the design principle.

Alternative:

(I) Design principle "use old over new"

Pick the application which is the best match for the strategy being applied, such as "nearness of functionality" or "business process/function coverage". This application replaces the other applications in the context of the functional redundancy which has been identified.

If an application which is singled out for replacement also supports other business processes or functions, a new to-be release must be produced of both the replacing and the replaced application. IT support of the business process or function is taken over by the new to-be application release.

(II) Design principle "new applications"

Produce a new to-be application which replaces all applications in the context of the functional redundancy. This new application takes over IT support – in the context of the functional redundancy which has been identified – for business functions/processes previously provided by the application which it is replacing.

For both cases:

If the replaced application does not support any other business processes or business functions, it is marked as "to be replaced" as its lifecycle status. All assignments linking this application with business landscape elements are removed.

Apply the conditions relevant to the components used in your enterprise.

Context or requirements for applying the pattern	Deliverables of analysis pattern R-A-Fct and R-A-BP (see download attachment A) Design principles predefined: "Old over new" (see Sect. 2.4.2) or "New applications" and "Avoid redundancies" framed by principle "Only one productive release of an application" Selection strategy predefined: (1) "Nearness of functionality" (2) "Nearness of functionality and good state of health" (3) "Nearness of functionality or high degree of coverage of business process or function" (4) "Nearness of functionality or high degree of coverage of business process or function and good state of health"

Table 4.9 (continued)

Business landscape model	Application landscape model	Technical landscape model	Infrastructure landscape model	Project portfolio
L-A-Red	Eradicate functional redundancies in business support			Version 1.0
	An application can be said to have nearness of functionality to a business cluster when it supports a large number ("large" is relative to the enterprise) or exclusively the business processes of a process cluster, or the business functions of a function cluster, or the products of a product cluster. Applications can be said to have nearness of functionality when they deliver similar functionality to the same business cluster.			
Dependencies	With patterns R-A-Fct and R-A-BP (see download attachment A of [Han09]).			
Outcome of applyingthe pattern	Set of to-be applications, with just one application supporting each business function or each business process. Preferred diagram type: landscape diagram. Alternatives: mapping table and business cluster diagram with superimposed applications			
Outcome of applying the pattern, illustrated by typical examples	1. Step 1 is to apply analysis pattern R-A-BP.			

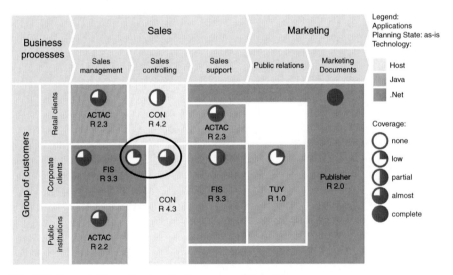

Fig. 4.26 Example illustrating L-A-Red: outcome of R-A-BP

Table 4.9 (continued)

Business landscape model	Application landscape model	Technical landscape model	Infrastructure landscape model	Project portfolio
L-A-Red	Eradicate functional redundancies in business support			Version 1.0

Figure 4.26 shows a redundancy in the coverage of the "sales controlling" business process for the "corporate clients" customer group. Applications FIS R3.3 and CON R4.3 both support the business process, whereby CON R4.3 provides a greater degree of functional coverage.

2. Define the to-be applications which will resolve the functional redundancies

Outcome of applying pattern as per (1) (Fig. 4.27):

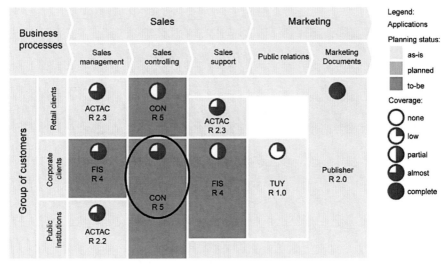

Fig. 4.27 Example illustrating L-A-Red: defining the to-be applications as per (1)

The new application release of CON, CON R 5, replaces application FIS in terms of its support for the "sales controlling" business process. Since application FIS R4 now has to be adapted, a new release is required: FIS R4.

Compliance with design strategy "Only one productive release of an application" is checked for each to-be application. If there is found to be another application release, it is replaced by the new application. In this example, application CON R5 will in future be used to support the "sales controlling" business process for all customer groups.

Outcome presented as a mapping table:

Application releases FIS R3.3, CON R4.2 and CON R4.3 are indicated in Fig. 4.28 as "to be replaced".

Application of pattern as per (2):

The to-be-application "NEW" is produced as a new application (see Fig. 4.29). New releases of applications FIS and CON are produced, without support of the "sales controlling" business process for corporate clients.

Table 4.9   (continued)

Business landscape model	Application landscape model	Technical landscape model	Infrastructure landscape model	Project portfolio
L-A-Red	Eradicate functional redundancies in business support			Version 1.0

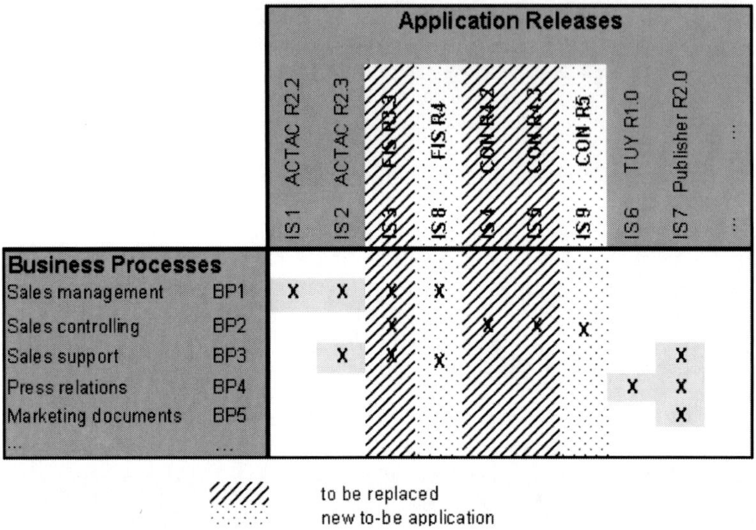

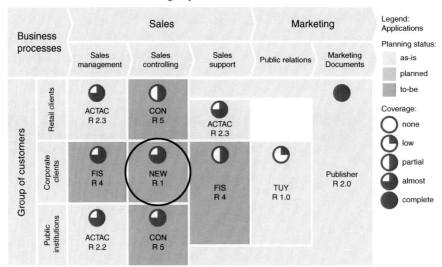

Fig. 4.28 Example illustrating L-A-Red: mapping table

In this case, it is not recommended to show the outcome in a mapping table because this does not permit direct representation of the dependency with the customer groups.

Fig. 4.29 Example illustrating L-A-Red: defining the to-be applications as per (2)

[Han09] provides further patterns which you can use for modelling the to-be IT landscape in your enterprise.

Modelling the to-be landscape: ground rules:

- Cascade IT-relevant aspects out of corporate goals and business requirements.
- Analyse the overall landscape model in terms of these IT-relevant aspects, also in terms of need for action or potential for optimisation. You can use the analysis patterns (see Sect. 4.4.2) to help you.
- Identify proposals for solutions, and assemble your to-be scenarios. The design patterns can help you here.
- Decide on a ratings system to appraise each of the to-be scenarios.
- And, last but not least, don't let the planning become an end in itself! Keep the effort in proportion to the benefit.

4.4.3.2 Deduce Implementation Scenarios

The to-be landscape model often differs from the current model in fundamental ways. In general, the gap between the two is so wide it cannot be bridged in a single step. The challenge is then to identify feasible, manageable implementation steps, appraise alternative planning scenarios and present the overall implementation roadmap such that the general direction is clear (see Fig. 4.19).

A planned landscape model is the planned state of a particular landscape model at a particular point in time. Frequently the plans are produced with annual time horizons. A planned landscape model describes one step on the trajectory from the as-is landscape model to the to-be model, or one step between two planned landscape models. In medium-term planning, you will typically map out the target landscapes for an extended period of time, but not too far into the future. A horizon of three to no more than five years is customary. Accordingly, medium-term planning is a milestone on the road to the to-be landscape model.

Each step in the implementation roadmap can itself comprise a range of steps which are implemented in one or more projects or maintenance measures. A planned landscape model is therefore essentially a set of tasks which are orchestrated to usher the landscape toward its to-be status. With each planned landscape model, the status gradually progresses toward the vision of the landscape which you have for the future.

Important:

When deriving your implementation roadmap, make sure that each step is consistent with the officially approved to-be landscape model, and can also be completed within a practicable timeframe. Draft out solutions and implementation steps, also making a rough estimate of time and cost.

In an iterative process of **analysis** and **design**, you identify and analyse implementation steps – individual steps or sets – and form them into alternative planning scenarios which are then subjected to a full appraisal (see Fig. 4.30).

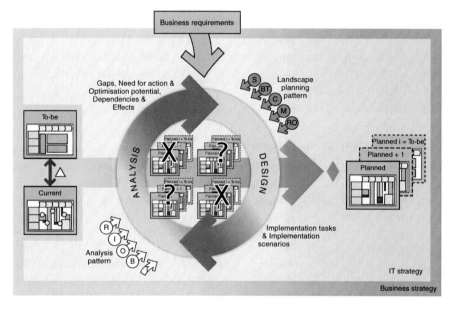

Fig. 4.30 Process of deriving the planned landscape model

Deriving the Planned Landscape: Analysis Activities

In **analysis**, you compare and contrast the current landscape model with the officially approved to-be landscape model in order to highlight the deltas. However, for the deltas to show through at all, the same business reference model must be used for both the current and to-be models.

Important:

The two landscapes must be compared using the same system of coordinates. You must use the to-be business landscape model as your reference model, since otherwise differences between the current and to-be models will not show through.

Detailed analysis is essential to identify all the deltas and their business impact. Figure 4.31 shows an example of deltas. Each row in the table shows a delta with identifiable differences in each of the landscape models, and the business impact of each difference.

		Landscape				Business effects	Barycentric activities
		Business	Application	Technical	Infrastructure		
G1	Order processing system	Automation of the business functions in order processing	New order processing system and new interface to the business partner system	-	-	Increased efficiency through elimination of manual tasks Consolidated customer master dasta	Master data management of customer data Introduction of a new order processing system
G2	CRM	Changing of CRM functionality, business processes, and business data	Changes on CRM system ACTAC Replacement of application FIS	-	Extended CRM infrastructure	Improved customer integration, especialliy fewer quality problems Harmonized product master data	Evaluating Master data management solutions Establiching a CRM infrastructure Expanding existing CRM application and CRM infrastructure
...	...						

Fig. 4.31 Example of deltas

More analysis is carried out once possible tasks or full or partial planning scenarios have been identified for the implementation roadmap. These planning scenarios are analysed and appraised by whatever criteria is relevant for the context. As shown in Fig. 4.30, the analysis patterns described in Sect. 4.4.2 can be used here. Figure 4.30 shows the categories of analysis pattern which were applied: "R", "I", "O", "B" and "T".

Deriving the Planned Landscape: Design Activities

Design activities largely comprise identifying and bundling implementation tasks and merging them into implementation scenarios. The alternative scenarios are each appraised, enabling a recommendation to be made for the planned landscape model.

Having identified the deltas by comparing the current and to-be landscape models, you now explore potential practical interventions to close these gaps. You can

	Correlation to barycentric activities						Coverage of business requirements						Dependencies between implentation tasks								
	H I	H II	H III	H IV	H V	...	BR I	BR II	BR III	BR IV	BR V	...	T1	T2	T3	T4	T5	T6	T7	T8	...
T1	✓			✓			✓	✓					☒	☒							
T2		✓	✓				✓		✓	✓			☒			☒	☒		☒	☒	
T3	✓			✓			✓			✓			☒				☒			☒	
T4	✓		✓				✓		✓	✓			☒			☒	☒		☒	☒	
T5		✓	✓				✓	✓	✓	✓			☒	☒	☒	☒	☒	☒	☒		
T6							✓						☒				☒				
T7	✓			✓							✓		☒							☒	
T8		✓					✓						☒				☒				
...																					

✓ complete coverage
✓ leveraged coverage
✓ low coverage

Fig. 4.32 Example of a list of implementation tasks

determine and document mutual dependencies and impacts of implementation tasks, and decide where to focus activities. Setting priorities helps make the potentially large number of tasks more manageable.

An example of a list of implementation tasks is shown in Fig. 4.32. For each task, the figure lists the action priority, the coverage of business requirements and dependencies between tasks.

Analysing implementation tasks in terms of dependencies, impact and urgency gives you an idea how to prioritise and bundle them (you might also choose to prioritise certain elements of tasks as appropriate). The urgency of a task is determined by the urgency of the need for action on operating and strategic levels. The resulting bundles of tasks and planning scenarios are then evaluated and analysed in terms of dependencies, and some will inevitably be culled at a very early stage. Figure 4.33 illustrates a scheme for evaluating individual tasks and task bundles.

Table 4.10 illustrates how planning scenarios can be evaluated. Unlike tasks and task bundles, each planning scenario represents a complete implementation roadmap. The scenarios can constitute alternative course of actions.

The key criteria for appraising the scenario are coverage, the time to implement business requirements, implementation risk, landscape fit, cost and benefit. You can also add other criteria of your choice (for example taken from project portfolio evaluation). As well as tabular format, you can also use portfolios to present the evaluation of planning scenarios.

The planning scenarios are then appraised and presented to a decision-making board such as the IT landscape management board (see Sect. 6.2), possibly with a recommendation on a course of action. Once the board has taken a decision, the new implementation planning must be documented and communicated throughout the company. The approved implementation roadmap serves as the basis for making project proposals and managing them in the project portfolio.

Evaluation of implementation tasks						
	Risk	Strategy fit	Landscape fit	Benefit monetary	Benefit qualitative	Urgency	Import-ance
T1	low	70%	100%	100T/Y	low	high	low
T2	high	30%	30%	20T/Y	middle	high	high
T3	middle	50%	50%	75T/Y	high	middle	middle
T4	high	70%	20%	60T/Y	low	low	high
T5	low	30%	90%	150T/Y	high	high	low
T6	high	50%	20%	200T/Y	middle	middle	high
T7	middle	20%	30%	125T/Y	low	low	middle
T8	low	90%	80%	10T/Y	high	low	low
...							

Fig. 4.33 How implementation tasks can be evaluated

Overview of the Process

Your route to deriving the planned landscape model:

1. **Decide which area you are going to plan, define a planning horizon**

   Determine what the area will comprise and define the planning horizon.

2. **Iteratively derive and appraise alternative planning scenarios**

   - If you have not already done so, produce the common business reference model for comparing and contrasting the current and to-be landscapes.
   - Analyse the deltas between the current and to-be landscape models, or between planned landscape models.

     Deltas can be caused by gaps in the current landscape model, by replacing and/or changing components, or through tidying up loose ends.

     To analyse the deltas, you may need to add more detail to the current and to-be landscape models. Break down the current and to-be application landscape models into finer-grained components (the breakdown should reflect the elements of the to-be business landscape model) and assign business objects and interfaces to the applications. This makes it easier to identify points where there is potentially a need to refine or change the to-be landscape model.
   - Having identified the deltas, determine where you are going to focus activity. You should not have more than 10 action priorities.
   - Decide on possible interventions to close the gaps, and appraise the urgency of these interventions by considering how immediately action on the issue in question is required at operating level. Determine content-related and chronological interdependencies between the implementation tasks.

Table 4.10 Example of an evaluation of planning scenarios

	Planning scenario I comprising M1, M3, M7 and M8	Planning scenario II comprising M2, M4 and M7 ...
Business requirement 1		
IT-relevant aspect 1.1	M1, M7	Not met
IT-relevant aspect 1.2	M8	M2
...		
Business requirement 2		
IT-relevant aspect 2.1	M3, M7	M7
IT-relevant aspect 2.2	Not met	M4
...		
...		
Coverage of business requirements	82%	88%
Fit with IT landscape plan	good	poor
Fit with strategy	medium	medium
Risk appraisal (occurrence, severity [4])		
Risk 1 – severity I	10%	-
Risk 2 – severity III	80%	20%
...		
Implementation risk	high	medium
Cost	Year 1: 300T – 500T Year 2: 400T – 600T	Year 1: 400T – 600T Year 2: 100T – 200T Year 3: 200T – 400T
Implementation period	2 years	3 years
Benefit	200T/year after first implementation stage	150T/year

- Package implementation tasks or sub-tasks into bundles and planning scenarios.
- Appraise each of these task bundles and planning scenarios.
- Formulate your recommendation.

---

[4] Classification: I lowest severity, II medium severity, III highest severity.

3. **Produce project proposals on the basis of the approved implementation roadmap and add them to the project portfolio.**
4. **Document and communicate the approved implementation roadmap.**

By this time, you might be wondering: how does one locate the deltas between the current and to-be landscape models? How does one define appropriate implementation tasks to close the gaps? What alternative planning scenarios can be formed by bundling these tasks? Which planning scenarios are suitable? The next section provides guidelines on answering these questions.

Pattern for Deriving the Planned Landscape Model

Designing the implementation roadmap is a creative process which requires in-depth understanding of the corporate strategy and business requirements, as well as how these requirements are mapped into IT. The creative design process can be made considerably easier by codifying this knowledge and experience.

Planning patterns are tried-and-tested, generalised templates for arriving at implementation tasks, action priorities and planning scenarios to close the gap between the current and to-be landscape models in a particular context. One example of a planning pattern is a guideline for defining an implementation roadmap for replacing core systems.

You can use all or some of these patterns, depending on your requirements. They help you quickly and easily produce proposals for analysing and designing an implementation roadmap.

Below is a summary of the various categories of planning patterns, consolidated from experience across many projects. Detailed descriptions of these patterns are provided in [Han09].

- **A**: Identify action priorities, define tasks and bundle into planning scenarios

  Comparing and contrasting the current and to-be landscape models and the various planning statuses shows up the deltas. These can be grouped into focal points for activities, to which you can add action priorities emerging from operational level.

  To implement the underlying business requirements, the next step is to identify appropriate implementation tasks and bundle these into one or more alternative planning scenarios. Each of these scenarios is then appraised, enabling planners to submit a recommendation on a particular course of action.

  The following planning patterns have been consolidated from project experience:

  - Compare and contrast various states of the application landscape model using a common business reference model
  - Analyse deltas and identify action priorities
  - Identify implementation tasks and group them into planning scenarios

- **RO**: Rollout strategy when replacing core systems: The key patterns for rollout strategies are the "big bang" and "evolutionary" strategies.

  - "Big-bang" rollout strategy: In a big-bang rollout strategy, new applications are introduced in one big step, generally coinciding with the retirement of core systems. The renewal is comprehensive, without interim steps.

    Big-bang rollouts usually address large, associated sections of the to-be landscape model such as an entire business cluster. Given the complexity of the undertaking, the rollout – whether of own-build or third-party software – has to be managed in a separate project.

    Evaluation: The big-bang approach does have considerable complexity and is a high-risk activity. However, it is the quickest way to achieve overall change. Projects are often lengthy, which increases the probability that business requirements or external constraints will change over the project. The success of a big-bang rollout depends on how well the complexity of the undertaking is understood and managed, and how well the organisation can take the strain.

  - "Evolutionary" rollout strategy: When a core system is replaced gradually, or when individual or component-based third-party software[5] is introduced as part of the future systems, the core system and to-be systems are divided into functional blocks to reflect the groupings in the to-be landscape model. Functional blocks are then segregated out of the landscape and developed in a set of feasible and manageable implementation tasks. Tasks tend to be prioritised on urgency and importance, so initial tasks will usually focus on the more urgent action priorities or areas which make a major contribution to the value proposition.

    Evaluation: Since an evolutionary approach involves introducing systems step by step in manageable portions, duration and risk remain manageable for each step. Changes to external parameters can be accommodated no later than the next implementation step. Each step should take no longer than one year.

    The drawback of the evolutionary approach is that it can necessitate highly complex interim solutions. This has to be taken into account in the overall evaluation.

Detailed descriptions of these patterns are provided in the download attachment to [Han09].

Important:

Each planning pattern can do no more than provide pointers on implementation tasks, action priorities and sections of the planned landscape model. It is up to you to decide which ideas to use.

---

[5]An evolutionary approach is frequently not feasible when you are introducing third-party software, since adaptive integration tends to involve far too much effort.

Deriving the planned landscape model: ground rules:

- Make sure the current and to-be landscape models use the same coordinate system.
- Pinpoint the deltas between the current and to-be models, and identify action priorities. This is the only way you will be able to manage the many differences.
- Identify the implementation tasks which can feasibly close the gaps. Evaluate the tasks, establish the urgency of each, and which dependencies exist between them. This is the key prerequisite for collecting tasks into bundles and forming planning scenarios.
- Decide on a ratings system to appraise implementation tasks and planning scenarios.
- And, last but not least, don't let the planning become an end in itself! Keep the effort in proportion to the benefit.

4.4.4 Governing the Further Development of the IT Landscape

Further development of the IT landscape has to remain on a trajectory that steers it toward the target landscape vision, and the measures orchestrated to develop the IT landscape must be consistent with the implementation roadmap. To make strategic IT management easier, it has to be possible to check progress toward the target landscape quickly at all times by reviewing how the outcomes of maintenance and projects actually measure up against the original planning. A synchronised plan provides an at-a-glance overview of planning snapshots and key milestones such as the go-live dates of applications. Figure 4.34 illustrates

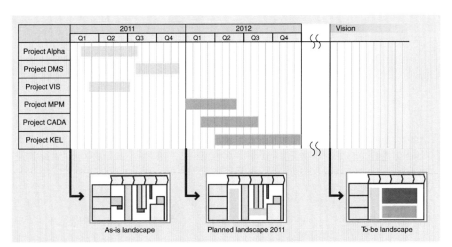

Fig. 4.34 A synchronised plan

a synchronised plan in which the planning status is presented on a year-to-year basis. A plan like this is a good tool to show up the changes in landscapes (business, application, technical and infrastructure) effected in connection with projects.

As well as the synchronised plan, another way to highlight changes or progress is to use a chronological sequence of portfolios (see Fig. 4.35).

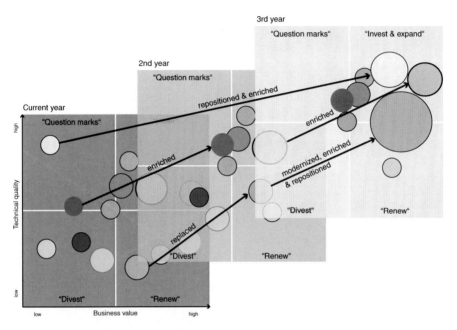

Fig. 4.35 Using portfolios to present changes

To manage the evolution of the IT landscape effectively, you need to define appropriate metrics and indicators, and to establish a control toolkit (see Chapter 6). This enables your enterprise to monitor the current status of the IT landscape and progress on development.

However, metrics and toolkits are not enough on their own. IT landscape management also has to be integrated into project and service management, and into decision-making processes across the enterprise. Even in the run-up to a new project, the project managers should be asking for input from IT landscape management. Likewise, this interplay is essential to manage the IT landscape effectively: without an awareness of new focal points in the enterprise, it is impossible to steer the development of the IT landscape and manage implementation. Further details are provided in Sects. 4.5.1 and 4.5.2.

Fact file:

- You can only influence the development of the application landscape by institutionalising IT landscape management in your IT organisation and decision-making processes (see Sect. 4.5).
- Install post-hoc controlling to verify that IT landscape management is working effectively. Make sure reviews consider the benefit cases presented for projects and for IT landscape management itself: have promised benefits genuinely materialised?

4.5 Establish Organisational Change

Key to making IT landscape management work effectively is to institutionalise it in the organisation. Unless practices are embedded, it will be impossible to ensure landscape database is consistently kept up-to-date and at a high enough quality, and that landscape plans are genuinely operationalised in projects and maintenance measures.

To embed IT landscape management in organisational structures, it takes:

- Clear roles and responsibilities in IT landscape management
- Integration of IT landscape management processes, particularly maintenance, into the processes in IT and decision-making
- An estimate of the maturity of IT in terms of IT landscape management.

Important:

Introducing IT landscape management instigates a process of change in the enterprise. How this change is orchestrated, and which processes are introduced, must be consistent with the maturity level within the organisation. Guidelines are provided in Sect. 4.5.3.

4.5.1 Roles and Responsibilities

IT landscape management requires a dedicated role, that of the enterprise architect, with clear-cut responsibilities, obligations, participation and execution rights.

How many enterprise architects a company needs depends on its size and how its IT is organised. In centrally organised IT (see Chapter 6), there is often a separate architect for each business segment, each responsible for the landscape cluster of the segment in question. One also finds enterprise architects in centralised IT – often in central corporate units – with more generalised tasks, such as developing methods, making tools available, consolidating IT landscapes and planning enterprise-wide IT landscapes.

> **Important:**
>
> Have an appropriate number of enterprise architects for your company size, and define their position consistent with your organisational structure. In general, a medium-sized company will need no more than one enterprise architect, and this individual can fulfil other roles at the same time.

An enterprise architect is responsible for executing all the processes in IT landscape management. However, the as-is IT landscape tends not to be documented by enterprise architects themselves, since they do not generally have the requisite detailed knowledge about applications and interfaces. In many cases, this task will be performed by application managers in application maintenance phases, or by project members (e.g. business enterprise architects) in projects. The task of the enterprise architect is then to provide application managers and project staff with appropriate methods and tools for the job and to quality-assure the documentation. Quality assurance should be an ongoing process, geared toward the need-for-action points.

Planned and to-be landscape models are usually kept up-to-date by the enterprise architects themselves. Decisions taken in project portfolio management are documented as planned landscapes. It is also usually the enterprise architect's job to document the officially approved to-be and planned landscape models.

By analysing the landscape models, enterprise architects can highlight points where there is need for action or potential for optimisation and show up evidence of areas meriting further analysis. They can use landscape information as a basis for design ideas and provide prompt, well-substantiated contributions on the feasibility and impact of ideas in both the business and IT camps of the enterprise.

With strategic and operating-level business requirements framing their considerations, enterprise architects work out alternatives for the target application landscape and its implementation roadmap, and appraise each of these alternatives by the enterprise's chosen criteria. These alternatives are then submitted to the decision-making board for IT landscape management (perhaps also with a recommendation on a course of action).

As well as documenting, planning and quality-assuring the landscape model, enterprise architects also give direction. By designing the target application landscape model and its implementation roadmap, they ultimately stake out the objectives for future development of the application landscape. The possibility of measuring progress toward the target and planned landscape models (overall or project-based) is an effective tool in steering development. For this to work, however, enterprise architects must be part of official processes for developing strategy, managing projects, maintenance and taking IT decisions, as well as being on the relevant boards.

The skill profile of an enterprise architect is daunting – but it does take finely-honed capabilities to achieve the benefits discussed in Sect. 4.2:

- **Highly experienced employee, in the company for many years, with good business and IT knowledge**, with an overall understanding – in technical and in functional terms – of the application landscape and a good network within the company.

  Enterprise architects must act as sparring partners for the business and IT camps in order to pull together salient information for documenting and planning the IT landscape. They have to speak the language of IT, and be able to ask the right questions.
- **Ability to grasp new concepts quickly and find workable solutions; good conceptual thinking skills**: An ability to pull and place information correctly, distinguish what is important and derive meaningful answers from the plethora of information available.
- **High level of commitment, good communication skills, and ability to present a compelling case**: Particularly in the first few years after introduction, IT landscape management is an uphill struggle. Architects have to persevere, reinforcing the case to application managers, project managers and business users, and achieve a consensus in a group of individuals with highly diverse professional backgrounds.
- **Innovative, enterprising, far-sighted**: Enterprise architects must have the innovative thinking skills to spot potential for optimisation in business and IT. Thinking like an entrepreneur is also essential to identify strategic implications which cut across every segment of the business, and to appraise each course of action. Enterprise architects also have to be far-sighted enough to keep short-term, medium-term and long-term planning horizons in view.

Fact file:

- Enterprise architects document, plan and quality-assure the IT landscape; they also give direction.
- Enterprise architects are responsible for documenting, analysing, planning and directing the application landscape model. By analysing the entire model – or by zeroing in on particular sections – they can uncover the points where there is need for action or potential for optimisation,

and highlight evidence of issues warranting further analysis. With actions directed to implementing business and IT goals, they design the target landscape model and implementation roadmap.

- In many cases, application managers are tasked with documenting the current application landscape model. However, enterprise architects remain responsible for the content of this documentation and – fulfilling their quality assurance function – must make sure the data provided is of sufficient quality.

4.5.2 Integration into Processes of IT and Decision Making

IT landscape management touches on the following strategic and operating-level management processes:

- IT strategy development: The IT strategy maps out general principles such as "make or buy", application strategies and strategic IT goals as objectives for IT landscape management, creating a basis for modelling the to-be and planned landscape models and documenting the outcomes in the IT strategy document (see Sect. 2.5.2).
- Strategic controlling: IT landscape management forges links between structures in business and in IT, enabling objectives for business structures to be linked with structures in IT. Information on these structural connections and objectives are a key contribution to strategic IT controlling.

    What strategic IT controlling does is review whether strategic objectives are genuinely being enacted. Information from strategic IT controlling is channelled back into landscape planning to adjust the to-be and planned landscape models.
- Technical standardisation: This prescribes the IT standards for components such as databases which the enterprise has elected to use in developing the IT landscape. In determining how and where technical components are utilised in landscapes, the technical standards make an important contribution to IT landscape management.

    Information also flows in the opposite direction: analysis of the landscape database serves to identify points where there is a need for action or potential for optimisation, and this is input for the technical standardisation process.
- Project steering and maintenance: Projects and maintenance are the vehicles by which the to-be and planned landscape models are operationalised. IT landscape management supports projects and measures in a variety of ways:

    - IT landscape management provides valuable contributions as early as the project definition stage, with the documentation of the as-is, planned and to-be landscape models enabling the content and scope of projects and measures

to be defined more sharply. It is also easier to identify points warranting more detailed investigation. Projects become far quicker to define and get underway.
- Timely, well-founded analysis which specifically addresses the areas of concern in a project provides valuable input to the project or measure, particularly at the early scope-setting stage.
- IT landscape management documents the content and implementation times of all projects, enabling them to be consolidated where necessary. By revealing potential conflicts, IT landscape management makes a key contribution to project synchronisation.
- The modelling guidelines help people working on projects and measures to document the IT landscape, also simplifying the quality assurance process.

• Service management (infrastructure): The coarse-grained units in the infrastructure documentation and planning form the infrastructure landscape model. These units are utilised in IT landscape management. Vice versa, IT landscape management also provides input to infrastructure landscape modelling by identifying the points where there is possibly a need for action or potential for optimisation.
• Delivery management and vendor management: Analysis of the entire landscape model can provide valuable input for managing sourcing and vendors, provided the relevant metrics and indicators are included in the documentation of the IT landscape.

Integrating Update Processes

Important:

Without integrating landscape database maintenance into operating-level and strategic IT management processes, it is doubtful whether the documentation of the IT landscape can be kept adequately up-to-date and consistent.

Maintenance of the current landscape model (as-is and planned) should be made part of project portfolio management and project management, as shown in Fig. 4.36. The as-is and planned landscape models should be updated at predefined milestones in project management, at the very latest before systems go live. The outcomes of project portfolio management must also be documented promptly to ensure the planned landscape model is kept sufficiently up-to-date. The same goes for maintenance measures: changes which arise during maintenance and upkeep can be integrated at predefined times in the update process; the latest possible point is before systems go into productive operation.

As soon as a to-be or planned landscape model has received official approval, the relevant landscape planning data should be entered or updated. Landscape planning

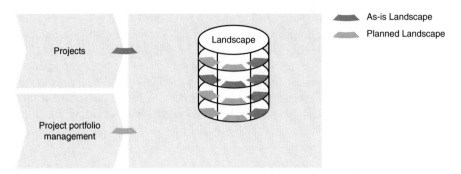

Fig. 4.36 Maintenance of current landscape model, integrated into IT processes and decision-making

entails developing, analysing and appraising planning scenarios – in some cases alternatives – for both the to-be and planned models. The most suitable scenario is submitted as a recommendation to the decision making board. Once the board has given its official go-ahead – but not before – the officially approved planning is integrated into the landscape database (see Fig. 4.37).

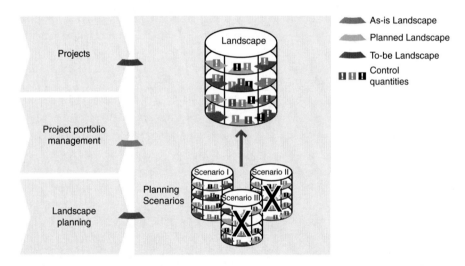

Fig. 4.37 Maintaining the to-be landscape

Important:

If it is impossible to integrate data maintenance into IT processes right away, you must ensure that modified data is updated at regular intervals, e.g. monthly.

Consistency checks and quality assurance of the documentation should be a fixed part of the regular update process, ensuring data quality is sustained over time. These rules and policies are part of the maintenance concept (see Sect. 4.4.1).

Involvement in Decision-Making Boards

It is difficult to influence IT decisions without membership or involvement in the boards which actually take these decisions. Each enterprise will have different boards and entities for IT governance – at least a general group for IT investment decisions and strategic IT planning (see Chapter 6). Decisions relating to the evolution of the IT landscape and business landscape model require a separate board, termed the "IT landscape management board" in the following. This board sets out planning assumptions, appraises alternative planning scenarios and makes a recommendation for the to-be landscape model or its implementation roadmap. These outcomes are required for developing the IT strategy and serve as input for the IT board and project portfolio management.

The IT landscape management board consists of the CIO and – key to the board's composition – enterprise architects (see Sect. 3.4.1). Other members can be IT or business managers or individuals with specialist expertise from the business units.

IT implementation of business requirements can be planned efficiently and effectively in an interdisciplinary team comprising application, business and IT architects. The business enterprise architects are often members of the business segments.

What matters here is to ensure IT landscape management dovetails closely with business planning and can influence project portfolio management. It can contribute by:

- Verifying consistency of projects with the to-be and planned landscape models
- Providing information for evaluating and prioritising projects in terms of the entire portfolio
- Providing prompt, well-substantiated statements on feasibility and the impact of ideas in business and IT, e.g. through "what-if" analysis
- Highlight potential conflicts between projects.

Fact file:

Integration into processes in IT and decision-making is vital to ensure the documentation of the IT landscape is kept sufficiently up-to-date and consistent. Ultimately, the entire benefit of IT landscape management hinges on the quality of this information.

If it is impossible to integrate update processes into IT and decision-making right away, you can for an interim period have data maintenance carried out regularly at fixed times.

4.5.3 Maturity Level of IT Landscape Management

The organisation and processes of IT landscape management must be aligned with its maturity level – as must the rollout of IT landscape management in the enterprise. If maturity is low, for instance, you should not begin IT landscape planning at the first stage.

Landscape planning requires a base of data which must be sufficiently up-to-date and of adequate quality for analysis and for designing the target landscape. You need a maintenance concept (see Sect. 4.4.1) which sets out the code of practice for building the repository of landscape database, and maintenance must become an institutionalised part of processes in IT and decision-making (see Sect. 4.5.2). Many stakeholders have to be brought on side – and all need convincing that this is the right way to go. As a rule, it can take several years to get functioning update processes hardwired into IT processes and decision-making – even with relentless commitment on the part of enterprise architects and the CIO.

Brian Burke, Gartner [Gar08] expresses this succinctly: "EA programs typically take 3 years to-become mature. Start small. Pick low-hanging fruit. Build credibility. Develop the EA program through multiple iterations. Speed before breadth, breadth before depth."

Maturity models such as Cobit or ITIL (see [Joh07], [itS08] and [Luf00]) help unearth the latent possibilities for process improvements, and identify the gaps, particularly in critical processes, which can help you make a case to management.

Estimating maturity in IT landscape management requires a more detailed investigation. To obtain a complete picture of the status quo, the appraisal must include content, processes, organisation, steering and tool support. The following aspects are important:

- **Content of enterprise architecture (level of documentation, documentation method)**

  - Completeness
    Have all landscape models and the interactions between them (e.g. business alignment) been addressed? Have all parts of the enterprise or just sections been documented?
  - Granularity, up-to-dateness, quality and consistency
    Are there objectives and guidelines for documentation?
    Has the right granularity been used for all landscape elements and for the relationships between them (see Sect. 3.3)?
    Are documentation and landscape database adequately up-to-date, coherent and consistent?
  - Ease of maintenance
    Can the structure, metrics & indicators and extended data prescribed by the enterprise architecture be maintained without undue effort?

- **Processes**

  - Completeness of IT landscape management processes
    Have all IT landscape management processes (see Sect. 4.4) been defined?
  - Landscape planning horizon
    If IT landscapes are being planned at all, is there any medium-term planning?
    Is there a strategic plan which serves as the vision?
  - Maturity of processes
    What is the status of process documentation? Are decision-making authorities
    and boards clearly defined? Are there clearly defined and communicated meth-
    ods? Is there regular process optimisation? How are stakeholders informed? Is
    there a communication plan?
  - Practicability
    How comprehensible, simple and efficient are the processes?

- **Organisation**

  - Roles and responsibilities
    Are there clearly defined roles and responsibilities for all IT landscape man-
    agement processes? Does the company have enterprise architects? Do they
    have the right skill level?
  - Integration into processes in IT and decision-making (process integration)
    Are IT landscape management processes integrated into workflows in IT and
    decision-making? Where has process integration already taken place? What
    boards are there?
      Examples of processes to be integrated with IT landscape management:
    IT strategy development, technical standardisation, demand management,
    project management, software development, change management, security
    management and service level management.
      Examples of IT decision processes: general IT management support, project
    portfolio management, project steering, vendor management, personnel devel-
    opment
  - Stakeholders
    Has a stakeholder analysis be completed? Who are the sponsors? In IT? In the
    business? What is their influence? Who are the beneficiaries? What agendas
    are people pursuing with EAM? Who is the provider of data?
    Is there any feedback from stakeholders? One-off or regular? In what way is
    feedback obtained?

- **Steering the future development of the IT landscape: governance**

  - Reach or influence
    What parts of the business (e.g. business units or processes) are being
    addressed? Which are already involved?
  - Verifying conformity
    Are projects or applications checked in terms of their fit with the landscape
    plan or with prescribed standards?

- – Performance management for controlling effectiveness and efficiency
  What metrics and indicators are used to steer the evolution of the IT landscape (see also Chapter 6)? Which measurement criteria are available? To what
  extent have these been operationalised?
  Are customers satisfied?
  Is the benefit of EAM presented in qualitative terms? Are at least parts of the
  benefit quantified?

- **Tool support**

  - – Extent of tool support
    To what extent are the processes of documentation, analysis, planning and
    control supported? What diagramming, analysis and simulation options are
    available?
  - – Usability
    How user-friendly is the tool? How simply and efficiently can it perform rou-
    tine tasks? Is there any support for routine tasks and consistency checks? Can
    even occasional users work intuitively with the tool? Is there a good level of
    user buy-in?
    Can the tool provide all possible beneficiaries promptly and appropriately with
    the information they need?
  - – Automation and integration
    To what extent is process, project and operating data and other data required
    for IT landscape management integrated? What possibilities are there for
    importing and exporting data? What types of automation or integration with
    other tools are there?
  - – Adaptability to enterprise needs
    Can the requisite structures and diagrams be represented with the tool? Is there
    a possibility of producing views for specific roles, users or groups (e.g. for all
    enterprise architects in a business segment)?

The appraisal of these individual aspects can be systematised using a unified
rating scheme, making them objective and comparable across the company. Each
of the aspects can be assigned a set of responses, creating a multiple-choice-type
survey for stakeholders to complete. The scores on each of the aspects are then
aggregated into an overall evaluation. The results are often represented in the form
of a spider diagram (see [Mül05]).

A qualitative evaluation is however also quite sufficient to determine the
maturity level. Developed on the basis of practical experience, the maturity
level model presented in Fig. 4.38 enables you to use your own qualitative
appraisal to estimate the maturity level of IT landscape management in your
enterprise.

Important:

Appraise your IT on each of these aspects. Even if you can only make a qualitative appraisal, you can still determine the maturity level.

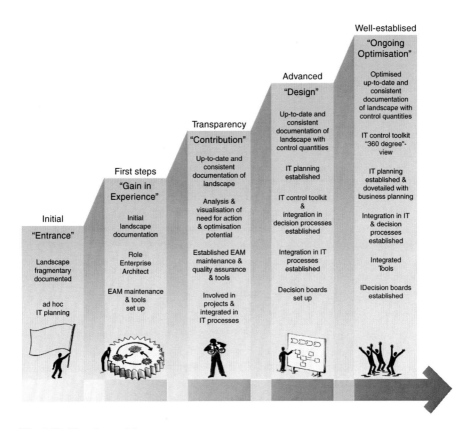

Fig. 4.38   Maturity model

This maturity model differentiates between the following stages:

- Initial: "Entrance"
- First steps: "Gain in experience"
- Transparency: "Contribution"
- Advanced: "Design"
- Well-established: "Ongoing optimisation"

If the maturity fails even to reach "initial" it will be difficult to introduce IT landscape management – perhaps impossible if there is no-one at senior management level prepared to champion the undertaking. With there as yet being no one who sees a benefit in IT landscape management, the CIO and IT managers have a lot of convincing to do. Worse still, the CIO and IT managers have only a slim budget and few resources at their disposal, yet must tackle all the maturity issues simultaneously in order to get IT landscape management going in the first place. It takes major personal commitment and perseverance to see this long change process through to completion.

The various stages in the maturity model are each discussed in detail below. The qualitative characteristics of each stage enable you to make your own estimate of maturity in your enterprise and to scope out possible steps to raise the level.

"Initial" Level

This is the level most enterprises start from. The following characteristics are indicative of "initial" maturity:

- Documentation of the IT landscape resembles more of a patchwork – produced as part of major projects, for instance, and not kept up-to-date once projects are complete. Granularity differs because sometimes only project-specific sections have been documented in detail. Documentation is often widely disparate and does not follow any standardised modelling guidelines.
- IT landscape management processes are generally neither defined nor integrated into other processes in IT and decision-making. The role of the enterprise architect does not exist, and nor do entities such as the IT landscape management board.

At the "initial" level, IT managers have recognised the need for an overall view of the application landscape, yet have no clear idea how to go about it. There may have been initial attempts at stocktaking and documenting the IT landscape, but managers will have met the typical early-phase problems:

- Which aspects are relevant?
- Unclear method, so non-uniform modelling
- No agreed terminology
- What granularity is most appropriate?
- No differentiation between as-is and planned landscape models
- Unclear who is to provide data, problems obtaining data
- Data quality shortfalls; information not up-to-date enough
- Inadequately qualified enterprise architects, or none at all
- Inadequate tool support

At this level, you have to try out IT landscape management using a few manageable, representative examples and carefully select and develop enterprise architects.

As the first step, you should plot at least sections of the IT landscape, tailoring your choices at this stage to the specific areas of concern which your enterprise is looking to address. This will give you a feeling for granularity and for the type of change process which will have to be instigated. It is also a good way to start getting people "on side". Tangible benefit is what determines success in terms of institutionalising IT landscape management in the organisation.

Ongoing projects are suitable vehicles for "test-driving" IT landscape management. For one thing, the content has already been defined, and in addition the results can be used directly for projects and for marketing. Without a concrete project, there is the danger that IT landscape management will fail to address the truly relevant areas of concern.

Once enterprise architects have acquired some initial experience, their insights should be consolidated into modelling guidelines and recommendations. It is important to choose representative examples, particularly for documenting and diagramming the application landscape. This is in itself a good basis for selecting appropriate tools.

Designing IT landscape management is an iterative process. You trial-run the concepts in real projects and then channel project experience back into refining and honing the methods.

> **Important:**
>
> Be sure to keep the development of the method completely separate from involvement in projects. Development and evolution of the method should be funded with a separate budget which is quite independent of projects.
>
> Make sure you are making a contribution to the project. The benefit must outweigh the cost. Otherwise you run the risk of failing to meet project expectations in terms of quality or time – and losing potential user buy-in for good.

When you first begin IT landscape management, the success of the undertaking stands and falls with the enterprise architects. Select these people carefully, and ensure they have the right skill sets for the job (see Sect. 4.5.1).

"First Steps" Level

At the "first steps" level, the enterprise has already acquired its first hands-on experience and made an initial standardised documentation of the application landscape, or at least for large sections of it. The following characteristics are indicative of "first steps" maturity:

- The IT landscape is documented, but the documentation might be outdated, inconsistent and/or is not reliably or continually updated.
- Enterprise architects have been appointed and update processes defined. However, the quality of maintenance is contingent on who is performing it:

Practices have not been codified, and nor are they integrated into processes in IT and decision making.

- Entities such as the IT landscape management board have not been set up or – if they already exist – are not established parts of the organisation.

Since the documentation of the IT landscape is not adequately up-to-date, complete or consistent, it must be completely overhauled before use.

Important:

If the documentation is not to end up gathering dust in a cupboard, it must be kept permanently up-to-date. However, this takes functioning processes for maintenance and upkeep. If these processes are not integrated into IT and decision-making, alternatives have to be established. For example, the enterprise architect can be tasked with updating the changed data on a monthly basis.

If data upkeep processes are not yet an institutionalised part of project management and maintenance, the results will ultimately be contingent on the discipline and commitment of the individual enterprise architect. Without integration into IT processes, actually pulling all this data together is no easy matter – which makes the personal commitment of the enterprise architect all the more important. If the architect is not an expert in the context in question and has no personal connection with the individual who is supplying the data, he or she has to put forward a compelling case to persuade people to co-operate. This can be a challenge – because the providers of the data might not see what's in it for them!

Outside a project context – without a specific project driving the task – collecting data can often be a hopeless undertaking. Yet getting enterprise architects on board project teams is no easy matter. Projects will often fend off attempts to put an enterprise architect in the crew or to enter into an obligation to provide input. The project team will naturally ask "what's in it for me", and a certain value has to be identifiable. Be sure to market the benefit exhaustively, backing your case with real-life project success stories. A little gentle pressure – perhaps from IT management – is also beneficial.

If enterprise architects are involved in projects, they do have to make a perceptible contribution. This of course makes some tough demands of the individuals in question, particularly in terms of their ability to contribute expertise in the project context. Projects should therefore be selected extremely carefully. Pilot projects, being so few and far between, are generally followed with close attention. At worst, negative feedback can bring IT landscape management to an abrupt end; at best, you may have a series of glitches to iron out, which will prolong the rollout phase.

While the project is underway, don't neglect consolidation of the method itself, particularly modelling guidelines and recommended diagrams, also the current landscape model and tool support. This is the basis for providing a solid contribution to other projects and measures.

If IT landscape management can make a perceivable contribution, people are more likely to buy into the concept. Active marketing – publicising all project successes, particularly to management – helps gradually raise the level of support.

Important:

Choose your pilot projects carefully. Put together a coalition of the willing and use tangible successes to convince the sceptics. Take care to market even minor successes.

"Transparency" Level

The transparency level is attained when the application landscape is at all times being documented consistently and kept up-to-date. Other characteristics of this level of maturity are:

- Update processes, including quality assurance of data, are integrated and established in IT processes with tool support.
- Enterprise architects are involved as a matter of course in at least the important projects.

When application enterprise architects are involved in projects, there is great opportunity for exerting influence (see Fig. 4.39). Yet IT landscape management then has to deliver on its promises: otherwise the architects will be sidelined again.

Depending on the size of the enterprise and how it organises its IT, data upkeep and maintenance can be distributed across several shoulders, possibly also involving business architects in projects or application managers. Business architects and application managers have to be trained, and tool support has to be extended and enhanced accordingly. Enterprise architects must quality-assure the data to ensure it is up to standard and kept up-to-date.

The better the contribution, the more likely it is that IT landscape management will be accepted. More and more stakeholders will want IT landscape management to be part of projects, with management and business departments now seeing the benefit. At "transparency" level, it is increasingly standard procedure for IT decision papers to include contributions from IT landscape management, documented need-for-action points and potential for optimisation. More and more use

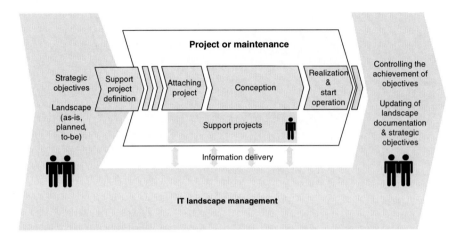

Fig. 4.39 Project integration

is made of landscape analysis. As stakeholders increasingly appreciate the clarity with which the application landscape is presented – with its range of analysis and diagram options – IT landscape management is integrated into project rollout phases.

In the long term, the survival of IT landscape management is contingent on the quality of the contribution it makes.

Important: sustainability and sufficient quality:

Getting people to actually use the landscape database is dependent on having a repository of information which is reliable, up-to-date and of sufficient quality. It is the task of enterprise architects to make sure the quality is right. Data upkeep entails effort. So enterprise architects must persevere to ensure the work is actually being performed. Integrating data upkeep into IT processes and decision-making also helps no end! It is essential to prompt sources to deliver data, and to check and verify that the data has actually been delivered. Regular quality assurance is also required to determine whether the quality of the data is up to scratch.

Even if the team of enterprise architects changes owing to staff fluctuation, the right skill set and experience must be permanently available. The personal skills and competence of the enterprise architects determines whether they can gain people's trust – all the more significant considering the architects also have to convince representatives in IT and business management and business segments.

If people can see demonstrable, lasting benefit to IT landscape management, it will become an established success factor for projects and measures. This creates the prerequisites for institutionalising IT landscape management in IT project management, in the development of implementation tasks and in the process model.

"Advanced" Level

"Advanced" level is attained when IT landscape management has become an integral part of strategic IT planning and control. The characteristics of this level are:

- The documentation of the IT landscape is adequately complete, consistent and up-to-date.
- Enterprise architects and update processes are established in the organisation. Update processes are integrated into IT processes.
- The company has commenced IT landscape planning and set up an IT landscape management board, but neither are truly established in the organisation.
- IT landscape modelling is enriched by strategic and operating-level metrics such as contribution to strategy or value proposition, cost or state of health.

As when establishing the documentation of the application landscape, IT landscape planning begins with acquiring experience, and this experience is then consolidated into practicable methods and procedures. You also have to be thinking of tool support at this stage, gradually refining it with each improvement cycle of the method for modelling the to-be landscape.

Integration into processes such as project portfolio management establishes IT landscape management as a fixture in IT decision processes. By delivering perceptible value, IT landscape management is assured the backing of management and of the majority of key stakeholders, provided the quality of the contribution can be maintained over time.

Paramount to success is to present the to-be and planned landscape models from the business perspective – in diagrams that single out salient issues and highlight mutual dependencies and impacts of ideas in business and IT. This means enterprise architects need a good sense of what's important for the business.

"Well-Established" Level

The "well-established" level is attained when IT landscape management is a success factor for business planning.

Even at this stage, it is key to continue enhancing IT landscape management. What matters are permanent efforts to optimise methods, organisation, processes and tool support, complemented by consistently high quality results, and enterprise architects with skills and experience in methods and business functionality, plus a good sense of what drives the business.

The maturity model at a glance:

- After deciding to begin IT landscape management, try first to get a sense for this complex topic by trying out representative examples, ideally in the context of projects.
- Locate and develop sponsors in management and among relevant stakeholders. To get people's backing, you need to show demonstrable success.
- Consolidate the experience and insights gained in practice, and continue to develop the method and tool support. Be sure to keep the evolution of the method and involvement in projects separate in order not to sacrifice acceptance in projects.
- Gradually establish update processes. Initially, maintenance and upkeep should be carried out by a small team of experienced enterprise architects. As buy-in increases and IT landscape management becomes more widespread, these processes must be integrated into other processes in IT and decision-making so as to institutionalise IT landscape management.
- The transition between "first steps" and "transparency" is the most critical phase. With enterprise architects now involved in projects, IT landscape management is out in the open, and architects are under observation.
- Establishing IT landscape management is a long process of change. What matters is that visible benefit is delivered early in this process, and that this benefit is actively marketed to stakeholders.
- IT landscape management only delivers benefit if it can genuinely make a contribution. This takes skilled enterprise architects and a critical mass of up-to-date, consistent landscape database and diagrams. Without this, it is impossible to demonstrate value and make a compelling case for IT landscape management.

Dependency Between Objectives and Levels of Maturity

The objectives which the enterprise has when introducing IT landscape management must be consistent with the maturity level. The nature of the objectives – ambitious or modest – also set the scope for the expectations of managers and users. Not all objectives are achievable at every level of maturity in a single step (see Sect. 4.6). Table 4.11 plots the objectives discussed in Sect. 4.2 against the maturity levels.

Table 4.11 Achievable objectives in correlation with maturity levels

	Maturity level				
	Initial	First steps	Transparency	Advanced	Well-established
Business alignment of IT					
Common business language		⊠	√	√	√
Transparency of business impacts/dependencies			⊠	√	√
Linkage between business and IT		⊠	√	√	√
Optimising of business through IT		⊠	√	√	√
Business-oriented control and direction of IT (objectives for IT, control of project portfolio)				⊠	√
Strategic planning and control of IT					
Overview of IT landscape	⊠	√	√	√	√
Strategic objectives			⊠	√	√
Optimisation of application landscape		⊠	√	√	√
Supporting technical standardisation		⊠	√	√	√
Supporting infrastructure planning		⊠	√	√	√
IT landscape planning (define target landscape and implementation roadmap)			⊠	√	√
Governing further development of IT landscape	·			⊠	√
Operational planning and control of IT					
Simplified documentation requirements	⊠	√	√	√	√
Reduced effort in initiation of projects and input for project management	⊠	√	√	√	√
Supporting operational planning and control of IT		⊠	√	√	√
Supporting internal service delivery and vendor management			⊠	√	√

A good way to get started with IT landscape management is to use overview presentations and consistent lists. Overview presentations make interdependencies visible at a glance – sometimes leading to an "epiphany moment" among stakeholders, who might see for the very first time how everything fits together. Lists can simplify mandatory documentation, e.g. associated with risk management, compliance or security requirements. With these simple means, you can deliver appreciable benefit without undue effort.

More advanced questions such as those associated with strategic IT management or landscape planning can only be answered with a far superior base of IT landscape data.

> **Important:**
>
> To get IT landscape planning established in the enterprise, you need functioning update processes backed by good tools – this makes sure there is a good enough base of data to work with.

New goals have to be approached step by step. This is indicated by "⊠" in Table 4.11. You can gradually extend the method to embrace a new goal through repeated feedback and improvement cycles. To give an example, to achieve the goal of a "common language", you will generally need to cycle through the feedback process many times before arriving at a consensus for the business reference model.

When you set a new objective, first focus on just one section of the IT landscape to see how things pan out, and involve just a few of the more receptive stakeholders. A "quick win" will always help, so be sure to use data of moderately high quality. For the "common language" goal, for instance, you can begin by compiling the names of business functions or business objects. Achieving a consensus on these terms, including their wording, can be deferred until you take your next pass at the topic. The initial collection in itself suffices to show what sort of questions can be answered. After the trials, however, you must make sure data quality is brought up to scratch.

> **Important:**
>
> - Be sure to set realistic goals. A goal is only realistic if it is consistent with the current or targeted maturity level.

4.6 Guidelines for Personalisation of IT Landscape Management in Practice

The introduction of IT landscape management is usually initiated by the CIO or IT managers. However the impetus can equally come from strategists, or from security or compliance representatives.

When it comes to customising IT landscape management for your enterprise, what matters first and foremost are the objectives and interests of your relevant stakeholders. What agendas do they have? IT landscape management has to be able to answer their questions.

Important:

Identify champions at management level or among valued stakeholders in the enterprise, and get these people involved. Champions are a critical success factor when it comes to introducing IT landscape management.

As a rule, IT landscape management is introduced in stages, each of which must be designed to fit the status quo and maturity level of your enterprise. Each introduction stage comprises three phases: conception, sampling and optimising, and anchoring in the organisation (see Fig. 4.40).

Designing and refining IT landscape management usually take place in a series of workshops over a period of several months, possibly with different participants depending on the subject matter under discussion. Structures, processes and organisational issues in each introduction stage must be pilot-tested and optimised before they can be embedded in the organisation.

Fig. 4.40 Customising IT landscape management for an enterprise: steps in the process

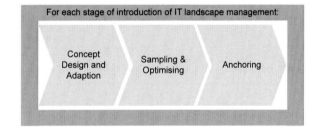

For each stage of introduction of IT landscape management:

Concept Design and Adaption → Sampling & Optimising → Anchoring

---

Important:

Keep each introduction stage to manageable proportions, and ensure it is achievable quickly. These quick wins are the only way to convince the sceptics and gain champions.

   Concentrate on the salient issues to accomplish declared objectives in as quick and straightforward a manner as possible.

Each of these introduction phases is described in detail in the following.

4.6.1 Conception of IT Landscape Management

Depending on where you are starting from, you will have to establish structures, processes, an organisation and tool support for IT landscape management and plan how to get it underway. The following activities are required (see Fig. 4.41):

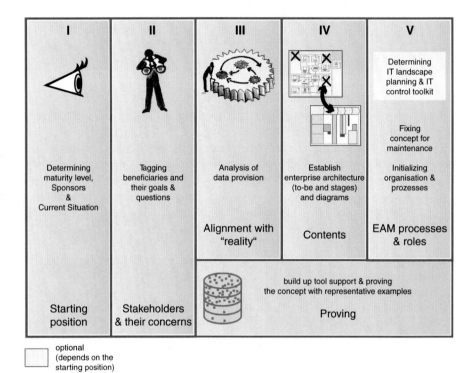

Fig. 4.41 Planning the concept of IT landscape management

I. Determine Status Quo

Determine the maturity level of your enterprise in terms of IT landscape management. Guidelines for estimating the maturity level are provided in Sect. 4.5.3.

This information gives you a picture of where you are right now.

> **Important:**
>
> You also need to decide at this point which stakeholder groups you wish to involve in the concept planning stage. This depends on the maturity level. If

maturity is still low, should keep the group small. If it is already high, you should involve all stakeholder groups (see Fig. 4.42).

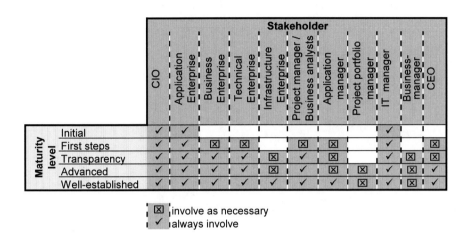

☒ involve as necessary
✓ always involve

Fig. 4.42 Integrating stakeholder groups depending on maturity

II. Identify the Relevant Beneficiaries, and Determine What Their Goals and Areas of Concern Are

(a) Find out who the relevant beneficiaries are and what objectives they have.

Guidelines for identifying beneficiaries and their agendas are provided in Fig. 4.43 and in Sect. 4.4.2. Agree objectives and priorities with the various stakeholders.

(b) Verify that objectives are in alignment with the maturity level.

This is a major element in defining the introduction stages. Guidelines are provided in Sect. 4.5.3.

(c) Document the specific questions which the beneficiaries you have identified are looking to address.

Document questions and areas of concern of beneficiaries, and be sure to achieve explicit agreement on content with beneficiaries and sponsors of IT landscape management.

Evaluate questions in terms of their relevance. Only questions which are genuinely relevant should be pursued. To answer each new question, you will generally need additional data which has to be kept up-to-date. If in doubt, weigh up cost and benefit on a case-by-case basis. Take care also to consider the effort for updating and possibly also consolidating data.

	Stakeholder										
	CIO	Application Enterprise	Business Enterprise	Enterprise Technical	Enterprise Infrastructure	Project manager / Business analysts	Application officer	Project portfolio manager	IT manager	Business-manager	CEO
Business alignment of IT											
Common business language	✓	✓	✓							☒	
Transparency of business impacts/dependencies	✓	✓	✓							☒	
Linkage between business and IT	✓	✓	✓	☒					☒	☒	
Optimising of business through IT	✓	✓	✓	☒					☒	☒	
Business-oriented control and direction of IT (objectives for IT, control of project portfolio)	✓	✓	✓	☒	☒			☒	☒	☒	✓
Strategic planning and control of IT											
Overview of IT landscape	✓	✓			✓	☒	☒	☒	☒		
Strategic objectives	✓	✓			☒				☒	✓	
Optimisation of application landscape	✓	✓			☒		☒	☒		✓	
Supporting technical standardisation	✓	✓			✓		☒	☒		☒	
Supporting infrastructure planning	✓	✓				☒		☒		☒	
IT landscape planning (define target landscape and implementation roadmap)	✓	✓		☒	☒		☒	☒		☒	☒
Governing further development of IT landscape	✓	✓			✓	☒	☒	✓	☒	✓	☒	✓
Operational planning and control of IT											
Reduce efforts in obligatory documentation requirements	✓	✓	✓		☒			☒	☒	✓	
Reduce efforts in initiation of projects and through delivering of input for project handling	✓	✓	✓		✓	☒		✓	☒		☒	☒
Supporting the operational planning and control of IT	✓	✓	✓		✓	☒	☒			✓	
Supporting the service control and vendor management	✓	✓			☒				✓		☒

☒ under circumstances

Fig. 4.43 Stakeholder groups and their objectives

Useful hint:

Use diagrams to illustrate the ways in which stakeholders' questions can be answered. A picture says more than a thousand words! Diagrams also put you on safer ground when it comes to selecting relevant questions, since you can be more certain whether aspects are genuinely relevant.

(d) Work out what landscape elements, relationships, core and extended data and control quantities are required.

Determine what information is required to address stakeholders' questions. You can use the list shown in Fig. 4.44 as a template.

III. Analyse Data Procurement

(a) Evaluate the effort for procuring data.
    Identify the providers of the data and assess the effort for data procurement. Examples of data providers in terms of IT landscape management are provided in Sect. 4.4.1.

		Enterprise architecture	Linkage	Attributes	Diagrams
Goal 1					
Q11	Question 1	...	...	...	...
Q12	Question 2	...	...	...	...
Q13	Question 3	...	...	...	...
...	...				
Goal 2					
Q21	Question 1	...	...	...	...
Q22	Question 2	...	...	...	...
Q23	Question 3	...	...	...	...
...	...				
...	...	...	...	...	...

Fig. 4.44 Template for compiling questions

Determine who will be providing the data on each landscape element, e.g. business processes, applications, also relationships and attributes. The underlying question you need to answer in each case is "who (which role) can provide the data with which quality, how up-to-date with what effort?" It is the combination of these three factors – quality, up-to-dateness and effort – that matters:

- **Quality**: Data can only be used effectively if its quality is up to standard. You can only derive meaningful statements from data if it is consistent and has been documented with uniform granularity.
- **Up-to-date**: Without ongoing updates that ensure changes are mapped promptly into landscape database, queries cannot be executed without first bringing the data into line – which takes time and effort. This calls the entire benefit of IT landscape management into question: there is no guarantee of reliability.
- **Effort**: The effort for ongoing data maintenance with sufficient quality must be in proportion to the benefit. If it is a major effort to keep information (e.g. infrastructure data) at a quality standard appropriate for IT landscape

management and the ensuing benefit is not particularly large, you should omit this from proceedings, at least at first. The greater the effort, the lower the user buy-in. The effort has to be justifiable in terms of expected benefit. Data procurement channels must be as efficient and simple as possible. For instance, if data provision can be automated, there is no need to enter information twice.

(b) Weigh the effort for data procurement against the benefits.

When defining your enterprise architecture, ensure there is a match between the information required to address stakeholders' areas of concern, and the information which can actually be obtained by the data providers.

Following analysis of data procurement, many enterprises elect to introduce this in stages, initially including only the questions which can be addressed with available data or with data which can be obtained with reasonable effort.

Useful hints:

It is often difficult to quantify benefit. Often, just working out the effort will be enough to estimate whether a question is really important. For this reason you should confront the beneficiaries with the efforts that will be necessary to answer their questions. This enables you to determine which questions are relevant.

When you first introduce new questions, it is often enough to begin with a basic data quality. For example, even with a rudimentary, incomplete list of business functions, you can present a reasonable picture of functional coverage in a landscape diagram. Often, it takes a diagram of this sort to show business segments and managers what the benefits are.

IV. Establish Your Enterprise Architecture

(a) Define your enterprise architecture in accordance with areas of concern you wish to address (to-be concept).

When defining the landscape elements in the to-be enterprise architecture and the relationships between these elements, all relevant stakeholder questions have to be considered – regardless of the estimated maturity level. Guidelines are provided in Sect. 3.6. Enrich the enterprise architecture with the core data, extended data and control quantities (indicators) you have decided to use.

As well as the structures, also decide at this point what diagrams you will be using to answer stakeholder questions. Consider who will be using each diagram, when, and to what purpose.

Guidelines on choosing diagrams are provided in Sects. 3.3 and 4.4.2.

(b) Produce your rollout planning.

Your rollout plan should take into account the maturity level you have identified, relevant questions and areas of concern, and the outcomes of the data document analysis. Define feasible steps, each with clearly defined benefit (see Sect. 4.5.3).

The first stage is the most important – IT landscape management might not get a second chance to make a good impression, and will only be taken further provided people can see benefit in it from the start. The enterprise will not be prepared to make an investment if it is not clear what the benefit is. Therefore, you must implement the first stage in a manageable timeframe and finish with a good cost-benefit ratio. A few months are usually enough.

The first stage is also where you define the structures, diagrams and tool support to address enterprise-specific concerns, creating greater transparency and testing IT landscape management (or sections of it) as part of a general stocktaking exercise. Update processes and particularly the role of the enterprise architect are introduced at this stage. Project stakeholders gain a feeling for the abstractions, granularity and necessary change process in the enterprise. Potential benefits are identified. Good results at this stage – such as landscape diagrams or information flow diagrams – can win over the first stakeholders, start to build user buy-in, and even create the first champions for the undertaking.

At the first stage, you must also document at least sections of the IT landscape. Besides helping you put forward your case for IT landscape management, this is also the rootstock of data for real-life projects or IT strategy development.

The first stage must be completed within a manageable timeframe and with a good cost-to-benefit ratio. Here are the ground rules to follow:

– **Focus on known, relevant areas of concern**: When defining structures, diagrams, processes and the organisation of IT landscape management, centre efforts on the objectives and interests of the enterprise – the questions which the enterprise is looking to answer. It is important only to consider questions which can actually be formulated in specific terms. Estimating the relevance is rather more difficult, seeing it is only when a question is asked and answered that its relevance can really be appraised. Be sure to explain – to yourself and others – exactly why each question has been included, since permanent downstream effort will be required to keep data for each question up-to-date. By appraising relevance at this stage, you can limit the number of questions.

- **Big picture rather than detail**: Create an overall view of the IT landscape, rather than detailed documentation for individual questions such as the cost situation with IT systems.
- **Holistic view**: At the design stage, you should explicitly attempt to include all landscape models across the entire enterprise architecture, as well as linkages with projects and maintenance. Even if it is impossible to implement everything in a single step, you should take the full picture into account in the concept. This ensures there are no inbuilt barriers to expansion at a later date.
- **No "nice-to-have" data collection**: Stick to the data you need to answer known and relevant questions. This ensures you will be documenting only the data which is genuinely required, and can keep effort for entering data to manageable proportions.
- **Sufficient data quality, sufficiently up-to-date**: Data must be of high enough quality and up-to-date enough to accomplish declared objectives. Don't overshoot your targets. Data only has to be able to answer the set of questions which have been defined.

  When you first introduce new questions, it is often enough to begin with rudimentary data quality. For example, even with an incomplete list of business functions, you can present a reasonable picture of functional coverage in a landscape diagram. Often, it takes a diagram of this sort to show business segments and managers what the benefits are – and get people on side as active supporters.

  Another example is performance indicators: if reports are only made once per month, the underlying data needs only be updated monthly.
- **Benefit/simplification for providers of data**: There has to be a benefit obvious for every stakeholder, particularly for the people who are providing the data. Without high-quality, up-to-date information to go on, analysis and evaluation cannot deliver meaningful results. So data entry has to be made as simple as possible for the people doing the work. Good tool support is important. At the same time, the people tasked with providing data must actually be in a position to do the job. There is little point asking application managers to update infrastructure units if they are not familiar with the mapping and have to obtain this information from others.

  Benefit for data providers can be enhanced by providing them with help in their daily work – for example, by simplifying the production of mandatory documentation to meet compliance or security requirements, by creating a better focus in project and maintenance work, or simply by clarifying issues through landscape model analysis.

(c) Introduce the enterprise architecture, explain why it has been designed the way it has, elucidate its potential to stakeholders, beneficiaries and data providers, and channel their feedback into optimising the architecture. Get people actively engaged in the undertaking.

V. Define the Maintenance Concept, Processes and Tool Support, and Determine How IT Landscape Management Is to Fit into Organisational Structures

Guidelines on this are provided in Sects. 4.4 and 4.5. IT landscape planning and support for strategic evolution of the IT landscape are required only for "transparency" maturity level and higher.

4.6.2 Sampling and Optimising

Each introduction stage first has to be tested in a representative section of the IT landscape. You can then optimise it before integrating it into the organisation at large. It is particularly important to take several passes at refining structures, processes and organisational integration, and to test their robustness. Results emerging at this stage can be deployed in real-life projects, in project portfolio management or in strategic IT planning to help show where changes or additions are required.

Often, practical testing is what makes the difference. A draft concept of structures, for example, cannot take into account technical aspects such as the properties of interfaces. Yet in real projects having this knowledge can be crucial. You can optimise your particular enterprise architecture by channelling such experience and feedback back into designs. Once trials are complete, it is clear which business and technical landscape elements, with which relationships and which core and extended data, are genuinely required to address the questions formulated at this stage.

The toughest challenge at the trial stage is getting participation in IT and decision-making processes. At this stage, enterprise architects will not automatically be brought into projects or IT strategy development. Architects are under pressure to prove their worth before they are given a say, and to demonstrate through professional competence or method skills that they can deliver value to projects or IT strategy. Commands handed down by top management tend not to work. Rather, architects have to make a valuable contribution quickly by providing answers to issues that matter to the project, "what-if" analysis or landscape diagrams. Guidelines are provided in Sect. 4.5.3, with a discussion of possible steps to sample and optimise IT landscape planning in line with the maturity level.

4.6.3 Anchoring IT Landscape Management in the Organisation

In essence, it comes down to a few basic tenets. Define quick wins, then expand breadth and depth through active involvement in projects. Continue to find sponsors, and signpost development by publishing visible successes.

Since establishing and developing IT landscape management is not something that can be shoehorned into a conventional project with a defined start and end, teams can lack the discipline typical of projects. Focus becomes hazy, work is less results-driven, and initiatives can lack professionalism. IT teams and senior management can easily begin to gripe and grouse. To build in project-type discipline, Gartner suggests writing project plans and establishing professional project managers (see [Gar05]).

Communication is also a key success factor. A formal communication plan and key messages must ensure relevant stakeholders are kept informed of value contributions and progress towards goals. Each issue must be communicated such that recipients understand what it is all about.

The enterprise also has to decide on the media which people will use to communicate, and stake out an action plan with timeframes and responsibilities. Feedback processes should also be established to check that the communication plan is working. According to Gartner, the EA team should spend approximately 30% of its time on communication and planning (see [Gar05]).

Despite the methodical approach, all stakeholders should be clear that this is an arduous undertaking which will demand change. Change generates fear. For many people, change means forsaking tried-and-trusted habits and is perceived as a threat to their interests. This often leads to resistance. Such a far-reaching realignment of IT takes discipline and perseverance. Success largely depends on people understanding change, actively shaping it and above all being willing to go along with it.

It is important not to forget the human factor in implementation. It is often anything but easy to drive issues through and persevere with the undertaking. Important stakeholders are generally all under pressure, and have neither the time nor inclination to perform additional work without recognizable benefit to themselves. Recognizable benefit, coupled perhaps with gentle pressure from IT management, is the only way to gain and retain the support of the essential stakeholders.

In this way, IT landscape management can be developed into a cornerstone of strategic IT management. It can contribute fundamentally to making the business a success and ensure the IT landscape develops in alignment with the business. It also helps direct IT investments and projects, and manage resources effectively.

IT landscape management must be continually evolved. Sustained data quality, information which is adequately up-to-date and, above all, experienced enterprise architects with a good grasp of methods, the subject, and good communication skills can all help establish IT landscape management and embed it in the organisation.

Important: Communicate! Communicate! Communicate!

The enterprise has to proceed through a lengthy change process before the opportunities of IT landscape management are genuinely understood and accessible, and all stakeholders have been convinced of the benefits. What matters in this change process is to win over early champions among management and users. Stakeholders first have to understand what IT landscape management is, and what benefits they can expect. Top management must be involved every step of the way. You have to turn passive recipients into active stakeholders.

Requirements for a successful rollout of IT landscape management:

- Make a realistic estimate of your current maturity level. This ensures user expectations will be pitched at around the right level.
- Take care to document data with the right granularity. If information is too fine-grained, you will not be able to see the wood for the trees.
- "Think big and start small"
  Slowly but surely elicit decision points and relevant areas of concern from potential beneficiaries. Put together an overall concept and implement this in a series of manageable steps. Prevent a "wish list" mentality – with unclear priorities and activities – from gaining the upper hand.
- Make sure structures are appropriate and easily maintained. Avoid the trap of "modellitis"! Stick to the data you really need to address relevant areas of concern.
- Establish simple update processes and good tool support [Pey07]. Integrate these as early as possible into processes in IT and decision-making. This ensures data will be kept up-to-date.
  Targeted analysis and planning options based on data which is both meaningful and current enable decisions to be taken rapidly and help ensure business success.
- Ensure data is kept up-to-date, and maintain high quality by introducing explicit quality assurance, regular tidying, and ongoing optimisation.
  Decisions are only ever as good as the data on which they are based. The reason why data is so often incomplete, outdated or of inadequate quality is that updates or quality assurance are performed inconsistently or not at all.
- Develop qualified enterprise architects who can deliver quality advice to projects and produce high quality material on which to base decisions.
- Consistently market even minor successes. Use every opportunity to present the benefit case.
- Put together a communication plan for yourself in order to enter into an intensive dialog with all relevant stakeholders. Be sure to involve top management every step of the way. Turn passive recipients into active stakeholders!

Chapter 5
Technical Standardisation

If you want to build a ship, don't drum up the men to gather wood, divide the work and give orders. Instead, teach them to yearn for the vast and endless sea.

Antoine de Saint-Exupéry

Technical standardisation is what sets out the enterprise-specific standards which frame the development trajectory for your IT landscape. Even if the landscape you have at present is a heterogeneous patchwork, you can gradually usher it toward your vision by defining which technical standards are to apply in projects and maintenance measures (see Fig. 5.1).

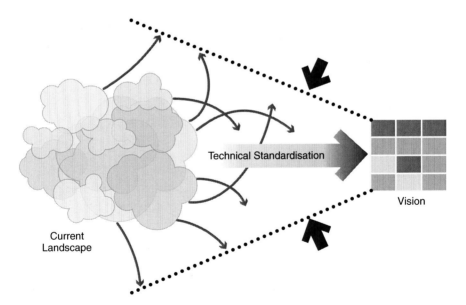

Fig. 5.1 Technical standardisation

I. Hanschke, *Strategic IT Management*, DOI 10.1007/978-3-642-05034-3_5,
© Springer-Verlag Berlin Heidelberg 2010

Questions answered in this chapter:

- What contribution does technical standardisation make to strategic IT planning?
- Which objectives are being pursued?
- What are the components of a standardisation catalogue?
- Which processes are required, and how can technical standardisation be embedded in the organisation?
- Which technical standards are appropriate for you?
- In which incremental steps can you introduce technical standardisation?

5.1 Scope and Definition

What Contribution Does Technical Standardisation Make to Strategic IT Planning?

Like IT landscape management (see Chapter 4), technical standardisation is fundamental to strategic IT planning. In this process, you take the objectives defined in the IT strategy, and out of them derive a combination of technical standards which are then shaped and fine-tuned to provide the best possible backing for your current and future business requirements.

By staking out the "permissible" technologies, databases, middleware solutions and reference architectures, technical standards are a key input for IT landscape management (see Fig. 5.2). They are the imperatives governing implementations of the applications and interfaces and – particularly importantly – the design of future application landscapes.

If technical standardisation shows what things should be like, IT landscape management provides information on how things are, showing which technical building blocks really form part of applications, interfaces or infrastructures. This information on the use of building blocks is valuable input for technical standardisation.

Technical standards can also be defined for productive operation as well as for infrastructure, with many enterprises electing to scope out service strategies and service designs (see ITIL V3 [Buc07]) that include specific standards on which hardware, operating systems and network components to use. For more information, please refer to relevant literature, including [Buc07], [Joh07] and [itS08].

Fact file:

- Technical standardisation prescribes enterprise-specific technical standards for projects and productive operation.

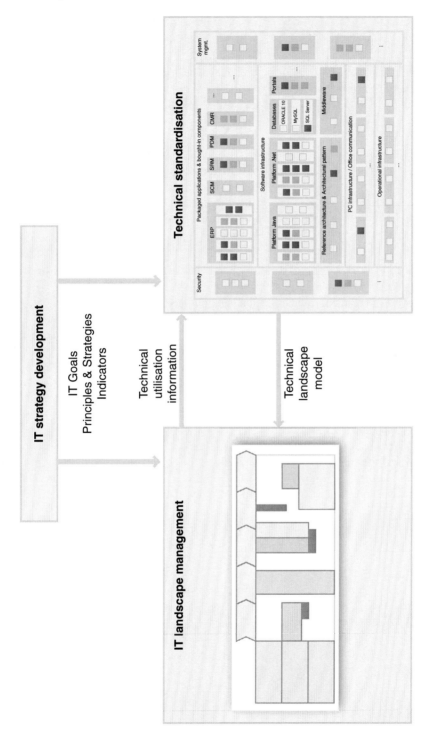

Fig. 5.2 How technical standardisation fits into strategic IT management

- IT landscape management provides a clear view on how and where technical standards have been applied in the IT landscape.
- Technical standardisation is operationalised by means of projects and maintenance measures.

5.2 Objectives of Technical Standardisation

The objectives an enterprise has in mind with technical standardisation will differ depending on the strategic positioning of IT in the organisation as a whole (see Sect. 2.3):

- **Cost savings** through economies of scale, with the opportunity of greater negotiating power when purchasing is centralised, and of more focused expertise as an outcome of technical standardisation and homogenising.
- **High technical quality** of applications and the operating environment, an outcome of reusing tried-and-tested technical components such as reference architectures, frameworks or third-party software within the enterprise.
  The technical quality depends both on where the system is in its lifecycle and on the degree to which quality requirements have been enacted concerning performance, security etc. The technical quality is important for creating sustainable systems.
- **Appropriate IT support** for business requirements, such as the agility of IT systems to adapt to evolving business requirements and external constraints or to fulfil security or compliance requirements.
- **Sustainability** of the IT landscape through explicit IT innovation management and strategic evolution of the technical standards; see also Sect. 5.4.

Fact file:

- The huge cost savings potential is in general a key incentive for embarking on technical standardisation.
- Having the right technical standards is vital to making the IT landscape robust enough and fit to underpin the enterprise's business operations into the future.

Important:

The only route to accomplishing the named goals is by planning and controlling technical standardisation – and by planning and controlling how technical standards are utilised in the IT landscape.

See also Sect. 5.4.

5.3 Elements of a Standardisation Catalogue

The bare skeleton of the standardisation catalogue has to be fleshed out with details specific to your enterprise. Ultimately, the catalogue is nothing other than the technical landscape model (see Fig. 5.3), also termed "blueprint" in the following. The technical landscape model comprises two levels:

- Technical reference model: the modelling equivalent of a cabinet with drawers;
- Technical components – the elements which fill the cabinet and its drawers.

The "drawers" in the model are the architectural domains. These domains can be organised into a hierarchy, i.e. each drawer can be subdivided into further trays.

The technical components can in turn also consist of subcomponents (i.e. hierarchical relationships can exist within component structures). There can also be other associations connecting technical components. For example, a Java application server has a "uses" relationship with a JRE. Technical components can be versioned, making it possible to manage multiple release states of a Java application server (e.g. Version 1 and Version 1.1) in the same blueprint. These version states can be linked by a predecessor-successor relationship.

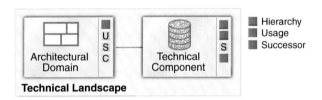

Fig. 5.3 Technical landscape

The blueprint can comprise the following categories of filler elements:

- **Technologies** (a kind of catch-all term here): Taken from the context of software engineering, third-party software or operation such as ".Net", "JEE", "SAP" or

"BS2000 host", these umbrella terms are a concise way of summarising both the technology target and the status quo.

- **Reference architectures and architectural patterns** (see also [Aie04], [Aie05], [Bas03], [Foe03], [Star08] and [Vog05]): Reference architectures and architectural patterns serve as solution templates either for a complete application category – such as templates for the rollout of standard software across multiple sites, or reference architectures for web-based JEE applications – or for a specific area, e.g. a data access tier.

It can also be useful to distinguish between reference architectures or architectural patterns which are tied to particular technologies and products, and those which are not. In practice, though, with the few reference architectures usually in use in a single company, this distinction tends to be unnecessary.

- **Third-party IT products**: These are software and hardware solutions which are sourced on the general market as "off-the-shelf" products with no enterprise-specific customising.

  Examples are:

  - Packaged business software such as SAP or Siebel, or bought-in components for specific functionality such as OCR
  - PC infrastructure and office communication products such as word processing, groupware and fax solutions, DMS or CMS
  - Runtime environments, including application or web servers such as Tomcat or JBoss
  - Databases such as ORACLE or SQL Server
  - Middleware such as MQSeries or CORBA
  - Security components such as firewalls or virus scanners
  - Hardware and network infrastructure such as servers and network components

- **Technical building blocks** that can be used to build applications: Technical building blockThese can be own-build frameworks to cover specific aspects of an application (e.g. security or logging) or third-party products such as workflow engines or rule systems.
- **Tools** for software development and system management

  - Software development-related tools such as development environments or test tools also belong in this category, as do version and configuration management tools, build and deployment tools
  - System management tools are tools for running applications, e.g. for system administration, monitoring and software distribution

The following sections describe architectural domains and technical components in greater detail.

5.3.1 Architectural Domains

A separate architectural domain is earmarked in the technical reference model (TRM) for each functional area (e.g. databases) requiring standardisation. With these domains representing the "drawers" in the cabinet-of-drawers model, you can locate the right sort of technical components for the context you are working in simply by looking in the appropriate drawer.

The following information is required to document an architectural domain:

- **Name**: The unique identification of the architectural domain, e.g. "software infrastructure"
- **Description**: Description of the content of the architectural domain
    Example: the architectural domain "software infrastructure" contains all the technical components for developing custom software.
- **Hierarchy**: Description of the hierarchical structure of the architectural domain; in other words, this defines which drawers and trays the architectural domain consists of, and in which drawer or tray the domain itself is located.

Many enterprises elect to structure architectural domains to reflect their own architecture conventions, using "tiers" and "layers" to organise a domain into suitable units. Tiers are the vertical subdivisions and structure an application in terms of logical functionality. Layers, on the other hand, are horizontal subdivisions. Each tier and layer has clearly demarcated responsibilities. Here are some examples of tiers:

- **The presentation tier** is responsible for composing and visualising data and other content.
- **The business tier** provides business functionality, e.g. as business services.
- **The data tier** delivers data to the application either directly from the database or indirectly from other interfaced applications.

In many cases, these tiers are complemented by integration tiers for front-end (e.g. via portals) and back-end integration (e.g. via EAI).

Figure 5.4 illustrates how an application might be organised into layers and tiers. Only two layers are used here: "functionality" and "technology", though in practice both would be subdivided into further layers. The technology layer would be organised into software infrastructure and hardware and network infrastructure layers; "functionality" would consist of "IT-functional" structuring units such as core business processes or functional blocks, to reflect the structures most appropriate for the enterprise. As well as the layers and tiers, other aspects which cut right across an application – system management, cross-cutting concerns or security, for example – can be used as architectural domains [Hor02], [IEE00], [Sch04] and [Sch07].

The technical reference model is presented in chart form using cluster diagrams (see Sect. 3.3.2). Figure 5.5 illustrates what a technical reference model could look like for a particular enterprise.

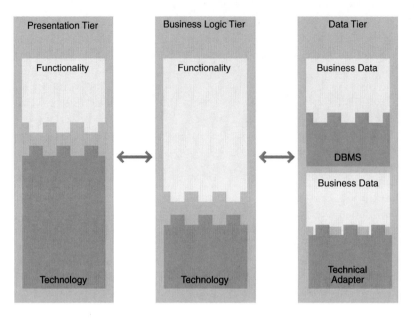

Fig. 5.4 Example layers and tiers

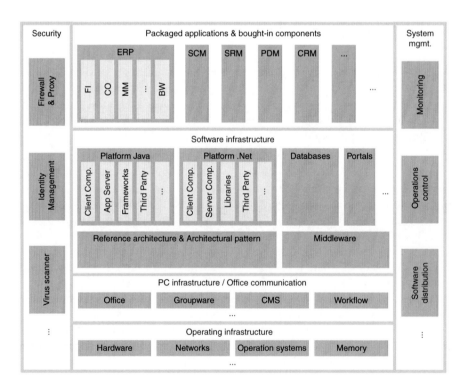

Fig. 5.5 Reference model for a blueprint: an example

In this example, the subdivisions are largely within the individual layers, with only "system management" and "security" cutting right across the model. The functionality is located on the top layer with "packaged applications and bought-in components". This architectural domain is subdivided into units such as "ERP", "SCM" and "SRM", reflecting the functional units with which IT operates.

The technology layer in this example is subdivided into software infrastructure, "PC infrastructure/office communication", and operating infrastructure. The software infrastructure comprises all the technical components for custom software solutions. The components are routinely grouped into platforms with compatible technologies, named after the key technology. One example is the Java JSF platform, which can be viewed as an entity. Platforms can, however, also be bundled into packages on code level, a means of ensuring that only components which really fit together will be used together. This approach helps drive down the costs of provisioning, support and consulting, also simplifying utilisation of the components in IT landscape management. Having clear categorisations in the model renders transparent the connections and interdependencies such as those existing between complementary technologies, substitution and competing technologies.

As suggested in the figure, the platforms can be refined as necessary into additional substructures. However, this is only a valuable exercise if there are enough technical components of sufficient variety to warrant more detailed grouping.

Useful hints:

- The architectural domains you define should have enterprise-wide validity.
- Choose names for the architectural domains which are easy to understand and make clear what the domain does. This makes it a lot easier for people to locate what they need.
- The structure you choose for the blueprint should reflect the structure you have decided upon for the architecture, e.g. layers and tiers.
- Where possible, group compatible components into logical platforms.

  A few suggestions: you can bundle components into software packages and thus head off dependency errors, reduce testing effort and make it easier to utilise the building blocks in IT landscape management processes.
- When defining the architectural domains you intend to use, you should make use of accepted standards, at least regarding accepted taxonomy. One commonly used standard is the TOGAF Technical Reference Model [TOG08].

  Elaborate the selected standard such that the resulting model is a reasonably accurate reflection of the scenario in your enterprise. Essentially, take care to use only the "drawers" which are genuinely relevant for your context.

  The functional and software infrastructure drawers in the TOGAF TRM are often not enough. Design these to fit your objectives.

5.3.2 *Technical Components*

Technical components are the elements which populate the technical reference model. For ease of use in landscape modelling each component must be adequately documented. Accordingly, each component definition must include the following information. Optional elements are enclosed in square brackets [].

- **Name**: Name of the technical component, e.g. "ORACLE"
- **[Release no]**: Release number of the technical component, e.g. "ORACLE 9.2"
  Together, the name and release number serve as the unique identifier of a technical component.
- **Description**: Description of the technical component, e.g. "ORACLE database system"
- **Position in architectural domains**: The architectural domains into which this technical component has been placed
- **[Planning status]**: The planning status of the technical component: This can be "as-is", "planned" and "to-be".

  - **"as-is"** is the current valid status of the component in the technical landscape model. In other words technical components with planning status "as-is" can be used in projects.
  - **"planned"** is the status attributed to technical components which are being planned or whose development is already underway, e.g. customised framework versions in the process of being developed, or third-party IT products for which purchase negotiations are in progress.
  - **"to-be"** describes the target vision of technical standardisation e.g. "SAP" and "Microsoft" in the "logistics" business segment.

- **[Compliance with standards]**: The degree of compliance with standards indicates whether or not the technical component has been set as an enterprise-specific standard. You might choose to have settings here such as "compliant", "conditionally compliant" and "non-compliant"
- **[Release status[1]]**: The release status indicates whether and under what conditions the technical component is available for inclusion in applications, interfaces and operating infrastructure units. The settings here can include: "unrestricted", "restricted to condition",[2] "individual release[3] and "not released"
- **[Status in lifecycle]**: This allows conclusions to be drawn on questions such as the stability of the component. The possible settings can include: "prototype", "pilot", "in production", "legacy"[4] and "decommissioned"

---

[1] Also termed standardisation status.

[2] Conditions should be formulated in text form, e.g. "For use in sales support business segment only".

[3] Released only in exceptional cases; separate authorisation is required in each case.

[4] Also termed "phase-out".

- **[Utilisation period]**: The period over which the technical component is used. For components with "as-is" status, this will be the period of time over which the component can be included in applications, interfaces and operating infrastructure units. For "planned" or "to-be" components, this is a statement on the planned period of use.
- **[Hierarchy]**: An indication of what the technical component consists of, e.g. "Application Server" consists of "Web Container" and "EJB Container".
- **[Interdependencies]**: A description of component interdependencies, e.g. "Application Server X" needs "JRE Version Y". The information here serves as the basis for later dependency analysis.
- **[Successor]**: A link with the chronological predecessor or successor of the technical component in question, e.g. successor release of a third-party IT product.
- **Guidance for use**: You must provide guidance on how each technical component is to be used. Requirements and dependencies – such as what is required in order to install an application – have to be stated; users also need guidelines for configuration, programming examples for frameworks and instructions for integrating into portals and migrating to new versions.

This core data can be enriched by additional information specific to your enterprise. For example, you might elect to categorise technical components, specify manufacturer details or component "owners" in your enterprise (see also Sect. 4.3.1).

The more optional information is used, the greater the overall complexity. To give an example, if you are making use of the planning status, period of use and the release status, you set up the following dependencies:

- If the planning status is "planned" or "to-be", the period of use must lie in the future.
- If the planning status is "planned" or "to-be", the release status must be "not released", because the technical components may not at the present time be included in applications or other entities.

Useful hints:

- You should include either compliance with standards or the release status in the definition of a technical component – but not both.
- Use the status in the lifecycle merely as an additional information field. Making it mandatory will drive up complexity unnecessarily in both use and maintenance.

- You can combine the planning status with the lifecycle status, using settings such as "to-be", "planned", "in-development", "prototype", "pilot", "in-production", "legacy" and "decommissioned".

  In such a case, though, the use of the technical components will have to be made contingent on their status.
- The period of use can be defined for each status in the lifecycle. However, since the meaning of the period of use can be different for each status, and periods can also overlap, you are setting yourself up for a huge increase in complexity. This makes use of the component difficult and also entails considerable maintenance and update effort.

When you are first embarking on technical standardisation, consider which information is likely to be the most appropriate way for your enterprise to describe the technical components. Bear in mind that certain information is essential if you want to effectively manage how technical components are used and integrated into the landscape models.

The following summary of the optional components provides valuable ground rules for your first venture into technical standardisation.

Getting started: ground rules for technical standardisation:

- **Your blueprint should include only as-is components which can be used directly.**

  If you are going to document to-be and planned components, you will need to stake out development trajectories clearly, also in terms of interaction with other aspects. Considerably more effort will have to be channelled into update and maintenance of technical landscape models.
- The **release number** is essential to highlight any dependencies between versions.

  Not all technical components need a release number – for example, programming languages or general technology terms such as SAP. However, be sure to specify release numbers for reference architectures, architectural components, third-party IT products and technical building blocks.
- The **release status** or alternatively **compliance with standards** is necessary to show the degree of standardisation.
- By specifying the **period of use**, you can show when particular components are going to be phased out (valuable for projects).
- By describing the **use**, you can ensure that dependencies between technical components show through in the blueprint. This is key in order to identify the technical flashpoints where there is a need for action.

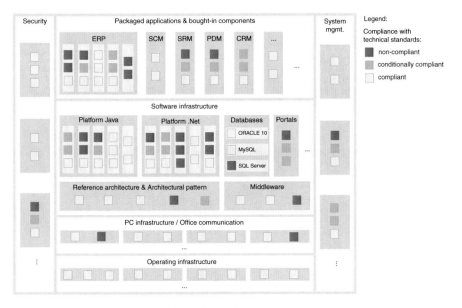

Fig. 5.6 Blueprint with contents (Cluster diagram)

The blueprint is generally presented in graphical form in a cluster diagram or a technical landscape diagram. Figure 5.6 shows the reference model presented in Fig. 5.5, enriched with technical components – for example, the "databases" drawer is shown containing the database systems ORACLE 10, MySQL and SQL Server.

Figure 5.6 provides additional information on the release status of the blueprint elements. Accordingly, the diagram shows at a glance which technical components can be used in projects and, if so, under what conditions.

Figure 5.7 presents the populated blueprint as a technical landscape diagram. Each of the technical components is placed to reflect its affiliation to architectural domains and tiers.

When a blueprint is presented in a technical landscape diagram, the x-axis generally shows the architectural domains (subdivided into sections as appropriate). What you choose to show along the y-axis depends on what correlations you wish to investigate. Common choices are locations,[5] release status, degree of standardisation, or responsibilities.

As in a cluster diagram, there are various ways to differentiate technical components in the technical landscape diagram. Components can be colour-coded, for instance, or have different border styles to indicate information such as the release status or degree of compliance with standards, also aspects such as locations, responsibilities, technical status, security level or cost.

---

[5]For example when there are different technical standards at different enterprise locations.

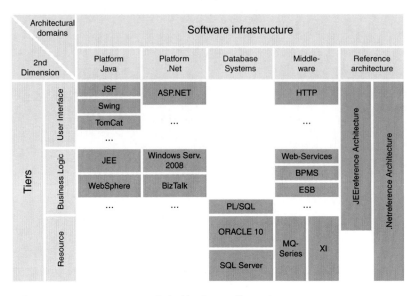

Fig. 5.7 Blueprint with contents (technical landscape diagram)

Technical landscape diagrams can typically also serve to show the utilisation of components in applications, interfaces or operating infrastructures. Unlike the blueprint in Fig. 5.8, "applications" are used here as the second axis. For each application, the diagram shows a row with the application's technical realisation,

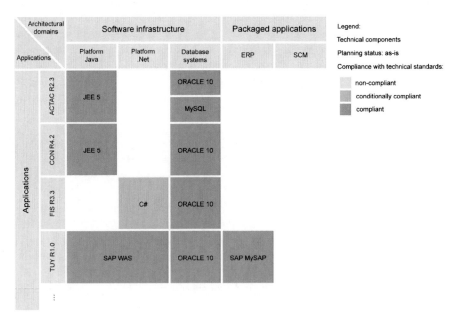

Fig. 5.8 Utilisation of technical components (landscape diagram)

sorted by architectural domains. To pick an example from the diagram, application ACTAC R2.3 uses the technical components "JEE 5" from the architectural domain "Platform Java" and databases "ORACLE 10" and "MySQL" for its technical implementation. The diagram can also present other information – the example here shows "compliance with technical standards".

Fact file:

- Each technical component should be placed in as few architectural domains as possible, ideally just one.
- When you first start working with technical standardisation, it is advisable to limit the number of information fields which needs to be gathered for each technical component. A few pointers are provided earlier in this section.

  By keeping things simple, you can get technical standardisation moving quickly and effectively, and also keep a firm lid on effort for initial and ongoing maintenance.
- Cluster diagrams or technical landscape diagrams are used to present a blueprint in graphical form.

  Technical landscape diagrams use architectural domains as their primary axis. What you choose for the second axis (and how you sort and arrange clusters in cluster diagrams) depends on what you wish to investigate with the diagram. You can choose to emphasise (e.g. through colour coding or border styles) aspects such as the release status or whatever is relevant for you.
- You will generally use a landscape diagram to present component utilisation (with architectural domains along the first axis and applications along the second).

5.4 Technical Standardisation Processes

This section describes the processes which are applied in technical standardisation. They include:

- **Maintaining, providing and communicating the blueprint**: This means making sure that the blueprint – the technical reference model and the filler elements – are published in up-to-date form, including the release status (see Sect. 5.4.1).

- **IT innovation management**: If you scan the market on an ongoing basis, you will be able to identify potentially relevant technological innovations and trends while they are still on the horizon, and to appraise them in terms of maturity, associated risks and practical feasibility (see Sect. 5.4.2).
- **Strategic evolution of technical standards**: This involves designing the to-be blueprint and deriving appropriate standardisation to reflect the requirements arising from IT landscape management and the operational side of the business. Technical innovations are also channelled into the evolution of technical standards (see Sect. 5.4.3).
- **Enacting standardisation**: This is all about creating or modifying technical components in accordance with strategic objectives and the specific requirements of your enterprise (see Sect. 5.4.4).
- **Directing compliance with technical standards**: Ensuring that the standards, once defined, are actually applied (see Sect. 5.4.5).

5.4.1 Maintaining, Providing and Communicating the Blueprint

Maintaining the blueprint has to be an ongoing process. Whenever a technical component is added or modified, you have to update and re-publish the blueprint. One option is to publish on the intranet, which you can also use as a platform for providing additional guidance for technical standards or as a resource for downloading software.

Important:

- **Communicate new and modified technical standards**: People can only apply technical standards if they know they exist. Take steps to ensure the blueprint is always up to date and that all relevant stakeholders are aware of its existence.
- **Make the blueprint simple to use**: The technical blueprint must be easily accessible, and the technical standards must be easy to locate.
- **Guidance for use**: Only if you actually provide guidance on how the standards are to be used – checklists, for instance, or a use-case concept – will you have any chance of making sure technical components are used for their intended purposes. At the very least, you should make sure there is a link to documentation or to the installation packages provided with the technical components.
- **Keep things tidy**: Also part of maintenance is the continuously checking if standards changed. Any standards which are no longer relevant should be clearly marked for decommissioning. Otherwise you will find technical standards extremely difficult to manage and maintain.

5.4.2 IT Innovation Management

The future relevance of technical standards – i.e. whether they are going to remain valid for an appropriate length of time – is a key aspect you will need to consider in the evolution of your blueprint. IT innovation management makes an important contribution here (see Fig. 5.9). Make it a principle to scan environments on an ongoing basis in order to identify and investigate trends, and be better able to appraise technological developments and the lifecycles of the technical standards you are using. This will help "future-proof" the IT in your company, enabling you to manage fast-paced technological change and ever shorter lifecycles of IT products.

Key elements of IT innovation management:

- **Technology scanning**: Keep your radar on at all times! This will help you perceive fledgling trends and technologies and new third-party IT products emerging onto the market, and to keep close track on their development.

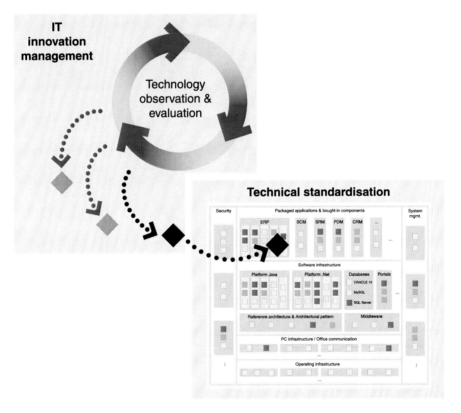

Fig. 5.9 IT innovation management

Since there are technological changes going on all the time (and in considerable numbers), you might have to scan a wide range of potential areas and topics.

- **Rough assessment of technologies**: Analyse the technological maturity and the potential of the likely-looking IT innovations in order to narrow down the scope somewhat. You can base your technology evaluation on either general or enterprise-specific criteria, e.g. available expertise in the market or company, or availability of solutions (IT or otherwise) and references. Making a rough estimate of the likely lifecycle is also paramount, particularly when you are looking into third-party IT products. In general, you will also make use of analyst reports, such as how a product is positioned in the Gartner Hype Cycle, to filter out some of the innovations.
- **Identify IT innovations which are relevant for the enterprise**: To identify the relevant IT innovations, appraise the technological maturity, the potential and the possible time of introduction in your enterprise, and weigh all this up in terms of opportunities and risks for the company. You can use a range of criteria – for example, to appraise maturity you can conduct trials with the technology or third-party IT products and obtain some hard, practical evidence. You might also like to consult expert opinion, either people in your own enterprise or outside consultants. Appraise the maturity and robustness of each IT innovation you consider relevant.

The time of introduction of an innovation in your enterprise depends particularly on your enterprise's attitude toward innovation. Of the categories shown here (see [Rog95], [MIT03]), which best fits your enterprise?

- **Innovators**: Fond of experimenting, innovators are among the first to engage with a new technology, despite all its risks and the lack of a practical track record. It is these people, with their enthusiasm, who spark off a new trend.
- **Early adopters**: are aficionados of technology and are quick to take up an innovation once an initial level of maturity has been reached and there are opportunity paths charted out. Despite potential early glitches, the early adopters see the new technology as an opportunity to carve out competitive advantage. They are the first real customers for the providers of the new technology.
- **Early majority**: customers have to be persuaded by the innovators and early adopters that there is a case for the technology. They draw on the experience of innovators and early adopters to reduce their own risks. Once the first positive reports are in and clear benefit can be identified, they jump on board before the technology has really picked up pace. As a rule, the early majority are looking to achieve benefits which are measurable in financial terms (faster, cheaper or better).
- **Late majority**: These customers adopt the technology only when the innovation has taken firm root and is already in widespread use. This group is more

conservative in outlook. They do not come on board until the new technology has been tested and has a proven track record. The risk is minimal and the benefit secure.

- **Laggards**: The laggards are more likely to look to the past and traditional values for their guidance. Often, any change is precipitated only after enormous pressure from outside.

The right adopter category for your enterprise will depend on your enterprise's strategic direction and its culture. If your company is striving for technological leadership, it will usually be an innovator, early adopter or at least part of the early majority. If it is committed to cost leadership, the company will usually be among the late majority or a laggard.

IT manufacturers tend for the most part to pursue early-adopter strategies. There are ramp-up programmes in the SAP field, for example, which have good effort-to-benefit ratios. Reduced licensing and maintenance fees, and training and coaching, make early adoption choices far easier for the customers.

The need to identify relevant IT innovations can easily be submerged by day-to-day business, so special groups such as think tanks and "innovation spearheads" can be instituted to ensure space and time is set aside. Another source of information is quite simply other people: just think of IT communities, consultants and universities.

It is essential to keep permanent track on how well your IT innovation management is working. Keep tabs on the number of issues you are scanning, or on what feedback you are receiving from markets. There is no point trying to number-crunch your way through innovation management. Unfortunately, there are no statistics testifying to a connection between research & development effort and corporate success. R&D capital is venture capital.

Irrespective of this, all the IT innovations you identify must be put under scrutiny: are they a good fit with your needs? Are they stable enough? As you go about technical standardisation, you need innovations which will be a good basis for technical implementation of your applications, interfaces or elements of your operating infrastructure. To appraise innovations, you should use the same criteria as for the strategic evolution of technical standards (see Sect. 5.4.3).

Fact file:

- By permanently scanning and monitoring emerging technological developments and keeping tabs on the lifecycle of the technical standards you are using, you can ensure the continuity of business operations.
- IT innovation management delivers key input for strategic evolution of technical standards.

- Deciding on whether a technology is future-sustainable often comes down to "gut feeling". Experienced software architects and tried-and-tested methodology help distil this gut feeling into fact-based findings.

Ultimately, only time will tell whether the assumptions underpinning your strategic IT planning turn out to be the right ones. However, you can help build in as much certainty as possible by careful evaluation, analysis, design and testing.

5.4.3 Strategic Evolution of Technical Standards

Over time, blueprints will need updating to keep them in line with business requirements and IT goals. The technical reference model, or rather the architectural domains, have to be brought into line with the changed situation, as do the technical components that fill the model. The following questions are of value:

- Which of the existing technical standards are still appropriate, robust and future-sustainable?
- For which technical trends and innovations are new technical standards to be produced for the enterprise? Which existing technical standards are to be phased out in their stead?
- IT landscape management and operational-level project work often reveal areas requiring action or improvement. For which of these action or improvement points are new technical standards to be developed or existing standards modified?

Technical standardisation requirements can be pulled from a variety of sources:

- **Information from IT landscape management: which technical standards are actually being used?**
  The use of technical standards – and any nonstandard technical implementation – shows through clearly in IT landscape management. IT landscape management also highlights particular points requiring action for improvement (e.g. to eradicate technical redundancy) and these action or improvement points serve as input for the technical standardisation process. IT landscape management can also be used to derive the requirement profile for technical components, e.g. in terms of flexibility or SLAs.
- **Operational-level sources**: Technical standardisation requirements can come from grassroots-level activities such as projects, maintenance measures or operation. For example, it might emerge in a compliance project that the enterprise requires some form of standardisation in its archiving solutions, or an own-build

software project might show up a need for technical standardisation for OR[6] mapping.

The standardisation requirements and strategic objectives are channelled into drafting proposals for the to-be blueprint. Figure 5.10 illustrates the result, showing in which architectural domains technical standards are to be produced, modified and phased out.

As shown in Fig. 5.11, the evolution of the technical landscape is an ongoing process. It entails defining the to-be blueprint, the planned blueprint and carrying out the interventions that will move the blueprint toward the plan. The to-be blueprint, which presents a vision of what the blueprint will look like some time in the future, is refined in an iterative analysis & design process which takes account of standardisation requirements.

The to-be blueprint can consist of elements such as reference architectures or architectural components, e.g. "Web 2.0" applications for the relatively new technology "Web 2.0" or also just be a more generalised statement of a need for third-party IT products for archiving solutions.

Once the to-be blueprint has been approved by the relevant decision-making entity (see Sect. 5.5.2), the next step is iterative development of the planned blueprint. Appropriate standardisation measures are derived, evaluated and prioritised for the new standards and for standards which are to undergo modification. The

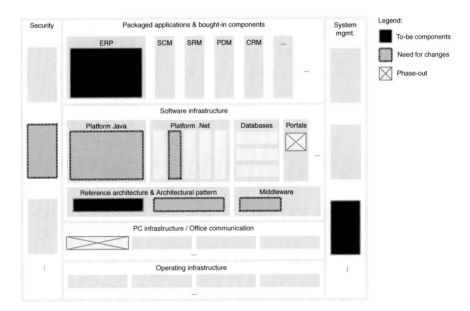

Fig. 5.10   Need for changes in the blueprint

---

[6] *Object Relational.*

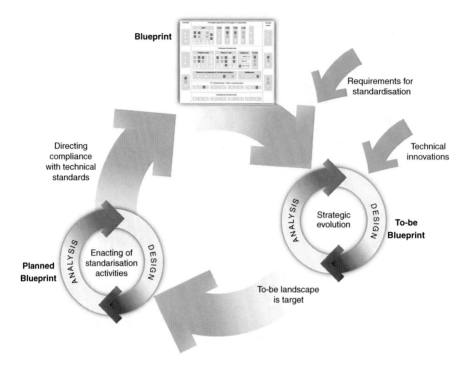

Fig. 5.11 Blueprint evolution process

process of enacting standardisation, i.e. putting the planned blueprint into action, keeps the blueprint in a state of permanent evolution.

Your appraisal of standardisation measures will of course consider cost,[7] benefit and operational urgency, but be sure also to apply criteria such as maturity level, consistency with strategy, and operational risk. Once standardisation measures have been be given the go-ahead by the relevant decision-making board, you can proceed with enacting them.

Fact file:

- Alongside technological trends identified in IT innovation management and standardisation requirements emerging from operational-level business, information from IT landscape management – details on how standards are actually in use – is the key input for the strategic evolution of the blueprint.

---

[7]One-off costs for producing the technical standard, including items such as licensing costs plus ongoing cost such as for maintenance, training or support.

- To evolve the blueprint, you produce a to-be landscape on the basis of strategic and operative requirements and derive standardisation measures from this.
- All standardisation requests should be appraised at least in terms of their maturity level, consistency with strategy, operational risk, cost and benefit – but you can of course use additional criteria if you wish.

5.4.4 Enacting Standardisation

Enacting standardisationThe blueprint is progressed by enacting standardisation measures which have been approved for go-ahead. Standardisation measures include activities such as:

- **Developing reference architectures or architectural patterns**: e.g. creating a reference architecture for JSF applications
- **Evaluating third-party IT products**: This entails determining what products are available on the market, and appraising them in terms of how they fit your company's requirements. A shortlist is then assembled and a recommendation given for one of the shortlisted products.

   Products routinely selected in this way are DMS, CMS or workflow engines.
- **Creating technical building blocks**: Technical building blocks are either developed from scratch, or adapted and configured to meet your company's requirements, e.g. enterprise-specific frameworks for business transactions or auditing
- **Provision of migration guidelines**: When your enterprise elects to phase out technical standards which are already installed in applications or interfaces, you will have to provide guidance on migration – e.g. how to update to successor components. You might choose to develop a complete migration concept, complemented by specific migration scripts. Such guidance is particularly important when you are introducing new releases of technical components.

Standardisation is often enacted as part of projects under the stewardship of technical specialists. For activities involving third-party products, the enterprise may be aided by product vendors.

There must be a dedicated release process in place to check the technical quality of all new or modified technical components, sign off on the components, define their release status and publish the components in the blueprint. Over time, this sequence of actions moves the blueprint gradually toward the to-be status.

Work does not stop once a new technical standard has been included in the blueprint. Rather, you have to keep close tabs on its fitness for purpose, cost and benefit, taking care to obtain feedback from users. After all, the benefit promised in the standardisation request might fail to materialise! If you find there is little or no demand for a technical component, if you feel it is unsustainable or its cost-benefit ratio leaves a lot to be desired, strip it out of the blueprint – quickly. Should the component already be in productive operation, you will have to find an alternative and scope out a migration path.

Fact file:

- Keep a close eye on the fitness of purpose, robustness and future sustainability of all new or modified technical components.
- It is by keeping a constant check on robustness and future sustainability, cost and benefit of each component, and the frequency of its use, that you can effectively steer the evolutionary development of the blueprint. A good way of obtaining such information is to invite feedback from projects or users.

5.4.5 Directing Compliance with Technical Standards

Even the best technical standards are no use if they are not applied! A proactive stance is what works best here, ensuring standards are actually carried forward into practice and enabling your enterprise to attain the goals it wishes to accomplish through its standardisation efforts (see Sect. 5.2). What matters here is that people actually adhere to the technical standards in their projects and maintenance measures and in routine productive operation. You can direct compliance with:

- Strategic controlling, using metrics such as the degree of standardisation or standards compliance as key criteria for investment decisions (see Sect. 6.3).
- Embedding technical architecture management into your organisational structures. This builds more effectiveness into the process of selecting and applying technical standards and enforcing their correct use (see Sect. 5.5).

Important:

- It will be impossible to direct compliance unless there is a possibility to directly influence the technical design stage of projects.
- To make standardisation enforceable, the overarching policy has to stake out precisely how much latitude people are allowed in decisions – there should be clearly demarcated trajectories which people cannot break out of without good reason.

5.5 Organisational Structures

The effectiveness of technical standardisation is due in no small part to how well it is embedded in the organisation. The following aspects are important:

- Clear roles and responsibilities in technical standardisation
- Integration into strategic and operational level IT processes, notably project management
- Decision-making entities and processes for

  - Strategic blueprint planning (to-be landscape and standardisation) and
  - IT investment decisions, including defining project portfolios and releases with due consideration of technical standards

- Maturity level of IT in terms of its technical standardisation

5.5.1 Roles and Responsibilities

A separate role with clear rights and remits is essential to move the technical standardisation processes forward. This role is termed "IT architect" in the following.

The IT architect is tasked with providing and evolving the technical standards, and for guiding and advising on their use. The architect also has the job of quality-assuring any technical standards developed by other parties, and of signing off on them.

Whether technical standardisation accomplishes its goals ultimately stands and falls with the people tasked with implementing it. Accordingly, IT architects have to have a persuasive, compelling manner – and be as convincing as the prescribed technical standards themselves!

The skill profile of an IT architect is daunting – but it does take finely-honed capabilities to accomplish the goals of technical standardisation.

- **Highly experienced employee, in the company for many years, with an excellent grasp of software architectures and technology and extensive project and business administration experience**: IT architects must be able to give prompt, realistic appraisals of new technologies and trends. As such, they need to be in touch with how things work in practice, and have experienced the issues that typically confront people in projects and productive operation – for example, by working for a spell as a software architect. Further details on the role of the software architect are provided in [Star08] and [Vog05].
- **Ability to grasp new concepts quickly and find workable solutions; good conceptual thinking skills**: To convince others that a particular technical standard, be it a reference architecture or third-party IT product, is the right way to go, the IT architect will need to place it in the context of its later use, e.g. in a project, and show how the standard will lead to requirements being fulfilled.

- **High level of commitment, good communication skills, and ability to present a compelling case**: Particularly in the first few years after introduction, technical standardisation has an uphill struggle. The IT architect has to persevere, reinforcing the case to application managers and project leaders and showing what value the standards deliver in specific contexts.

Fact file:

- A specific role, the IT architect, is tasked with delivering enterprise standards and ensuring their continual development over time.
- The skill profile of the IT architect is described in vivid terms in [Nie05]: "IT architects must work with their heads in the clouds and their feet on the ground".

5.5.2 Entities, Boards and Integration into Processes in IT and Decision-Making

In order to be effective, technical standards genuinely have to be applied in practice – and this means having authoritative boards in the enterprise and integrating technical standardisation into operational-level and strategic IT management and decision processes.

The impact of IT on investment decisions is fundamental. When project portfolio managers come to appraise project requests, they also need to include evaluation criteria and metrics to measure the degree of standardisation or deviations from technical standards, and channel these findings into their decisions.

Blueprint Board

Investment decisions also have to be taken on standardisation efforts themselves. There should be a dedicated board in place to define the to-be technical blueprint, appraise what each standardisation measure is about, and prioritise them. This board is termed the "blueprint board". In practice, blueprint boards can exist both with and without authority[8] to take decisions on investments. In addition, the blueprint board must ensure technical standards are monitored continually with regard to their appropriateness, robustness, future sustainability, cost and benefit.

The members of the blueprint board are generally the CIO and IT managers in charge of IT operation, application engineering and possibly also infrastructure provisioning. Other members – key to the board's composition – are experienced IT architects.

---

[8]Whatever authority the board has, its scope for taking investment decisions will usually be substantially restricted.

Project Support

Alongside the quality and benefit of the technical standards, the key driver of success is the guidance and coaching provided to projects to help them select and use standards and embed them into project management and commissioning processes.

Without qualified project support, there will be no way of actually ensuring that technical standards are being used to the purpose intended. Therefore, even while projects are at the high-level draft stage, appropriate technical components should be selected from the blueprint. IT architects must be proactive in delivering advice and guidance to project teams. The IT architect can either be involved in the project itself and play the part of the project's software architect, or take an external role as a coach or sparring partner.

Whether you take a light touch with project support or aim for more intensive involvement depends on the complexity or strategic significance of the project in question. Be sure always to provide appropriate support to all major projects!

Quality Assurance Measures

Once the conceptual IT design has been finalised, if not earlier, instigate quality assurance measures such as reviews or handover & acceptance assessments to verify that projects are consistent with standards and use the appropriate technical components to the purposes intended.

Reviews and acceptance assessments must at least verify proper use of the components at each of the major milestones. To build in the required pressure and motivation, this practice should be embedded in project management and also in maintenance and operating processes.

At the very latest before the software goes into productive operation, reviews must be conducted to verify compliance with the technical parameters drawn up in the conceptual IT design, notably that the agreed technical standards have been used to the purposes originally intended.

Fact file:

- Include the degree of standardisation (or noncompliance) as appraisal criteria to be investigated when making investment decisions.
- Work with the blueprint board to establish an entity to take decisions regarding evolutionary development of the blueprint.
- Be sure to provide qualified project support.
- Quality-assure the conceptual IT design and sign off on the implementation at least before systems go into productive operation.

5.5.3 *Maturity of IT in Terms of Technical Standardisation*

The way you organise structures and processes, and what approaches you take to technical standardisation, must fit with the current maturity level in your enterprise. To determine the status quo, you can use the following maturity model (see Fig. 5.12), which draws on project experience:

- **Entrance**: IT peripherals are standardised, and the resulting economies of scale and concentration of expertise deliver enormous cost savings.
- **"Black-box" standardisation**: Technologies, third-party IT products and tools are defined as mandatory objectives for projects, maintenance measures and operation.
- **"White-box" standardisation**: "White-box" standardisation has the objective of enhancing the technical quality of applications.

  Each level of standardisation builds on the preceding one. The levels are described in greater detail below.

Entrance

The huge cost savings potential tends to be the primary motivation for embarking on technical standardisation – which begins with commodity IT products

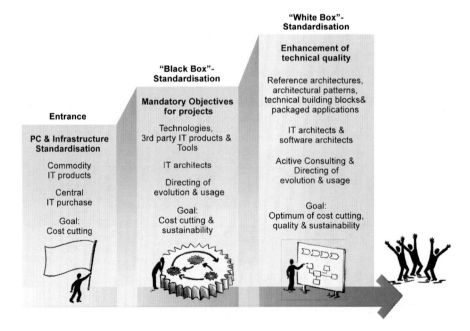

Fig. 5.12 Maturity levels in technical standardisation

such as PC infrastructure and office communication, also operating infrastructure. The enterprise can achieve economies of scale by standardising these peripherals. Standardised workstations and operating platforms simplify procurement, provisioning and operation, enabling major cost savings to be achieved with relatively little effort. A key lever for implementing technical standardisation at this level is that it enables IT procurement to be centralised (e.g. with technical buyers). There is no need for specific roles, boards or processes.

"Black-Box" Standardisation

Black-box standardisation expands technical standardisation to include technologies, third-party IT products and tools. Specific technologies – for instance SAP, JEE and .Net – create the technical cornerstones for evolutionary development of the application landscape and operation. Third-party IT products and tools are black-box components which can be used unchanged as self-contained units. Technologies, third-party IT products and tools are specified as mandatory objectives for projects and maintenance measures and for planning the operating infrastructure.

Black-box standardisation entails integrating the standardisation processes into IT processes and decision-making, establishing a board for technical standardisation (see Sect. 5.5.1), and grooming qualified IT architects (see Sect. 5.5.2) to guide the people in charge of projects and maintenance. Before new or modified applications go into productive operation – if not before – tests must be conducted to verify that technical standards have genuinely been applied.

Useful hint:

While you are moving ahead on black-box standardisation, you should actively drive technical homogenisation. It is only by retiring the non-standardised technical components that you can lessen the heterogeneity and achieve sustained cost savings.

"White-Box" Standardisation

White-box standardisation takes things a step further, also standardising reference architectures and architectural patterns, technical building blocks and packaged applications such as Siebel. White-box standardisation moves beyond slotting ready-made technical components into landscapes; it also sets out rules for the inner structure of applications, at least to some extent, in order to raise the applications' technical quality.

In developing a set of practice-tested white-box standards for projects, maintenance and operation, the IT architects take into account the technical innovations relevant for the enterprise (see Sect. 5.4.4).

By staking out particular reference architectures and architectural patterns, you are defining the software architecture of applications on the conceptual level, and giving people a set of practice-tested solution patterns for tasks such as data access, and particularly also for implementing non-functional requirements such as performance or security.

Technical building blocks such as framework components can be used for custom application systems. Off-the-shelf business software will as a rule be mandatory for particular purposes in the to-be blueprint. The introduction of packaged software can be made substantially easier by tools such as configuration templates (see also [Vog05]).

To ensure white-box standards are applied for the proper purpose, IT architects must be able to provide qualified guidance, particularly to projects. The IT architects should either take on the role of software architects themselves in the projects, or support the projects' own software architects.

Important:

- The appropriateness and the cost-benefit ratio of technical standards are what decides whether a technical standard will really remain in lasting use.
- Whether the white-box standards are applied as intended is largely determined by how simple it is to use them, and by the quality of the guidance provided by the IT architects. See also [Star08] and [Vog05].
- IT architects must have a high skill level and project experience in implementing standardisation measures. Train IT architects if you do not already have such highly qualified software architects on your team.

Drafting out the white-box standards to a high level of quality, and above all keeping them up to date, will generally be a lot of work. However, standardisation is not an end in itself – so be sure to keep a vigilant eye on the costs for providing and maintaining standards and ensure they do not outweigh the benefit.

Fact file:

- The entry point into technical standardisation is generally via the commodity IT products, with centralised IT procurement aimed at achieving cost savings.
No IT architects are required for this. Processes are simple to get underway, and this level of standardisation is easy to embed in the organisation.

- After commodity IT products, standardise the technologies, third-party IT products and tools, and present them as mandatory technical standards for projects and maintenance measures. This will help keep your IT landscape aligned with strategic considerations.

  While all this is in progress, actively drive forward the homogenisation of technical building blocks as a means to achieving sustained cost savings.
- Following black-box standardisation, you can, if appropriate, tackle the white-box standards.

  Since development of the standards takes so much time and effort, the white-box standardisation level may not necessarily be the right way forward for your enterprise. Please weigh up the costs and benefits carefully and keep a permanent check on them as the landscape develops.

Dependency Between Objectives and Degrees of Maturity

Not all objectives (see Sect. 5.2) can be attained at all levels of maturity. See also Table 5.1.

The "cost savings" objective can be achieved at all levels of maturity, with a different focus at each level. It is simple to standardise IT peripherals and operating infrastructure, and this also has substantial impact on costs. Particularly by standardising peripheral equipment, you can achieve enormous savings with relatively little effort.

Sustained reduction of operating and maintenance costs is achievable only by homogenisation. By "tidying up" server[9] or software elements or entire systems, you can cull the legacy elements. And you can also reduce the proliferation of maintenance contracts, push down integration costs, simplify workflows and concentrate expertise.

Actually putting homogenisation efforts into practice is no simple matter, in many cases progressing no further than good intentions. One of the reasons is that it means making changes to existing systems. As a rule, the effort then clearly outweighs the benefit. Plus, the benefits – in the form of reduced maintenance costs or faster time-to-system – tend to be long-term and difficult to quantify. As a result, all that happens is the gradual levelling via update measures (projects and maintenance) that would be taking place anyway, whereby effort and benefit have to be compared for each measure. For example, retiring a VAX operating system platform can drag on for many years. It takes perseverance and rigour to see it through!

---

[9]Such as homogenisation of operating locations by merging data centers.

Table 5.1 Achievable objectives in correlation with degrees of maturity

	Degrees of maturity		
	Entrance	"Black-Box"	"White-Box"
Cost savings			
Use of economies of scale and central negotiating power in procurement	√	√	√
Concentration of expertise	√	√	√
High technical quality			
Re-use of practice-tested black-box components		√	√
Standardisation of white-box standards			√
Appropriate IT support, e.g. flexibility			
Reference architectures and architectural patterns which support the principle of service and component orientation			√
Standard middleware and interfaces/API solutions such as an Enterprise Service Bus		√	√
Future security			
IT innovation management		(√)	(√)
Strategic planning and direction of technical blueprints, and use of building blocks in the landscape		(√)	(√)

Huge benefits are achievable by standardising and homogenising applications. However, this is also the greatest challenge. There must be genuine business reasons driving the move to standardisation. For instance, some enterprises, having investigated business process re-engineering or the likes, might be keen to standardise the IT support of their business processes or business functions. As a rule, implementing technical standardisation often goes hand-in-hand with the introduction of packaged software such as SAP, largely because this is an established way forward ("you can't make the wrong decision!"). Packaged software sets standards in terminology and in business processes. The process standards used in the software[10] can be rolled out across the enterprise.

Enforcing such standards is immeasurably easier than creating your own, because the former, being defined externally, are not changeable. At the same time, this can be a problem if functionality is inappropriate or the structures in packaged software are not really a good fit for the enterprise, meaning substantial modifications have to be made. Changes to packaged software – quite apart from the upfront effort – make life difficult when you move to a new release or install bug

---

[10]Possibly customized for your enterprise.

fixes. In other words, before standardising on applications, you should make a thorough investigation of the business needs to decide whether a standard solution or a custom-build is more appropriate to map the uniform to-be business processes and functions.

Homogenisation is in any case an ongoing task. Each technical standard which has reached the end of its lifecycle must be marked for retirement. This helps stem the heterogeneity which would otherwise inevitably grow with every new technical innovation.

Useful hints:

- Use the business requirements to make your case for gradually homogenising the IT landscape.
- Explicitly carry out lifecycle management for your technical standards and mark the ones which are likely candidates to retire.
- Common in many enterprises is a range of retirement projects which are "90% complete". This is best avoided!

  Make sure your retirement projects undergo regular controlling. This ensures they can actually be brought to an end and deliver the envisaged cost savings.
- Standardising or homogenising on application level should always be motivated by business reasons. Genuine business benefit is the only justification for the huge effort involved.

To achieve the aims of improving quality or providing appropriate IT support, you need to extend technical standardisation to include basic technologies or even application or operational architectures. For both these objectives, you should prudently select at least technologies, third-party IT products and tools, design sustainable reference architectures and architectural patterns as necessary and ensure there are high-quality technical building blocks available. Standardising at this level engages far more effort than just standardising peripheral equipment.

You can achieve business manoeuvrability by installing flexible, service-oriented and component-oriented architectures, and standard middleware solutions such as an Enterprise Service Bus.

If you are looking to increase the technical quality or build flexibility into an outmoded application landscape which has proliferated over time, you may seriously have to consider complete replacement of at least parts of your application landscape. There is no immediately obvious business benefit to this course of action, and the reduction of high maintenance and operation costs (on systems that have been "maintained to death") is the only real savings potential you can name. Even so, the rollout costs often exceed the savings. Nor do the danger of inflexibility, or

the unreliability of the IT, add more credence to the case. These arguments are often
not enough to win the right stakeholders over. A quantifiable business benefit has to
be found!

Anticipatory scanning of technological innovation, which is part of the IT
innovation management process (see also Sect. 5.4.4), is key to the objective of
"future-proofing" the IT landscape – as are strategic planning and control of the
landscape and of which building blocks are used. The future sustainability of the IT
landscape is largely dependent on the core applications and their operating environment, i.e. it is determined by high-level technical standards and as such correlates
with the higher levels of maturity.

Important:

Be sure to set realistic goals.
A goal is only realistic if it is consistent with the current or targeted maturity
level.

5.6 Guidelines for Technical Standardisation in Practice

Under the stewardship of the CIO, the enterprise team makes a first pass at
developing the blueprint, organisation and processes for technical standardisation
in line with the IT goals and current standardisation requirements. This initial
version is then adjusted constantly to bring it into line with changed environmental parameters. As a rule, the initial version is drafted as part of IT strategy
development (see Sect. 2.5) in a series of workshops over a period of several
months, possibly with different participants depending on the subject matter under
discussion.

Important:

Be sure to involve at least one representative of the executive board, and all
IT managers for all core IT areas.

This section provides a guideline for developing technical standardisation to fit your
company. Introducing technical standardisation essentially comprises four steps, as
shown in Fig. 5.13:

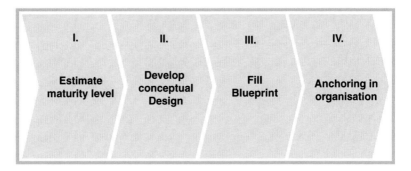

Fig. 5.13   Four steps to introducing technical standardisation

- **I. Estimate the maturity level of your IT in terms of technical standardisation**: Work out where you stand right now regarding technical standardisation.
- **II. Develop conceptual design for technical standardisation**: Define your objectives, the technical reference model, the organisational processes, and tool support.
- **III. Fill the blueprint**: Define the initial blueprint, filling it with the technical building blocks which are already in use. Determine the to-be landscape and the standardisation you will need to introduce in order to get there.
- **IV. Anchoring technical standardisation in the organisation**: Establish the role of the IT architect, and the blueprint board as an authority in your enterprise. Integrate the technical standardisation processes into the IT and decision-making flows and initiate the change process.

These steps are described in greater detail in the following.

I. Estimate the Maturity Level

The maturity model described in Sect. 5.5.3 is used to estimate the maturity level. To determine your current level of maturity in terms of technical standardisation, it helps to answer the following questions:

- What is already technically standardised today?
- Who is in charge of producing the technical standards?
- How is technical standardisation enforced?
- How and by whom is technical standardisation monitored?

Below is a table for each level of maturity which you can use to answer the questions. Determine your current maturity level, and the level you would like to work towards. A maturity level is considered attained when all aspects mentioned in the table are covered (Tables 5.2, 5.3 and 5.4).

Important:

- Set a realistic goal for the maturity level you are aspiring to.
- Do not have too many irons in the fire at once!
- A level is only realistically attainable once the predecessor level is anchored and demonstrable benefit has been delivered.

Table 5.2 Entrance

Maturity level: Entrance	
What is already technically standardised today?	*Commodity IT products* *PC infrastructure and office communication (standardisation of peripheral equipment)*: Standardisation of items such as PCs and notebooks, PC workstation software such as office products and communication platforms *Operating infrastructure*: Homogenisation and standardisation on hardware and network level in operation, e.g. standardisation of servers and network components
How is technical standardisation enforced?	Centralised IT procurement
Who is in charge of producing the technical standards?	IT managers
How and by whom is technical standardisation monitored?	No specific roles, boards or processes are necessary

II. Conceptual Design

Define a reference model for the blueprint, organisational structures and processes in accordance with your enterprise's specific objectives, also factoring the current and target maturity level into your decision. The following activities are required here:

- **Select the enterprise-specific objectives**: From the set of possible objectives (see Sect. 5.2), select those which are relevant for you, or elaborate them to fit your requirements.

  Make sure they fit with the level of maturity you are aiming at. See also Table 5.1.

- **Define the reference model**: Next, bearing in mind your selected objectives and the standardisation requirements, define the "drawers" and "trays" in the model (considering the principles and strategies of the IT strategy, see Sect. 2.4), and refer the outcomes back to your initial stakeholder group.

Table 5.3 "Black-box" standardisation

Maturity level: "Black-box" standardisation	
What is already technically standardised today?	*Commodity IT products* *Technologies*: General technology objectives, e.g. JEE or .Net *Third-party IT products*: Standardisation of third-party IT products in application engineering and in operation, e.g. runtime environments, database systems or middleware *Software and system management tools*: Defining unified tools for software engineering and system operation, e.g. software development or monitoring environments
How is technical standardisation enforced?	Mandatory objectives for projects and maintenance measures, and for planning the operating infrastructure; set by a technical standardisation board
Who is in charge of producing the technical standards?	IT architect
How and by whom is technical standardisation monitored?	Involvement of IT architects in rolling out projects Reviews and handover assessments, integrated into IT processes Permanent monitoring of cost to-benefit ratio

Table 5.4 "White-box" standardisation

Maturity level: "White-box" standardisation	
What is already technically standardised today?	*Commodity IT products* *Technologies, third-party IT products and tools* *Reference architectures and architectural patterns* (see also Sect. 5.3) e.g. SOA reference architecture as vision for further development of applications *Technical components* (see also Sect. 5.3): Standardisation of technical components in the context of custom development of applications, e.g. frameworks for security aspects, troubleshooting or monitoring *Packaged business software*: Standardisation and homogenisation of packaged business software in terms of business support, e.g. a single predefined application for a specific business function
How is technical standardisation enforced?	Mandatory objectives for projects and maintenance measures, and for planning the operating infrastructure; set by a technical standardisation board
Who is in charge of producing the technical standards?	IT architect, possibly collaborating with software architects
How and by whom is technical standardisation monitored?	Involvement of IT architects in rolling out projects Qualified consulting and guidance Reviews and handover assessments, integrated into IT processes Permanent monitoring of cost to-benefit ratio

Useful hints:

- The potential standardisation points you identify when analysing the maturity level must each be categorisable into an architectural domain.
- In choosing architectural domains, stick to those which are consistent with the maturity level you are aiming for. Try to keep the number down, and use no more than eight main structural elements.
- Each architectural domain should be filled with at least one technical building block.
  Remove the domains to which you are unable to assign building blocks.
- Make use of best practices and standards such as TOGAF TRM, as described in Sect. 5.3.1, to define your architectural domains.
  Go through all the architectural domains in the selected standard (e.g. TOGAF TRM) or in the best-practice approach, and deliberately ask whether there is a requirement for standardisation in this context.

- **Define processes, organisation and tool support**: Define processes, organisational structures and tool support in accordance with the maturity level you are aiming for and the objectives you have selected. See also Sects. 5.4 and 5.5.

III. Filling the Blueprint

Once you have decided on the drawers and trays for which technical standards are to be offered, you have to fill them – by assigning each drawer and tray initial contents.

Proceed as follows:

- **Determine which technical building blocks are currently in use (status quo)**: If there is no documentation available giving an adequately up-to-date picture, you will have to stock-take the technical components which are currently in use. You can use information from IT landscape management, findings of earlier inventory processes or items such as purchase lists for third-party IT products.
  The existing technical components are possible candidates for inclusion in the blueprint. Evaluate whether you wish to include these in the blueprint as pre-existing de-facto standards.
- **Design the to-be blueprint (see 5.4.3)**: Design this in accordance with your IT goals, principles and strategies, and what you require in terms of standardisation. You have to identify potential to-be components for each architectural domain. Describe these components in relatively general terms such as "embedded workflow component for JEE applications".

Evaluate the importance of each to-be component on the basis of your standardisation requirements and information from IT landscape management. You
can then make a selection from the to-be components. Consolidate the proposals
and integrate them into the reference model you have already created.

Submit the to-be blueprint to the blueprint board if existing, otherwise to the
CIO or head of IT for a decision (see 5.5).

- **Derive your standardisation measures**: Using IT landscape management and
operational-level business requirements as input, you now derive appropriate
standardisation measures to move the blueprint from its present status (as-is)
toward your planned status. Elaborate and assess the measures you develop. This
is the basis on which the blueprint board or project portfolio board will take an
investment decision and thus move the blueprint to the next stage of development
(see also Sect. 5.5.2).

IV. Embedding in the Organisation

"Isn't it nice, when things just work" describes succinctly the ultimate target status
of technical standardisation. The benefits of technical standardisation far outstrip the
costs – at which point (and not before) technical standardisation will be embedded
in your organisation.

Keep a close eye on the appropriateness, robustness, future sustainability, cost
and benefit of all technical standards, and how often each is used. You can then be
sure that the prescribed technical standards are actually delivering on their promised
benefit!

When calculating effort, however, do not just consider the initial work of preparing and publishing standards. Prior to unrestricted release of such standards for
reference architectures and architectural patterns, third-party IT products and technical components for projects, there has to be clear evidence that they are fit for the
purpose and up to the job. Trial-run a technical standard in at least one project or in
all relevant application cases. The time taken for such trials must also be considered
in your cost-benefit estimate, as does all maintenance and advisory work.

It will generally be impossible to fully quantify the cost and benefit of technical standardisation. Nonetheless, you should try to determine potential costs and
benefits and at least make a rough estimate of figures.

Useful hint:

Deliberating the cost and benefit aspects at least helps you work out the decision case. If you are unable to find enough arguments in favour, there is in
general not enough need to go ahead with the standardisation!

Before including a new technical standard in the blueprint, you should answer
the following questions:

- What costs will arise for producing and providing the technical standards?
  What one-off costs can we expect for the development of technical standards, including licensing costs and effort for producing guidelines on use?
  What one-off costs can we expect for piloting the technical standard?
  What costs will arise in project(s), e.g. for learning or customising? Are there any risks we need to consider?
  What costs[11] or what savings can we expect in operation per year or per project? Are there any other costs (such as for coaching, consulting or training) to consider?
- What benefit will ensue when the technical standard is used in productive operation, in various project types or in a specific project, possibly depending on the number of use cases or the number of entities in the data model?
  Which of the following benefit aspects are relevant, and how should these be evaluated for the technical standard?

  - Business benefit, e.g. by simplifying business processes or paving the way to new business models
  - Shorter time-to-system
  - Higher flexibility
  - Greater productivity through efficiency gains (e.g. fewer employees)
  - Higher quality through practice-tested technologies and architectures
  - Cost savings through fewer licences, less training or less maintenance (owing to reduced system complexity)
  - Use of synergy effects as an outcome of reducing technical diversity, e.g. economies of scale through more clout in purchasing, more efficient operation, and concentration of expertise.

Important:

- Each technical standard and each recommended technical innovation has to be demonstrably appropriate, fit for purpose and sustainable into the future.
- Stick to the technical standards that are important and essential for your enterprise. Each standard you introduce brings with it extra work for producing guidance on use, provisioning (particularly updates and maintenance) and guidance for projects.
- Each technical standard must have a clear reference to business requirements and a clearly defined benefit.
  A particular challenge is providing for flexibility in applications, which tends to involve major one-off and ongoing effort. Only make provisions for flexibility where it is genuinely required.

---

[11] For example maintenance contracts.

It is essential to have technical standards which are suitable, fit for purpose and future-sustainable if you are going to embed standardisation in your organisation. Apart from making sure the standards themselves measure up, you also need to complete the following activities:

- Identify highly qualified IT and software architects, or train them if you have no one with suitable skill profiles on your team (for details on the skill profile, see Sect. 5.5.1).
  You need to do this if you are working toward the maturity levels of black-box or white-box standardisation.
- Establish technical standardisation processes, and integrate them into your IT and decision-making workflows (see Sect. 5.5.2).
- Put the tool support in place and communicate this appropriately to relevant stakeholders.
- Appropriate tool support in line with the conceptual design (see Sect. 5.4.1) helps reduce the scope of communication measures to get technical standardisation underway. Announcements, training and project guidance are essential to get the new technical standards really established.
- Offer guidance and coaching, and ensure these services are a fully integrated part of IT processes.
  Ultimately, you need the active involvement of IT architects, at least in key projects, to ensure compliance with technical standards. Proper guidance and coaching, plus reviews and handover & signoff assessments integrated into IT processes, are the only real way to ensure technical standards are being applied properly (see Sect. 5.5.2).
- Get standardisation metrics established in decision-making processes. The boards with enough clout to drive through decisions are the groups which must enforce compliance with the technical standards. These boards must also use the degree of standardisation (or noncompliance with technical standards) as criteria for appraising proposals and taking investment decisions.

Technical standardisation prerequisites for success:

- You have to strike a balance between the competing goals of flexibility, economy and innovation.
  Flexibility: the basis for responding quickly to trends and changed requirements.
  Economy: planned and executed IT projects have to make economic sense.
  Innovation: the ability to make new business products and processes possible and optimise existing ones impacts substantially on the competitive strength of any company.

- Make sure you have the backing of your executive board.

  Win board members over by making your case on the basis of business benefit (see Sect. 5.2), and be sure to keep up the dialogue. You are then more likely to have the board's backing when it comes to enforcing technical standards.
- Produce high-quality, appropriate technical standards and processes, and train qualified IT architects and software architects with the right skill profiles (see Sect. 5.5.1) and outstanding communication abilities.
- The change process is a long road and you need to be persuasive– and gather up and convince all relevant stakeholders along the way.

Chapter 6
EAM Governance

Knowing is not enough; we must apply.
Willing is not enough; we must do.

Johann Wolfgang Goethe (1749–1832)

To institutionalise Enterprise Architecture Management in your company, you have to define EAM governance practices appropriate to your organisation and breathe life into these practices. Figure 6.1 shows the main components of EAM governance.

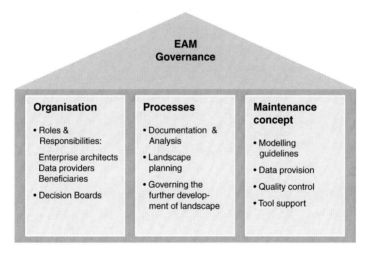

Fig. 6.1 EAM governance

EAM governance comprises the following elements:

- **Organisation**: An appropriate IT organisation with clearly defined roles and responsibilities and functioning boards is essential to provide business and IT intelligence promptly to stakeholders. It also enables decisions to be taken fast and efficiently. This chapter describes best practices for organisational structures to help you install and establish Enterprise Architecture Management. For further

information on roles and responsibilities in business landscape management, IT
landscape management and technical standardisation, please refer to Sects. 3.4,
4.5 and 5.5.

- **Processes**: Business landscape management, IT landscape management and
technical standardisation are the disciplines of which Enterprise Architecture
Management is comprised. Each of these disciplines requires appropriate processes. More information is provided in Sects. 3.4, 4.4 and 5.4. This chapter
(Sect. 6.3) explores particularly the control aspects in greater detail.
- **Maintenance concept**: A maintenance concept lays out the guidelines for documenting the business and/or IT landscape. The concept comprises modelling
guidelines to ensure documentation is standardised and has appropriate granularity, and also defines the procedures and practices for data collection, quality
assurance and tool support.

  A maintenance concept is essential to ensure your landscape data is kept up-
  to-date at all times, with sufficient quality and appropriate granularity. For more
  information, refer to Sect. 4.4.1.

This chapter discusses best practices for organising and establishing a control
toolkit to help direct the strategic development of the IT landscape. You might also
like to refer to further literature (see [Küt06], [Kel06] and [KüM07]).

Questions answered in this chapter:

- What are the main elements of EAM governance?
- What is the correlation between EAM governance and IT governance? Can
CobiT be applied without modification?
- Which model of collaboration between business and IT is appropriate?
- Which boards and decision-making processes are necessary?
- How can IT planning be dovetailed with business planning?
- How can you ensure you accomplish your goals and cover the core areas
of EAM governance?
- What indicators do you need to effectively steer the evolution of the IT
landscape?

6.1 Scope and Definition

EAM governance is a key element of IT governance. IT governance comprises the
principles, procedures and methods which ensure that an organisation's IT is actually aligned with corporate goals, that resources are being deployed responsibly and
risks adequately monitored (see [Mey03], [Fro07] and [IGI08]).

As well as enterprise-specific approaches, dedicated frameworks have become established to help define structures, tools and practices in IT governance. The generally accepted framework is CobiT (see [ITI08]). CobiT (Control Objectives for Information and Related Technology) is an international IT governance standard. It integrates international standards such as the technical standards EDIFACT, ISO 9000 and SPICE (see [Joh07]).

CobiT provides a guideline for management and control tasks. In the third version of CobiT, 34 IT processes are identified which are measured through 314 control objectives.

The current version of CobiT , 4.1, expands the framework to provide enhanced performance measurement, simplified description of goals, and better alignment of processes to enterprise and IT goals. The framework answers to the need of managers to make IT controllable and measurable. For further details, please refer to the relevant literature (see [Mey03], [itS08], [Joh07] and [IGI08]).

IT governance is the overall responsibility of senior managers such as the CIO, although its various focus areas can be under the stewardship of different managers. The following areas have emerged as being significant (see [itS08]). The CobiT terms are used here:

- **Strategic alignment**: IT is to be aligned with business requirements.
- **Value delivery**: IT must keep business operations up and running, and deliver its services appropriately and affordably. The IT service and product portfolio should also make a contribution to the enterprise's value proposition and strategy (see Section 2.2).
- **Resource management**: All IT assets such as applications, computers, also employees and vendors (see Sect. 2.2) must be managed responsibly.
- **Performance management**: IT processes must be regularly assessed to oversee compliance with strategic objectives, IT landscape objectives and technical standards; monitoring must also investigate the management of projects and maintenance, and the efficiency of service delivery (see Sect. 6.3).
- **Risk management**: With the growing dependency of businesses on their IT assets, and business data under greater threats through security gaps or crime, the awareness of risk issues has sharpened; it is essential to have consistent practices in place for managing risk and security.

  Compliance has also emerged as a key issue in recent years. In the wake of management scandals such as WorldCom and Enron, new statutory and regulatory frameworks were established. To enforce fulfilment of legislation such as the Sarbanes-Oxley Act (SOX), MaK (German legislation on credit exposure), Basel II, KonTraG (German legislation on control and transparency in business) and Solvency II (see [Joh07]), compliance is now part of corporate governance (see [Wei04] and [Wei06]), and this entails a complex series of activities. The company must be able to demonstrate appropriate, orderly procedures both in system development and in system operation.

Fact file:

- Your IT governance model must address all the focus areas discussed above.
- Use CobiT as a basis when you come to define your own IT governance and EAM governance. You will need to adapt the framework to the circumstances of your company.
- The documentation of CobiT is essentially generic and cannot be used directly without modification.
  A few pointers on operationalising the framework are provided in the following sections.
- Before mapping out an IT governance strategy, you have to know where you will be starting from. You can gauge the potential of your IT processes using the CoBIT maturity model, and determine the standing of IT in your company with the guidelines in Sect. 2.2.

6.2 IT Organisation

It is the changes in the way our work is organised
which will make the biggest differences to the way we live
C. Handy (1989)

IT organisation and processes have to be brought into line in all focal areas of EAM governance, and your enterprise is going to have to orchestrate an explicit change process to drive this continuous optimisation through. Critical for success is good collaboration between business and IT, appropriate boards and IT decision-making processes, and the right form of organisation for IT. In this continuous change process, you have to regularly adapt and adjust your IT organisation and processes to evolving external conditions.

6.2.1 Collaboration Model Between Business and IT

A key goal of Enterprise Architecture Management is to align IT with the business (see also Sect. 4.2). Good communication and collaboration are essential to define a common language for the two camps, render transparent the interdependencies between business and IT and the level of IT support, to optimise IT support and align the development of IT to business requirements.

IT must fulfil its function as a service provider to the business segments (see Fig. 6.2) and remain competitive. Service delivery must be transparent, reliable and of high quality. In general Service Level Agreements (SLAs) are contracted for basic

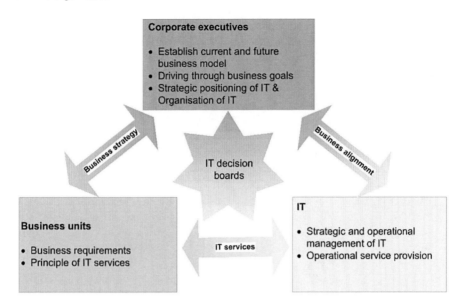

Fig. 6.2 Integration of IT

operations, and these are the foundation for managing and measuring performance (see [Ber03-1], [Küt06] and [Küt07]).

It takes an adequate understanding of what the business is about, as well as good contacts to the executive board, to align IT to the business. IT has to render transparent the impact of business requirements and proactively suggest solutions. The greater the understanding of the current and future business model, the more likely it is that IT can play an active role in strategic enterprise development, perhaps also providing its own ideas on new business models or helping drive forward the standardisation of business processes.

IT will only be able to support the business properly if the touchpoints between business and IT have been codified and the two camps use a common "language" (see Sect. 4.2). IT has to collaborate closely with business segments and promote an active dialogue.

If business requirements are merely tossed over the fence separating the two camps, IT will have no awareness of the context: people in IT will simply not know the reasoning behind business decisions or priorities. Despite much back-and-forth between business and IT, the misunderstandings and lack of information will keep IT support suboptimal. Providing solutions that fit properly takes a genuine understanding of operating and strategic business requirements.

Representatives must be appointed in IT and business segments to take on the bridging function and act as spokespersons for their respective groups. For example, by introducing IT coordinators with an adequate IT background into business departments, and IT consultants with business knowledge on the IT side, an enterprise can bridge the distance between IT and business. The IT coordinator can actively advise business users, collect and prioritise business requirements and forward them to the IT consultant in qualified form. The IT consultant coordinates IT implementation and oversees the outcome. With this approach, IT can provide proper support for business requirements and achieve sustained improvement in customer satisfaction.

IT consultants have to spend time in the business departments and engage actively with whatever it is the department does. They have to experience the day-to-day workings first-hand. Without this hands-on experience, they will be unable to put themselves in their customers' shoes and provide IT solutions which are genuinely tailored to what the business needs to do.

The IT coordinator on the business side and the IT consultant on the IT side collaborate closely. They consolidate and prioritise business requirements, translate them into IT proposals expressed in business language, negotiate with the business units regarding SLAs and pricing, and assist business and IT in the planning, prioritising and budgeting processes.

By working so closely with the IT coordinator, the IT consultant is better positioned to understand the goals and needs of customers, or rather business departments. This helps short-circuit the many unnecessary iterations when business and IT are trying to agree on an issue. It also avoids the wasted expense of inappropriate developments. Optimisation on the demand side delivers the greatest business benefit and incurs the least cost.

> **Fact file:**
>
> IT has to enter into an intensive dialogue with the business to build a relationship of trust with business departments. What matters here is to have clearly defined and established roles on both the business and IT sides, and to institutionalise collaboration based on regular exchange and dialogue.

6.2.2 Form of Organisation

EAM governance must be designed to fit the way IT is organised. In a centralised IT organisation, all IT areas can be influenced directly. In decentral IT organisations, on the other hand, it is immensely more difficult to influence activities or enforce strategic objectives. So it's worth exploring the various forms of IT organisation and their impact on EAM governance in the following. Sourcing and globalisation questions are also discussed.

The form of organisation for IT must be consistent with the structure, organisation and culture of the enterprise, and it is a matter for executive management to take these decisions. What the form of organisation does is create the structures to promote collaboration between the various business units and IT and optimise IT service delivery.

How IT is organised is also crucial to whether it can adequately support the current and future business model. The speed of decisions, the transparency of the IT landscape or the possibilities for standardisation are all substantially dependent on the choice of the organisation form.

Central or Decentral IT Organisation

Regardless whether the organisation is central or decentral, IT resources and capabilities must be distributed so as to maintain the balance between the enterprise as a whole and the individual business units.

In general, business unit autonomy goes hand-in-hand with the use of disparate IT systems and technologies, and autonomy of the decentral IT. This makes for a better fit and greater flexibility in meeting the business requirements of each unit. However, the lack of standardisation drives up overall cost for the enterprise as a whole.

The opposite of autonomy is centralisation, with IT services often bundled in a separate unit (a shared service centre), and IT systems and processes standardised to leverage economies of scale and reduce costs.

Traditionally centralised organisations often find there is a mismatch between their generic infrastructures and the needs of new and smaller business units, and as a response they are gradually moving IT competences to local levels. Traditionally diversified companies, by way of contrast, are increasingly centralising activities to leverage the benefits of standardisation.

In many companies, the IT organisation swings like a pendulum between central and decentral forms, with each swing of the pendulum aiming to use the strengths of the new form of organisation while avoiding its drawbacks. However, it is not until the new organisation form has settled down that benefits and drawbacks can properly be appreciated. Ongoing organisational changes are part of continuous change management in enterprises.

Figure 6.3 shows central IT, decentral IT, and a hybrid form with the central IT and Competence Centres (CC) and operating functions that cut across all divisions.

The hybrid form comprises central components such as central operation and IT services, plus overarching planning and control of IT, where the overall view of the IT landscape is produced and performance is managed. Competence centres, such as for EAM, are present both in central IT and in the decentral units. The competence centres form a virtual, distributed organisation, as indicated by the arrows. The central IT services oversees methods and is tasked with consolidating EAM issues. The decentral competence units have stewardship of matters relating directly to business, owing to their proximity to processes and markets.

Corporate groups are often organised as shown in Fig. 6.4. The structure in this example reflects the hybrid form depicted in Fig. 6.3.

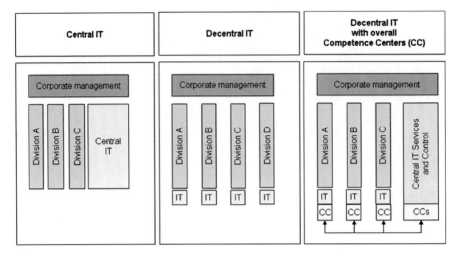

Fig. 6.3 Examples of central and decentral organisation forms in IT

Fig. 6.4 Example of an
organisational structure in the
corporate group

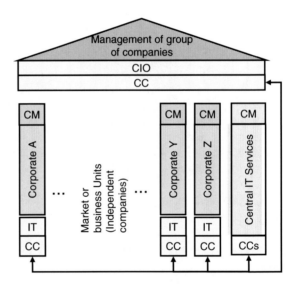

Figure 6.5 illustrates how a hybrid organisation such as the one presented in Fig. 6.3 might be structured.

This example has central IT organisation which provides central operation and centrally used components and systems such as controlling systems, plus standard components which can be used for individual developments. Central IT is also tasked with driving forward and consolidating the overall IT landscape and developing and consolidating methods and procedures. This example organisation also has separate business unit Its (BU IT), each generally structured along the same lines

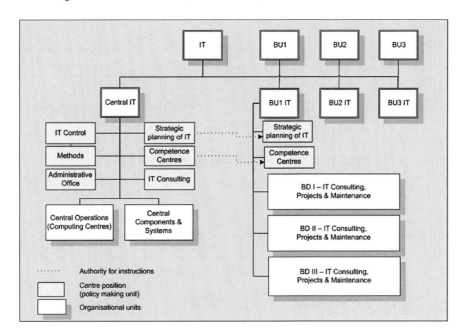

Fig. 6.5 Example of an IT organisation

as the BU divisions. Like the corporate IT centres, each BU IT has its own policy units for strategic IT planning (IT strategy development, IT landscape management and technical standardisation) and competence centres, e.g. for technologies or for packaged software such as SAP.

A hybrid organisation is generally a way of striking a compromise between standardisation and autonomy. To what extent there should be a stronger pull in either direction has to be decided to suit the circumstances of the enterprise.

The central and decentral forms of organisation each have their specific advantages and drawbacks. These are summarised in Fig. 6.6.

Each enterprise must decide for itself which form is right. Choose the approach which is the best fit for the maturity of your organisation (see [IGI08] and [Joh07]), its culture, strategy and structure.

The form of organisation must be able to sustain the strategic direction and positioning of IT, and fit with external circumstances. Innovative companies or companies experiencing strong growth often favour large-ish decentral units. An emphasis on centralisation is more likely to be found in efficiency-oriented companies in which the IT focus is low-cost, reliable operation of basic services.

Central IT units ensure that investment and changes are in alignment with the IT strategy. These units are often responsible for developing IT objectives, overseeing compliance with these objectives, and for defining and evolving standards. Decentral IT units then act within the parameters and constraints defined by their central IT.

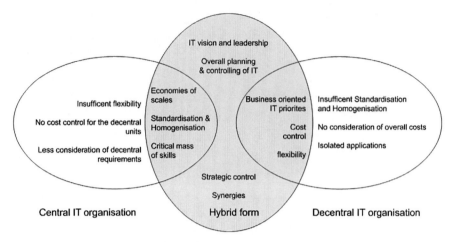

Fig. 6.6 Advantages and drawbacks of central and decentral IT organisation, as per [Mar00]

> **Important:**
>
> Central IT governance, and by association also central EAM governance, is required both to implement overarching strategic objectives in IT and to ensure across-the-board standardisation. It is up to executive management to embed the relevant practices in the organisation: it takes authority at the centre to enforce them.

Purely federal models often prove unwieldy in practice and slow to react. The danger of so many stakeholders is that decisions end up mired in discussion and outcomes are over-compromised. To head off this risk, decision processes must be managed carefully, for instance by having a set of agreed criteria for prioritising or escalation, and by installing appropriate escalation instances.

> **Fact file:**
>
> • Choose an appropriate form of organisation for your enterprise. Weigh up the advantages and drawbacks of the central, decentral and hybrid organisations.
> • Enterprise Architecture Management cuts right across business segments, and right across the corporate group. EAM governance therefore has to be under the stewardship of central IT units, endowed with corresponding authorities by top management. Generally this involves establishing boards with representatives from business units or – in a corporate group – affiliated companies.

At present, the pendulum in IT organisation choices is swinging more to the decentral organisations. Business units are granted a certain degree of autonomy. On the other hand, IT organisations are downsizing, focusing for cost reasons on core business. The basic IT functions or areas which do not add value are often outsourced to specialised providers, particularly when the functions are not part of IT core competencies.

Sourcing Strategy

Not all services can or should be delivered by internal IT itself. What about Enterprise Architecture Management – how does that fit into sourcing strategies?

Sourcing involves working out what IT can do itself (the IT "performance potential"), and carefully selecting and managing vendors. A clear distinction needs to be drawn between strategic and non-strategic elements of IT. The non-strategic portions can be bought in as commodities, freeing up internal resources and capital for strategic tasks. It is the strategic elements which differentiate the enterprise from its competitors.

Essentially, it comes down to the classic sourcing question: make or buy? Which IT services can or should the company deliver itself, and which should it source from elsewhere?

IT can use outsourcing to vary its own vertical integration, to respond flexibly to fluctuating demand, obtain quality and price advantages and gain access to specialist skills which are seldom required. By building alliances with vendors and involving them in the innovation process, IT can contribute more to enterprise value – benefiting from the additional competencies and ideas which vendors bring in at no extra cost.

Apply your strategic and operating criteria in deciding which services to outsource. Look at things from a strategic perspective – no short-termism! Core business competencies and strategic mandates generally remain in-house. When it comes to other function areas, decisions are based on comparisons, particularly of the transaction costs of internal and external service delivery. As well as the cost itself, remember to factor in the effort for coordination and controlling.

In outsourcing, an enterprise makes use of external resources and moves IT processes to an external provider in order to reduce cost, particularly by using economies of scale. Examples of services which are routinely outsourced are document printing, payroll, facility and fleet management, data centre operation (e.g. of SAP systems), billing, customer care and information.

The standardisation of IT processes through frameworks such as CobiT and ITIL (see [Joh07] and [itS08]) makes it easier to compare different external service providers.

Insourcing is the process of offering in-house products and services which were previously purchased from external vendors. This expands the value chain to include more competences. Insourcing is often prompted by a need to reduce costs, but particularly also a desire to build competences for exploring new business segments.

Offshoring means relocating IT services to low-wage countries such as India or Romania (the term "nearshoring" is used for relocations to closer countries), the idea being to exploit differences in wage costs and reduce payroll expenses. Each enterprise will have to consider the potential savings of such a move for itself. Many enterprises who opt for offshoring set up offshore development centres. IT functions are then moved to low-wage countries and external resources bundled in a separate company or joint venture.

After identifying the possible areas for insourcing, outsourcing and offshoring, you have to analyse the strengths and weaknesses, opportunities and threats of each, paying particular attention to core competencies, resources, cost and risk.

The basis for deciding on the sourcing strategy (see Sect. 2.4.3) is to analyse and appraise the performance potential of IT. The analysis has to take in all operating and strategic IT management functions and all IT assets, in order to identify potentially appropriate areas for sourcing, outsourcing or offshoring. One possible approach to estimating the competencies of IT is discussed in Sect. 2.2.

Figure 6.7 shows an example of findings of the analysis of current and future core competencies. Changes are shown by arrows.

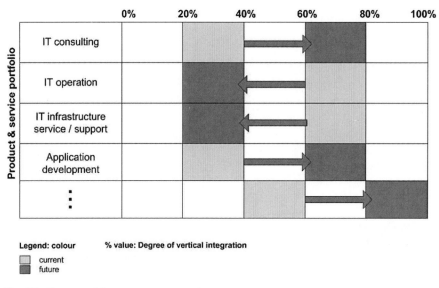

Fig. 6.7 Current and future core competencies

An appropriate sourcing strategy improves cost structures, reduces operating risk, and delivers greater flexibility and controllability (see [Bal08] and [Keu08]). However, outsourcing, offshoring and insourcing all have to be planned carefully in order to ensure continuity of operations. Efforts should be taken to mitigate risks where appropriate – e.g. the risk of dependency on a single vendor, loss of competence, and also of course contract and quality risks.

Having defined what core IT capabilities will remain in the enterprise and worked out your sourcing strategy, you have an effective basis for managing vendors, i.e. for developing and directing a vendor portfolio.

IT must have a full awareness of what its core competencies are, and expand these competencies with a committed focus on business goals. As more and more services are outsourced, leading and overseeing internal and external vendors is increasingly becoming one of IT's key assignments.

The major criteria for choosing external providers are increasingly characteristics such as reliability, flexibility on contracts, and also the willingness to take on some of the risk and provide management competencies. There are a variety of decision models for selecting partners, e.g. cost comparison or scoring models. These models are not described further here; for details, you should refer to relevant literature (see [Bal08] and [Keu08]).

Figure 6.8 gives an example of a sourcing strategy. In this portfolio, the in-house IT services are classified by current performance potential and business value (contribution to strategy, contribution to value proposition). A service's position within the matrix is an indication of what sourcing strategy is most appropriate.

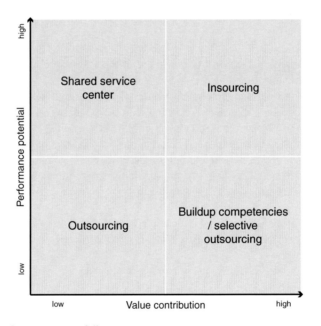

Fig. 6.8 Sourcing strategy portfolio

Enterprise Architecture Management tends to be in the right-hand quadrants, because the entire goal and purpose of EAM is to raise the contribution to strategy and value. Accordingly, Enterprise Architecture Management is either a strong candidate for building competencies/selective outsourcing, or for complete insourcing.

Sourcing at a glance:

- Work out your performance potential and core competencies.
  Define your future performance potential and vertical integration in your IT strategy.
- Define your sourcing strategy – this is part of the IT strategy development process.
- General rules:
  Core competencies – including Enterprise Architecture Management – should remain in the company.

Resources should only remain in the company if they create sustainable value. By assigning business value to the various IT services, and assigning services to resources, you can create a basis for taking decisions. You of course also first have to look what's on offer on the market. If there is no provider on the market of the service in question, there is no point making the analysis.

Globalisation

Another trend is globalisation. As discussed in the following, this has substantial impact on IT organisation and EAM governance.

With more and more enterprises globalised, often through mergers and acquisitions, IT in these companies has to contend with new challenges such as the need to deal with a range of disparate legal and cultural parameters. One-size-fits-all central IT is being replaced by a globalised IT organisation form that aims to utilise all the competencies and cultural characteristics. Alert to whatever opportunities are available, and able to network their global knowledge and competencies, these global organisations can pull together virtual teams of employees, consultants, vendors and customers to suit the situation in hand.

The term "glocalisation" has been coined to describe this process, and does a good job of describing what happens. "Think global – act local" is the principle here (see Fig. 6.9).

In an international corporate group, managers must decide how IT functions and parts of the IT landscape are to be distributed across the globe. IT can be organised such that its functions are globally distributed, but IT standardisation, planning and control, competence centres and central services such as data centre operations are kept central.

With this sort of approach, the enterprise can strike a balance between the requirements of the business as a whole for controllability and cost efficiency, and the requirements of local operating companies. IT services are provided at the best possible location, leveraging the benefits of being a global operator. One of the advantages is that the company has recourse to international recruitment markets, particularly in developing countries.

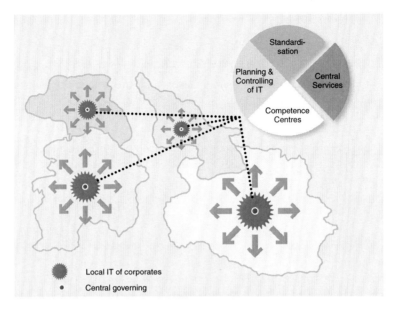

Local IT of corporates
Central governing

Fig. 6.9 Glocalisation

Pointers for globalisation:

- Create the organisational and technical structures which promote collaboration and knowledge-sharing. In decentralised IT operations, virtual teams and a good collaboration & knowledge management platform are essential to prevent knowledge from seeping through the cracks. Travel time can be reduced by using modern videoconferencing systems.
- EAM governance should be performed centrally in the local IT organisations. The same method must be deployed across all the local ITs, and the outcomes must be consolidated.
- Make sure the team has the requisite skills, including inter-cultural competence, the ability to work in teams, and a willingness to travel. Train your teams accordingly, and start early: development is a long-term measure.
- Introduce global methods and tools for all core project activities, such as project and demand management, and for Enterprise Architecture Management. Also verify that the methods and tools are genuinely being used, perhaps by introducing a certification scheme.
- Establish global leadership and create incentive systems, e.g. via goal agreements.

6.2.3 Decision Boards

To ensure IT has the requisite influence in the enterprise, it must be integrated into the overall enterprise organisation. IT can contribute to business development by participating in interdisciplinary planning teams. It is only when people are involved in this way that they understand what is driving business planning and IT planning, and why decisions are taken the way they are. Paper documents can't achieve this level of understanding.

If your IT is not yet integrated into business planning, this is often due to its current positioning (see Sect. 2.2): your IT is not yet perceived as a partner or enabler of the business.

Useful hint:

Change the perception which the business has of IT by actively involving business representatives in IT investment decisions and in budget planning. Close communication will create a common understanding.

Decisions on priorities and budgets pertaining to business matters must be taken by the business camp. If IT attempts to get involved here, it will merely end up caught in the middle. Of particular importance are proper budget planning and service-based charging. This is essential for IT to juxtapose cost and benefit and present this to business segments and management.

To ensure IT has a say in what happens, the responsibility for IT, and the boards for strategic and operating IT control, must be at top management level. The CIO can be a member of the executive management, or head a central function which reports to the board. Likewise, establishing boards and decision processes such as for project portfolio management must be a matter for executive management.

Boards and decision-making processes have to be installed for all areas in which IT decisions are taken. The following areas must be considered:

- Strategic IT objectives: (including IT goals, principles and strategies and IT organisation)
- Business architecture: (including business processes, products or business functions)
- Application architecture: (including to-be and planned landscape models for the IT landscape)
- Technical architecture: (including technical standardisation and innovation management)
- Infrastructure architecture: (including service management)

- Business requirement: (including demand management and project/programme management)
- IT investments and prioritising: (including determining the project portfolio and IT budgets)
- IT resources: (including employees, vendors and partners)

In each of these fields, planning and control of IT must dovetail closely with relevant business departments and top management, with close collaboration helping drive forward the implementation of strategic and operational business requirements in alignment with goals.

The "technical architecture" and "infrastructure architecture" decision areas are often under the stewardship of IT itself. The business can influence IT in this respect through specific objectives (such as to reduce operating costs by 20%) and SLAs.

The following boards cover all the important IT decision areas as they relate to strategic management of the IT landscape:

- **IT board**: The IT board is generally composed of the CIO and representatives from executive management, and is convened at regular intervals (e.g. quarterly). The IT board is where decisions are taken on strategic IT issues. The board decides on and approves the IT strategy, IT costs and investment planning and is responsible for defining and overseeing goal accomplishment and IT-relevant aspects of governance.
- **IT landscape management board**: The IT landscape management board consists of the CIO and – key to the board's composition – enterprise architects (see Sect. 3.4.1). Other members can be IT or business managers or individuals with specialist expertise from the business units.

  IT implementation of business requirements can be planned efficiently and effectively in an interdisciplinary team comprising enterprise architects (application and business) and IT architects. The business enterprise architects are often members of the business segments.

  The IT landscape management board takes decisions on further development of the business and technical IT landscape. It sets out planning assumptions, appraises alternative planning scenarios and makes a recommendation for the to-be landscape model and its implementation roadmap. These deliverables are required for developing the IT strategy and serve as input for the IT board and project portfolio management.
- **Project portfolio board**: The project portfolio board (see Fig. 6.10) is generally composed of the CIO and other IT managers, and managers from the business units (see [Ber03-1], [Blo06] and [Buc05]).

  This board is tasked with steering the project portfolio. It appraises and prioritises project requests and decides what will go into the portfolio. The board starts and stops projects, puts projects on hold and takes relevant investment decisions, sometimes also involving the IT board. The project portfolio board takes

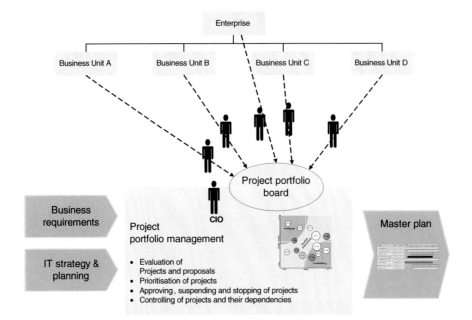

Fig. 6.10 Project portfolio management

its decisions based on information on the requested projects, and on progress and performance once projects are underway.

The main criteria for appraising projects are typically cost and benefits, contribution to strategy and to the value proposition, and an estimate of risk. When appraising whether a project is consistent with the target landscape and technical standards, board members can also consider criteria such as the degree of coverage of business processes or business functions, consistency with strategy, degree of standardisation, criticality or the state of health of applications. This information can be obtained from IT landscape management and strategic IT controlling (see Sect. 6.3.1).

- **Blueprint board**: The blueprint board comprises the CIO and IT managers who oversee operations, application engineering, possibly also PC infrastructure provisioning. Also essential to the board's composition are experienced IT architects and application enterprise architects.

  The blueprint board takes decisions on how the blueprint will be developed. It evaluates and prioritises standardisation requests and decides on implementation. It also defines the blueprint and oversees standardisation efforts (see Chapter 5).

Figure 6.11 summarises the composition of each of these boards. Mandatory representatives are indicated by "X"; optional members by "(X)". The coverage of IT decision areas is shown in Fig. 6.12.

Fig. 6.11 Example illustrating board composition

Member of \ Decision boards	IT board	IT landscape management board	Project portfolio board	Blueprint board
Corporate management	X		X	
Management of business units	(X)	(X)	X	
Business enterprise architects		X		
CIO	X	X	X	X
Management of IT units		(X)	(X)	X
Application enterprise architects		X		X
Technical enterprise architects		X		X

Fig. 6.11 Example illustrating board composition

Decision boards \ Decision areas	Strategic Objectives	Business architecture	Application architecture	Technical architecture & Infrastructure	Business requirements	IT investments	IT resources
IT board	D	I	I	I	I	D	I
IT landscape management board	C	D	D	C	I	I/C	I
Project portfolio board	I	I	I	I	D/I	D	I
Blueprint board	I	I	I/C	D	I	I/C	I

D - Deciding, P - Performing, C - Consulting und I – Informed

Fig. 6.12 Example illustrating how IT decision areas are allocated to boards

> **Important:**
>
> Establish boards and decision-making processes for all IT decision areas. For all steering tasks, ensure there are authoritative definitions of processes and boards, roles and responsibilities both on business and IT sides, and of rights and obligations in terms of decision-making, participation and execution.

How to Arrive at a Decision Structure Appropriate for Your Enterprise

You can define and document your decision structure in a matrix which plots the eight IT decision areas against the decision boards (see Fig. 6.13). You can then determine which boards are required.

Decision areas							
	Strategic Objectives	Business architecture	Application architecture	Technical architecture & Infrastructure	Business requirements	IT investments	IT resources
Corporate management	X					X	
business		X			X		
IT			X	X			X

(Decision rights — shown along the left vertical axis)

Fig. 6.13 Example of decision-making authorities

You also have to determine participation and execution rights. To do this, you could replace the "X" in the matrix by letters to represent the various levels of involvement, for example D – deciding, P – performing, C – consulting and I – informed. An example is provided in Fig. 6.14.

The decision structure must be a good fit for the environment, the company organisation, its strategic direction and the positioning of IT. In every good IT decision structure, it is clear for all areas who is ultimately in charge of taking decisions, and who is accountable if things do not work as they should. For example, IT investments are often decided as part of enterprise-wide budget planning which has been signed off by top management.

There is no generalised recipe for instituting these boards. How they are structured must be consistent with the maturity of your organisation, its corporate culture and business strategies. You may also choose to give the boards different names.

Decision areas						
Strategic Objectives	**Business architecture**	**Application architecture**	**Technical architecture & Infra-structure**	**Business require-ments**	**IT invest-ments**	**IT resources**

Decision rights	Strategic Objectives	Business architecture	Application architecture	Technical architecture & Infrastructure	Business requirements	IT investments	IT resources
Corporate management	D	I	I	I	I	D	I
Business units	C	D	C	I	D	C	C
Central IT	D	I	C	D	C	C	D
Decentral IT	P	C	D	C	D/P	C	D
IT vendors	C	I	C	I (C/P)	I/P	I	I/P

D -Deciding, P - Performing, C - Consulting und I – Informed

Fig. 6.14 Example with detailed decision-making authorities and participation rights

Large enterprises may have multilevel board structures, with middle management at the first level and more senior management at the next level.

> **Useful hints:**
>
> - The boards should be small enough to take decisions quickly and effectively, but large enough to ensure there are members representing all the areas on which the board decides.
> - From the word go, determine the frequency of meetings (perhaps in "jour fixe" format), and set a fixed agenda. This makes transparent what the board is doing.

Figure 6.15 illustrates how IT governance bodies might be put together. Each business unit has its own decentral IT (BU IT), which is a contract partner of IT. BU IT representatives, for example IT coordinators and IT consultants, represent their units on IT governance boards.

The CIO heads the IT governance boards, represents the interest of IT at executive board level and ensures enterprise decisions are enacted in IT.

Whether business and IT have a good alliance with strong mutual trust is largely contingent on the people involved on both sides. Suitable individuals must be appointed to the roles. As its points of contact for the business, IT should designate competent, committed individuals who have the requisite grasp of what

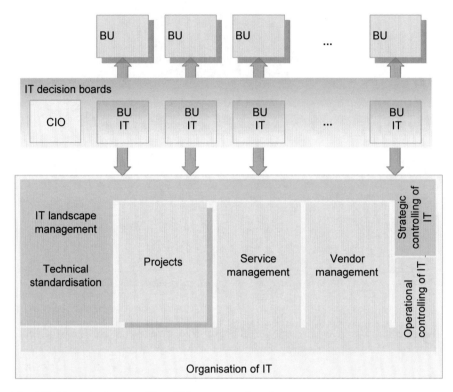

Fig. 6.15 Example of composition of IT governance boards

drives the business. This helps raise the image of IT. Good technical abilities, plus communication and leadership skills, are essential for all key roles.

The IT organisation boards should be established in alignment with the current and future business model of the enterprise and its value culture (see [Mas06] and [Vah05]).

Fact file:

- There is a direct correlation between the influence of IT and its integration into decision-making processes and boards.
- Establish boards and decision-making processes for all IT decision areas. For all steering tasks, ensure there are authoritative definitions of processes and boards, roles and responsibilities both on business and IT sides, and of rights and obligations in terms of decision-making, participation and execution.

> **Important:**
>
> Install boards and IT decision-making processes at the right level to ensure
> your executive management commits to IT goals and investments. This is the
> only way to strengthen the influence of IT in your organisation.

6.2.4 Changing the IT Organisation

Introducing EAM governance generally goes hand in hand with changes to the
organisation and culture of the company. New competences have to be established
and developed in IT. This starts with the CIO, who becomes an entrepreneurial-
minded leader with an understanding of technology. A good network of partners,
and understanding of the business, customers and competitors are equally as important as communication skills, the ability to think strategically and put forward a
compelling case – not to mention drive, tenacity and of course IT competence.
The CIO has to be able to appraise technologies and technical statements from IT,
however he or she does not need in-detail expertise in technology.

Business enterprise architects and experienced project managers are becoming
just as important as software architects; they enable IT to provide competent advice
to business departments, helping transform IT into a partner or even an enabler of
the business.

It takes a lengthy change process to transform the culture and build up the previously missing competencies. This change process is essential to turn IT into a
business-oriented partner which shapes and drives the business and generates value
for the enterprise. IT managers must alter perceptions of IT, ensuring business users
see IT as part of the lifeblood of the business and a contributor to the enterprise's
value proposition.

As part of the change management process, you have to align your IT governance to the changing parameters and anchor this in your organisation (see
Fig. 6.16).

Maturity models such as the CobiT model (see [Joh07], [itS08] and [Luf00]) and the
model for determining the standing of IT (see Sect. 2.2) help you work out where
you stand right now, and decide what your next steps should be.

The CobiT maturity model enables you to explore the potentials inherent in your
business processes, and identify gaps (particularly in the critical processes). The
result can be used for presenting to management.

When an enterprise decides to align its IT consistently to its business interests
and thus move to a higher level of maturity, the challenges it initially faces differ
depending on its starting point. Challenges are widely disparate, ranging from the
introduction of operating-level IT controlling through to comprehensive strategic IT
management.

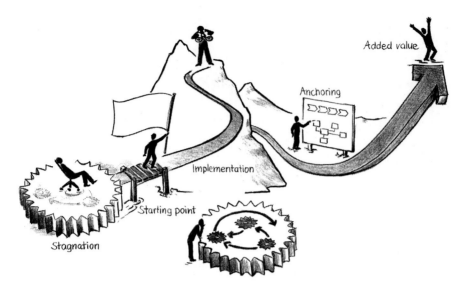

Fig. 6.16 Change process to embed new practices in the organisation

Stubbornness, consistency and perseverance – and the willingness to bid farewell to dearly-held habits and customs – are vital to institutionalise effective IT governance. Common pitfalls are unclear objectives, inability to measure goal accomplishment, lack of a big-picture view (resulting in islands of optimisation right across the company), a tendency to rush at things, and lack of personnel development.

The actors in this process must understand and identify with the change if they are to actively shape it and – above all – give it their support. So it is essential to involve all stakeholders and ensure there is proper communication between them!

A project to introduce strategic IT management functions generally starts in a spirit of euphoria. The first concepts, at this stage still theoretical, are soon mapped out. Yet as concepts are elaborated and people come to address the question "how does one ensure long-term effective IT governance?" it becomes evident it will take a lot of work and above all communication to convince stakeholders at executive board level, in business departments and IT functions.

For more information, please refer to relevant literature (see [Dop02] and [Bae07]).

Fact file:

- Work out your status quo and establish and initiate a change management programme from there.

> • Raise the qualification levels of your IT! Business expertise, communication skills and powers of persuasion are just as important as technology expertise.

6.3 Strategic Control Toolkits

Where there's a goal, there's a way – or so it's said. And if one can't find a way, the goal should be to build it!

Willy Meurer (∗1934), aphorist and commentator, Toronto

As well as having the right IT organisation, what is also essential in effective EAM governance is the control loop illustrated in Fig. 6.17. All the parts of this control loop are important. Strategic IT planning stakes out parameters, objectives and planning values such as the target landscape. By comparing planned values with actual operational metrics, strategic IT controlling can clearly identify any deviations, providing substantiated evidence on which IT governing bodies can take decisions.

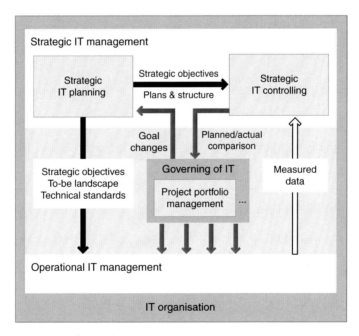

Fig. 6.17 Control loop of strategic IT governance

Strategic management of the IT landscape comprises a variety of controlling tasks such as ensuring that planned landscape models are enacted, or that standards are applied in projects. Each control task requires dedicated information as the basis on which to take decisions. A specific control toolkit must be provided for the requirements of the task or stakeholder group in question.

The classic controlling instruments, which ensure transparency on resource consumption in IT and assignment to cost centres, are indeed extremely important, yet nowhere near enough on their own. The strategic toolkit has to dig deeper, also showing up content and strategic aspects – as illustrated by the following quotation from [Bie07]:

> Successful business action entails taking decisions on how best to employ scarce resources. It is one of the key preparation tasks up front of decisions to make available to decision makers information which they need to make their choices. At best, this will include complete information about alternative courses of action, possible states of the environment at the time of the decision, appraisal criteria and how they are associated, and the possible outcomes of selecting one or the other alternative courses of action in a given context.

Tailored to the functions of the individuals in question, the strategic toolkit helps provide information enabling people to take decisions based on hard facts and evidence. Strategic IT controlling collects and consolidates the current values of operational metrics and compiles a salient presentation of the data required for a particular control task.

Different stakeholders, both inside and outside IT, with different agendas must be considered when designing this control toolkit. As well as the IT managers responsible for investment decisions, strategic IT planning and IT service delivery, managers in IT and the IT team also need some support, e.g. current status and planned/actual comparisons. Nor may one forget compliance and security representatives and other stakeholders who bear responsibility for risk. These individuals need a system with which they can set and monitor relevant checkpoints.

Alongside security, compliance is an important aspect in corporate and IT governance. Implementing compliance requirements such as the Sarbanes-Oxley Act (SOX), MaK, Basel II, KonTraG or Solvency II nearly always has significant impact. Enterprises cannot afford to compromise on the correctness of financial reporting, and need to provide evidence that both system development and system operation are conducted in an appropriate and correct fashion.

Strategic IT Controlling

Here are just some of the methods available in the strategic IT controlling toolbox:

- **Balanced Scorecard (BSC)**: The Balanced Scorecard is a management tool that uses "leading" and "lagging" indicators to investigate and present the vision and strategy of an enterprise, relevant internal and external aspects and how they interrelate. The enterprise is viewed from several perspectives, ratings being provided by metrics on each of these perspectives. The traditional perspectives of the Balanced Scorecard are "Finance", "Customer", "Internal Process" and "Learning & Development" (see [Blo06]).

- **Lifecycle analysis**: Technical standards and applications have a finite lifecycle. Lifecycle status (see Sect. 4.3) is decisive for planning the strategic evolution of the IT landscape (see [Ker08]).
- **Portfolio analysis**: Portfolios can be used to illustrate the as-is status, or to show the to-be or planned status or a combination of the two, illuminated from particular perspectives. For example, you can develop planning scenarios which serve as a roadmap for the further development of the IT landscape (see Sect. 2.4 and [Buc05] and [Ker08]).
- **SWOT analysis**: SWOT analysis is a tool for strategic management. The strengths and weaknesses, opportunities and threats in a particular context are analysed. By plotting strengths/weaknesses against opportunities/threats, managers can derive strategies for aligning or developing IT. Strengths and weaknesses are relative quantities and should always be considered in comparison with the competitions (see [Min05] and [Ker08]).
- **Scenario mapping**: Scenario mapping is a method used in strategic planning. By analysing possible developments in the future, the enterprise is better able to identify possibilities for change at an early stage. In general, you develop different scenarios for the relevant cases, also worst-case and best case scenarios. Scenarios can be developed both for a particular point in the future or as general trend predictions (see [Min05] and [Ker08]).
- **Benchmarking**: Benchmark is the process of comparing two companies or organisations on the basis of usually standardised metrics. Care must be taken to ensure that metrics are comparable. Often standards are set by using values from the strongest organisations as best practices and measures (see [Min05] and [Ker08]).
- **Resource & capability analysis**: An analysis of all IT assets, particularly the capabilities of employees and vendors, shows what competencies IT has at present, and what development opportunities there are (see [Min05] and [Ker08]).

The tenet of strategic IT controlling is "do the right things." Strategic controlling has to be effective and set the right objectives. It underpins progress toward long-term goals and helps bring about the conditions which will frame the operating-level service delivery processes. It helps IT management in formulating, implementing and overseeing strategic objectives and planning. Leading indicators alert the company promptly if a development looks to be veering off track.

Operating-level IT controlling, on the other hand, is largely concerned with efficiency. Its tenet is "do things right". Key measures for operating-level controlling are cost savings or increased profit or profitability in the company. Appropriate performance metrics and reporting provide input for operating-level control of service delivery.

Strategic IT controlling must help render transparent the degree to which strategic objectives and planning have been enacted. To enable effective progress monitoring, appropriate indicators must be selected and linked with operating metrics from projects and general operation.

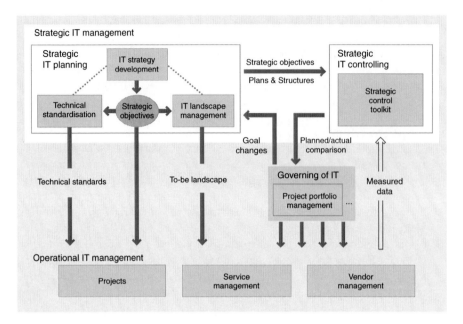

Fig. 6.18 Control loop for strategic controlling (detailed view)

Figure 6.18 illustrates the control loop, comprising strategic IT planning ("PLAN"), operational IT management ("DO"), strategic controlling ("CHECK") and IT governance ("ACT"). A control loop is the universal basic pattern for every control process. It consists of the steps planning, implementation, analysis and correction, and is repeated until the goal is accomplished or a predefined period of time has elapsed (see [KüM07]).

What strategic IT planning does is set out the strategic objectives, technical standards and target landscape for operational IT management. These objectives also served as the target values for comparing with the current values and metrics from the operating business. Usually, a performance measurement and management system creates the linkages between control quantities and the actual values from the operational business, and shows up any deviations. This provides an overall view of IT performance, makes the value of IT visible, and shows up the points to address in order to achieve sustained improvement.

The links between the various levels can be forged using the structure and relationship information from IT landscape management. These associations enable you to cascade business-oriented objectives into IT. For example, the goals associated with business processes can be used as objectives for the applications which support these business processes.

A robust foundation for controlling and directing IT is created through the linkages between indicators at the strategic IT control level and the basic metrics from operational level in accordance with the structures and relationships set out by IT landscape management. Basic measures are entered by users (e.g. in

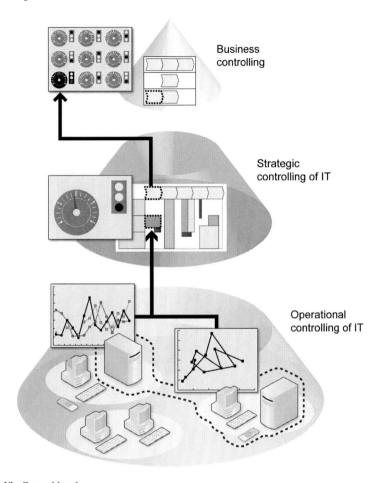

Fig. 6.19   Control levels

system monitoring at the infrastructure level), aggregated into meaningful information, condensed into a few indicators and presented in a cockpit-style management intelligence system (see Fig. 6.19).

Depending on what is being monitored – e.g. evolution of the IT landscape, or IT costs – the information and control toolkits needed in each case are different. Operating-level IT controlling often uses cost or SLA fulfilment as its metrics, whereas strategic IT controlling would tend to investigate cost, benefit, contribution to strategy and to value, state of health or compliance with standards.

Costs play a central role both in strategic and operational IT management levels. We will therefore explore IT cost control in greater detail.

IT Cost Control

IT cost control requires transparency in cost and service charging in IT. This enables precise, transparent linkages to be defined between IT costs and control objects, e.g. the cost contribution of individual products. Ultimately, the point of the exercise is to determine a monetary value for IT services. Apart from quite simply taking the heat off IT – letting users know what they're paying for – cost transparency helps managers control IT, direct its future development, and make its cost calculable for business departments. Cost-benefit comparisons can be performed on the basis of known costs, and IT costs can be channelled into business process and product costing. Complete transparency can only be achieved, however, when IT costs can be charged completely and correctly to the entities which incur them.

The service and product portfolio serves as a basis for naming and also pricing the IT services in the company. The IT service catalogue can include both infrastructure services and consulting. The performance of each IT service must be measured and appraised on relevant metrics such as SLA fulfilment or availability. This enables IT performance potential to be estimated.

Costs are planned as part of the IT budget planning process. This scopes out the investment required in the coming years to maintain and extend IT service delivery. IT budget planning considers both innovations and ongoing costs such as maintenance and staff expenses.

What happens particularly in large companies is that even though IT costs are measured and controlled at a range of detail levels, the actual business benefit of IT is unknown. This leaves the door wide open to typical negative preconceptions about IT – that it's "far too expensive", "too inflexible and slow", or "just an additional cost factor".

Transparency on the benefit and value contribution of IT operations and projects is a key decision and control instrument for CIOs, CFOs and customers of IT. CIOs need information to back their case in discussions with customers and vendors. CFOs have to see precisely what benefit will derive from the IT investment. Customers of IT, in turn, need to see evidence that requirements are being met, SLAs fulfilled and improvements made to process support.

> **Important:**
>
> When planning IT budgets, take care not to focus only on costs. All too often, what happens is this: every year IT budgets are planned. If they are too high, the typical response is to deprioritise items until the budget has been whittled down to an acceptable level. Break out of this thinking mode and compare the cost and benefit of each outlay!

Governing the Further Development of the IT Landscape

The evolution of the IT landscape is controlled on the basis of contributions from IT landscape management and technical standardisation, which frames the definition of technical standards, the target landscape and implementation roadmap, as well as other planning values such as SLA requirements. The connections between structures in business and IT, and between IT structures on the strategic and operating levels are what forge links between as-is values and planned outcomes. By comparing the planned and actual values, you can obtain a good picture of progress toward objectives.

Managing the IT landscape entails a variety of steering and control tasks. These tasks include the following:

- Comparing planning (to-be and planned) landscape models with the landscape model as it is at present. This can be measured by appraising factors such as the fit with the landscape plan (see Sect. 6.3.1).

Important:

The "real" landscape model can only be determined by analysing the current operating situation. Ultimately, the truth – the IT reality – lies on the operating level.

- Comparing the technical implementation of applications, interfaces and infrastructure units with prescribed technical standards: this shows up the degree of standards compliance (see Fig. 6.20).

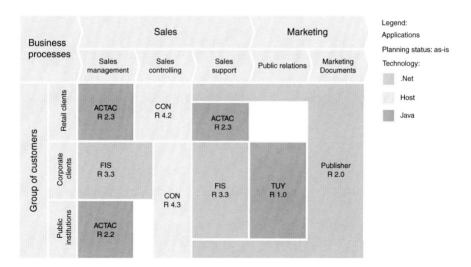

Fig. 6.20 Example of a landscape diagram emphasising compliance with standards

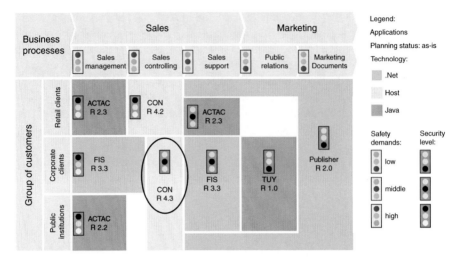

Fig. 6.21 Example of landscape diagram emphasising security aspects

- Over the course of IT landscape management and technical standardisation, requirements are formulated for the various IT components, e.g. applications. Accordingly, another control task is to verify compliance with these requirements. For example, the linkage between business processes and applications enables managers to determine whether the security required in a particular business process is in fact consistent with the security level which can be provided by the applications assigned to support this business process (see Fig. 6.21).

Fact file:

Work out what control tasks have to be performed, and what information each needs. Guidelines on establishing a control toolkit for managing your IT landscape are provided in the following sections.

6.3.1 Control Indicators

If you can't measure it, you can't manage it.
                        Peter Ferdinand Drucker

Given the difficulty of keeping checks on IT, a compact, at-a-glance overview of essential performance metrics can certainly add to clarity. By presenting precisely the information which the recipient needs, each control toolkit helps people discharge their control and governance responsibility is more effectively.

It is vital to have the right indicators. For example, if IT costs are presented in unstructured form – with cost items all rolled into one – it is easy for people to say that costs are too high. Overrun project budgets are also a prime candidate for debate of this type, above all when there is no analysis of why the discrepancies have arisen. If it is unclear what business benefit is being targeted with the introduction of new software, attention focuses all too easily on the rollout costs. The lack of transparency means it is difficult to assess whether the criticism is justified. And the disputes get in the way of day-to-day business and prevent improvements being enacted.

When choosing indicators, not only does one have to consider how to present the data effectively, but also how indicators are to be underpinned with operating-level metrics.

> **Important:**
>
> Ensure that it is possible to collect and assign data to give a measure on each of the indicators you have elected to use. The measurements must be accurate, easy to collect, provide meaningful information and be adequately up-to-date. Focus on the key indicators, and on steadily expanding the control toolkit. In this way, you will soon have strategic IT controlling up and working.

What matters is selecting the right things to measure from the plethora of possible indicators. You have to identify appropriate measures for all strategic objectives and planned values, and for all core tasks of IT (see Sect. 2.2) such as ensuring continuity of business operation.

Relevant for operating IT control are indicators such as SLA fulfilment, reliability and availability, customer satisfaction, cost, risk estimate or cost-efficiency. For strategic IT control, you will be more likely to use indicators such as a contribution to strategy or value proposition, consistency with the landscape model and standards, risk estimate or costs. These indicators must be integrated into planning and control processes in order for you to effectively direct IT service delivery.

Selecting the right indicators is key. Enterprises often have a lot of information, some of it in considerable detail, but end up not being able to see the wood for the trees. Wrong or inappropriately selected information can lead to wrong decisions which have far-reaching negative impact.

Yet how does one choose the right things to measure?

Relevant indicators are those which are essential for operating and strategic IT control. In other words, from the abundance of possible or obtainable measures, you need to select those which shed most light on the performance and progress of IT in terms of goal accomplishment, and are adequately up-to-date and reliable.

What exactly are indicators?

An indicator makes a statement of the planned or actual state of a control object at a particular point in time, or over a particular period of time. An indicator can take on different values (see [Küt07]), and is calculated from a quantitative, reproducible and objective measurement of a particular quantity.

We differentiate the following types of indicators:

- **Qualitative and quantitative indicators**: Quantitative indicators are measurable, e.g. the availability of a system. Qualitative indicators such as customer satisfaction, strategy contribution or code quality must be quantified. Values can be determined empirically or by applying rating schemes with multiple choice values for users to select. Individual appraisals can be obtained through surveys or similar means.

  Table 6.1 illustrates one way in which the strategy contribution can be determined. For each project or application, a quantified value must be obtained (e.g. through a survey) of the contribution to the various business drivers. The weighted average of these values gives the overall strategy contribution for each project or application.

Table 6.1   Quantifying strategy contribution

	Weighting	Object I	Object II	Object III	Object IV	Total
Business driver A						
Business driver B						
Business driver C						
Total						

Figure 6.22 illustrates how "conformity with strategy" can be calculated. Each project proposal is evaluated in terms of applications, vendors and technical standards, the project proposal being scored on each of these three control objects separately. The weighted average of the scores then establishes the project's conformity with strategy.

- **Absolute numbers and ratios**: An indicator can be either an absolute number or a ratio. Absolute-number indicators present situations or outcomes without reference to other indicators, e.g. investment sums, project duration, total IT cost, number of IT employees or project rollout costs. Ratios use a second value in addition. A ratio is a mathematical expression of quantity A in proportion to quantity B – for example, a degree of completion or degree of innovation.

  These indicators include:

  - **Indices**: An index is a single number calculated from a set of values over time, showing the development of a particular quantity over an interval of time, e.g.

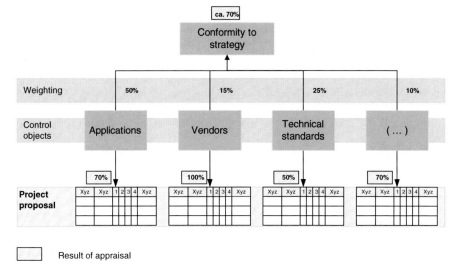

Result of appraisal

Fig. 6.22 Example for quantifying a qualitative attribute (multi-level appraisal)

the development of the IT budget or the number of users of an application. Historical data can also be included in indices.

– **Relationship ratios**: This ratio expresses one quantity in terms of another, e.g. IT costs to turnover, or cost to benefit.

– **Proportion ratios**: This ratio expresses a quantity as a fraction or percentage of the overall quantity or another sub-quantity. For examples: infrastructure costs expressed as a percentage of overall IT costs, or IT costs as a proportion of the overall costs.

• **Benchmarks**: Benchmarks require comparative indicators from the same industry or from other segments of the company. The company's figures are compared with the figures from other segments or the wider industry. Benchmarks can be internal and external.

Important:

Benchmarks can only really provide meaningful intelligence when the content and logical context compare with those against which you are measuring. Check the context – and how meaningful the information is – before going ahead. This way, you can avoid comparing apples with oranges!

A common basis is essential to ensure comparability. One approach is to use standards such as CobiT or ITIL.

Indicators create transparency, and are also used to check and verify goal attainment. Which indicators are relevant for managing your IT landscape?

Indicators for Managing the IT Landscape

Various control tasks have to be performed in managing the IT landscape. One task is to verify that the IT landscape is developing in line with the business. Another is to ensure IT remains oriented to strategy. Operating-level IT service delivery also has to be monitored. For each of these control tasks, you have to determine which "control objects" are going to be most valuable in your enterprise context. Control objects can include the following:

- Business control objects

  - Business processes such as product development process
  - Products such as vehicle models or liability insurance
  - Business functions such as calculating commissions
  - Business objects such as customers or orders
  - Business units such as sales, marketing and production, also sales levels

- Project portfolio
- IT control objects

  - Product and service portfolio such as SAP-based operation or process modelling consulting services
  - Application portfolio and individual applications
  - Information objects – the data managed by the applications
  - Blueprint and individual technical standards (see Chapter 5)
  - Infrastructure units such as data centres or portal infrastructure
  - Resources, i.e. employees, groups of employees and vendors

You must work out what can usefully be measured for each of the control tasks. Table 6.2 surveys the indicators which have proved valuable in practice for the various categories. Particularly important indicators are shown in bold type.

The indicators listed here show up both the current status as well as progress compared to the original situation. It is also possible to evaluate the method for managing the IT landscape. Indicators such as completeness, comprehensibility, usability, ease of maintenance and extensibility can be used for this. You can find more information on indicators and identifying suitable measures in [Küt06], [Küt07], [Lei07], [Mas05] and [KüM07].

Important:

You should select indicators in line with the maxim proposed by Lord Kelvin "The degree to which you can express something in numbers is the degree to which you really understand it".

Table 6.2 Examples of indicators grouped by control task

Control task: business alignment of IT Aligning IT with corporate goals and business requirements		
Objective	Objects to investigate (control objects)	Indicators
To create transparency of business interconnections	Business processes Business functions Products, business units or business objects	*Competitive differentiation* Changeability *Criticality* Turnover or cost contribution *Cost* *Risk* Need for protection Flexibility
To create linkage between business and IT	Applications	Degree and quality of business process support Degree and quality of function coverage or function fulfilment Business ownership *Contribution to value and strategy* Degree of utilisation
To identify points where there is need for action and potential for improvement to enhance the support IT provides to the business, and provide prompt, well founded statements on the feasibility and impact of business ideas	Applications and application portfolio	Degree and quality of business process support Degree and quality of function coverage Adaptability/flexibility Customer satisfaction index *Degree of satisfaction* Degree or number of redundancies and inconsistencies Degree of automation Degree of utilisation
	Business processes and business functions	Degree of standardisation Degree or number of redundancies and inconsistencies Degree of automation Degree of utilisation
To steer IT in alignment with the business with a view to selecting the right projects, steering the project portfolio and multiproject management	Applications and technical standards	*Strategy contribution* or strategic fit *Contribution to value proposition* or business value Differentiation from competition Customer satisfaction *Technology fit for compliance with standards* *Fit with landscape plan* *Risk* *Costs* (projects, maintenance, operation, etc) Proportion or degree of innovation
	Projects	Goal accomplishment (content, cost, time) Degree of implementation Degree of difficulty or complexity

Table 6.2   (continued)

Control task: business alignment of IT Aligning IT with corporate goals and business requirements		
Objective	Objects to investigate (control objects)	Indicators

		Costs
		Benefit or ROI or cost-effectiveness or degree
		    to which business case was realised
		Risk
		Contribution to strategy and value
		    proposition

Control task: strategic IT control		
Objective	Objects to investigate (control objects)	Indicators

To achieve technical
standardisation of the IT
landscape and
infrastructure
	Applications
	Interfaces
	Technical standards
		Future sustainability
		Degree of standardisation or compliance
		    with standards
		Complexity
		Adaptability, extensibility or integration
		    ability
		Scalability
		Reliability and availability
		Ease of maintenance
		Lifecycle
		Degree of automation
		Required resourcing

To plan applications
strategically and
strategically align the IT
landscape (IT landscape
management)
	Applications
	Interfaces
	Technical standards
		Future sustainability
		Effectiveness of resource deployment
		Degree of coverage of business requirements
		Degree of standardisation
		Technical quality or state of health
		Degree of integration or modularisation
		Freedom from redundancy, consistency
		Degree of modularisation or service
		    orientation or component orientation
		Adaptability, extensibility or integration
		    ability
		Scalability
		Flexibility
		Reliability and availability
		Ease of maintenance
		Lifecycle
		Degree of automation
		Required resourcing

	Information objects and business objects	Degree of freedom from redundancy, consistency of business objects

Table 6.2 (continued)

Control task: business alignment of IT Aligning IT with corporate goals and business requirements		
Objective	Objects to investigate (control objects)	Indicators
Sourcing and vendor management	Applications Interfaces Technical standards	Vertical integration Core capabilities Performance potential (overall and for individual IT services) Skill level
Control task: operating-level IT control		
Objective	Objects to investigate (control objects)	Indicators
To steer application and infrastructure operation	Applications Interfaces Technical standards Infrastructure elements	*IT performance* Downtime or failure resilience *Reliability* *Availability* *Performance* Response times Solution and service quality *Degree of SLA fulfilment* Efficiency/productivity of operation/service provision Implementation and provisioning time Process quality Efficiency of resource deployment Ergonomics Adherence to promised schedules *Risk* e.g. by means of resource availability – number of resources available for maintenance of an application or (in context of business continuity management, BCM) security or compliance Number of errors, error quota and severity Degree and quality of implementation, of security and compliance requirements and statutory directives Delivery ability Delivery reliability Response times *Service quality* *Costs* (projects, maintenance, operation, etc.) e.g. benchmarked *Benefit* Degree of documentation Number of annual releases per application Number of annual releases per technical software component

Table 6.2   (continued)

Objective	Objects to investigate (control objects)	Indicators
Control task: business alignment of IT Aligning IT with corporate goals and business requirements		
Internal service management and vendor management	Applications Interfaces Technical standards Infrastructure elements	Number of resources per application or per consulting, support or operation units *Delivery ability* *Delivery reliability* Solution, product and service quality

Describe all indicators precisely. Provide a template for this purpose. An example template is provided in Table 6.3.

Table 6.3   Template for describing an indicator

ID: <unique ID>	Name: <descriptive term > Control objects
Definition	Brief description (Underlying object and context, e.g. underlying strategy)
Type	Describe the type of the indicator, e.g. qualitative/quantitative; absolute number or ratio, and its unit of measure, e.g. units or %
Target value	Target values or – with benchmark indicators – the external values with which to compare
Limit or tolerance value	Target values are often not met exactly. By specifying limit and tolerance values you define what deviations are tolerable
Presentation	Format and scope of graphic or numeric presentation, e.g. traffic-light indicators into which measurements are mapped
Quality of data source, how up-to-date, and at what intervals is updated (provided/refreshed)	From what source is the raw data obtained? From which existing reporting systems or from which data repositories can the data be extracted? Document the availability and quality of the data, and how up-to-date it is (e.g. online, daily, weekly or monthly) Expected effort to determine values on the indicators
Calculation	How values for the indicator are calculated, e.g. by formulas or scoring models
Validity	Period of validity of the indicator
Target audience	To whom are the values of the indicator reported?
Archiving	Archiving/ retention obligations and the reasons for them Possible reasons can be statutory requirements, audit requirements or timeline analysis
Responsibility	Who is responsible for goal accomplishment?

Procedure for Selecting Indicators

Selecting the "right" indicators is one of the major challenges when you introduce a performance measurement and management system. From the plethora of potential indicators for IT – there can be over 100 available – you have to choose the most suitable. Given that you need to keep information intelligible, clear, obtainable and verifiable, you should select no more than 20 indicators from the many which are available.

The following approach is a good way to get the number of indicators down to manageable proportions:

1. Put together a long list of all potentially relevant indicators by determining what is valuable for control in terms of strategic objectives, strategic IT planning and operating-level business requirements.
2. Critically evaluate the long list, coordinating closely with IT management, to determine which indicators are relevant for control. Going by experience, over a quarter of the contents of the long list can be culled at this point.
3. Check whether indicators are balanced in terms of their coverage of business requirements and IT goals. Once you are finished, there should be just a few (ideally one) meaningful indicators remaining for each of the goals you wish to monitor. Another, albeit if not even the most important criterion, are the objectives set by decision maker groups, which must be analysed very carefully in advance.
4. Now consider how easy it is to obtain data on the indicators: will the underlying information be available in adequate quality and in adequately up-to-date form? Or must new information be obtained? If so, can sufficient up-to-date information be collected in sufficient quality by surveying business and IT managers, or does it have to be extracted from existing systems, or even entered in the systems in the first place? Ultimately, this step is about estimating the effort for providing the data, and seeing how the effort measures up against benefits.
5. Compile a precise description of the indicators using a standardised template (see Table 6.3).

Since data and reports can easily have unsure validity or be simply not available, you have to make a detailed exploration even at this early concept stage.

The precise description ensures that all the requirements can genuinely be fulfilled with the indicator in question. If an idea cannot be actioned, this will show through no later than now – when you make the description. Many potential indicators fall at this hurdle. A target value also has to be defined for each indicator, e.g. cost reduction by 30%. In some cases you may also opt to define a limit value at which some intervention is required.

The central metrics for operating-level IT indicators derive chiefly from IT operations (e.g. event monitoring in system management), cost calculation and project portfolio controlling, and internal service accounting. Strategic metrics come largely from evaluations conducted by business departments, executive management and IT managers. It must be possible to call up and analyse all the requisite information (ex post/ex ante) instantly. This can only be achieved by integrating information from existing systems such as internal service charging, early warning, risk management, strategic and operational planning, performance monitoring and operation monitoring systems.

New indicators for which data is not yet collected in reporting systems are often difficult to implement, or the quality of and frequency of measurements falls short of what is required. In many cases, introducing new indicators means adjusting reporting systems or even OLTP systems. For this reason, it is key to use only genuinely relevant indicators, particularly if you consider the permanent, ongoing effort for collecting measurements.

You also need to specify how often fresh data is to be provided. If values on indicators are to be determined by opinion survey or input of views, there has to be a process to ensure the relevant practices are carried through. For instance, decisions on the strategic classification of applications can be made by the relevant enterprise architects as part of the strategic IT planning. Incentivisation is also important: goal agreements are a good vehicle by which to incentivise people to update indicators. There also have to be appropriate quality assurance measures to make regular checks on the quality and consistency of the data being channelled into performance metrics.

Individual indicators have to be aggregated into overall measures in performance measurement systems. Individual figures often merely indicate the status of particular elements, saying little about overall contexts and phenomena that cut across a number of issues. Quite the opposite in fact: individual figures can tend to be ambiguous, limiting the extent to which they can provide meaningful information. To give an example, it makes no sense to look at the indicator "IT costs to turnover" in isolation. A far more specific picture emerges when we examine this in terms of the degree of business support or innovation, depending on the industry (see [Küt06], [Küt07] and [KüM07]).

The goal is to aggregate values into meaningful business intelligence in a performance management system, to exclude the possibility of ambiguity and take into account possible dependencies.

Fact file:

- Stick to what is really important!
  Given that you need to keep information intelligible, clear, obtainable and verifiable, you should select no more than 20 indicators.
- Document each indicator using a uniform scheme; clearly designate what statement the indicator is making and its significance in the context of strategic and operating-level IT control.
- The indicators you choose must be appropriate to answer the questions your stakeholders have. The content must be correct, they must provide meaningful intelligence, be easy to obtain and be verifiable, and also be adequately up-to-date.

- Following the precept "I can only control what I can measure intelligently", measurements have to be available or easy to obtain. You shouldn't need to build an entire new information world first. Information has to be extracted from existing systems or be easy to compile by consolidating views.
- Group indicators into control quantities and integrate them into a performance measurement system. This enables you to determine aspects such as degree of business alignment by a combination of the degree and quality of business process support and the degree of utilisation (see [Küt06]).

6.3.2 Decision-Making Groups and Their Information Needs

The decision-making groups which participate in strategic management of the IT landscape have different information needs, depending on what their special area is, and how far up the leadership chain they are:

- **Executive board perspective**: The executive board needs transparency on factors such as goal accomplishment, cost, risk and benefit of IT. IT costs are often also benchmarked against those of external IT providers or IT departments in comparable companies. Risks have to be made transparent, particularly in terms of projects and business operations, security and compliance, and in the implementation of business requirements. A statement on business benefit is also required, often expressed in terms of savings and optimisation potential, contributions to strategy and value proposition, also by the degree of business-oriented innovation.
- **Business segment manager perspective**: Business segment managers need to know their business requirements are being supported optimally, reliably and cost-efficiently by IT. Indicators such as the coverage of business processes or customer satisfaction are used to evaluate the degree of business support. SLA fulfilment and cost serve as criteria for monitoring reliability and cost efficiency.
- **IT manager perspective**: IT managers need indicators to check up on cost, status and reliability of operating activities and business support. Indicators are also required for strategic and operating-level control of development in accordance with IT goals and with strategic and operating planning.

Important:

Match the content, level of detail and presentation of indicators to what the target audience needs to know.

Which indicators are important for which decision-making group?

Table 6.4 shows which decision-making group is charged with which control tasks. The most appropriate indicators have to be selected to address the concerns and issues on which each group needs information.

Table 6.4 Control tasks performed by decision-making groups

	Decision-making groups		
	Executive board	Business segment managers	IT managers
Business alignment of IT			
Transparency of business impacts/dependencies		√	√
Linkage between business and IT		√	√
Optimising of business through IT		√	√
Business-oriented control of IT	√	√	√
Strategic IT control			
Strategic application planning, aligning IT landscape (IT landscape management)			√
Technical standardisation of applications and infrastructure			√
Sourcing & vendor management			√
Operating-level IT control			
Controlling application and infrastructure operations			√
Controlling service delivery and vendors			√

The following indicators from Table 6.2 are relevant for these three decision-making groups:

- Executive board

  - Cost (absolute, historic, and benchmarked)
  - Risk (per project, business operation, compliance, security)
  - Benefit (savings and optimisation potential, contribution to strategy, contribution to value proposition, degree or proportion of innovation)
  - Other relevant indicators: Competitive differentiation, changeability, criticality, turnover or cost contribution, strategic fit, customer satisfaction, cost efficiency, ROI and flexibility

- Business segment managers

  - Degree and quality of business support (e.g. business processes, business functions or products) and customer satisfaction

- Segment-relevant costs (project, implementation of business requirements, maintenance and operation of applications, infrastructure costs, e.g. for operation, PC and network infrastructure)
- Reliability of business operation via indicators such as criticality and SLA fulfilment in risk (project, business operation, compliance, security)
- Other relevant indicators: Degree of dependency, functional ownership, degree of standardisation, degree and number of redundancies and inconsistencies or degree of automation, degree of utilisation, contribution to strategy, contribution to value proposition

- IT managers: IT managers need the indicators of the other perspectives in order to ensure business alignment, plus other indicators to produce trend analysis, to-be/as-is comparisons and reliable forecasts. They also need to plan investments precisely and manage IT proactively. The following additional indicators serve as the basis for these tasks:

  - Strategic level: Future sustainability, degree of standardisation or compliance with standards, degree and quality of business coverage, technical quality or state of health, degree of integration or modularisation of applications, freedom from redundancy and consistency of business objects, applications, process support and technical landscape model, degree of modularisation or service orientation or component orientation, adaptability or extensibility or integration ability, effectiveness of resource deployment, vertical integration, core capabilities, potential performance (overall and for individual IT services) and skill level
  - Operating level: IT performance, costs (per project, maintenance, operation) e.g. benchmarked, also benefit, degree and quality of implementation of security and compliance requirements and statutory frameworks, complexity, ease of maintenance or adaptability or extensibility or integration ability, performance, scalability, reliability, availability, downtime or resilience, lifecycle, degree of automation, required resourcing and efficiency of resource deployment, response times, quality of solutions, products and services, degree of SLA fulfilment, efficiency/productivity of operation/service provision or number of resources per application for consulting, maintenance, support or operating unit, implementation and provisioning time, process quality, ergonomics, adherence to promised schedules, delivery ability and delivery reliability, risk, number of errors, and severity of errors, degree of documentation and number of releases of applications and technical components

For each stakeholder group, you should define no more than five to eight strategic and operating performance measures and map these in charts, traffic light type systems and diagrams. Alerts, triggered when a value exceeds a particular limit (e.g. traffic light indicators) indicate that immediate action is required. With this sort of information at their disposal, the stakeholders in the various decision-making groups always have a complete overview of what is happening in their area.

Key to the effectiveness of the strategic control toolkit is to choose the right indicators for the target group, and to present them appropriately. Indicators are required for all strategic and operating-level IT management functions. The information has to be provided regularly, pulling together a wide range of input which is consolidated into a compact display such as a cockpit. The salient intelligence has to be presentable in a few charts and indicators which gives stakeholders an at-a-glance overview of complex interdependencies and trends. The resulting transparency helps satisfy the need for information from multiple perspectives and creates a solid basis for decisions.

Useful hint:

Do not define more than five to eight indicators for each decision-making group. Otherwise it will be difficult to keep the overall system comprehensible and manageable. If you use more than 10 indicators, there will often not be clear demarcations between them, and this can lead to wrong decisions.

Establishing a Control Toolkit

A customised control toolkit has to be established for each perspective. In general performance management systems such as the Balanced Scorecard and cockpits are used to present the data.

A CIO needs an overall view of IT. A CIO strategic control system can comprise all the indicators for operating and strategic control of IT, giving the CIO a comprehensive overview of conformity with planning, and of the status of service delivery, also on fulfilment of compliance and security requirements. A cockpit such as the one shown in Fig. 6.23 can be used for presentation.

A cockpit creates a structured, compact overview of the status of control objects. It compiles all the relevant planned, as-is and forecast values from the various operating and strategic IT management functions. Commercial, technical and organisational information can all be presented as graphics and indicators with good visual clarity, making it easier to cut through the overall complexity.

The CIO cockpit in Fig. 6.23 uses both strategic indicators such as business coverage and application classification, and operating indicators such as IT performance, cost overview, vendor and project status, also SLAs for the various locations. The magnifying glass symbol is a drill-down tool for obtaining more detailed information in a particular category. The entire cockpit is a good aid for controlling and directing IT and enables the CIO to respond quickly in the event of changes. However, it should be remembered that the cockpit will only be of value when it is actually using the right indicators – in other words measuring the right things.

A business segment manager needs different information. Figure 6.24 uses the business cluster graphic as its basis (see Sect. 3.4.2) and relates control information

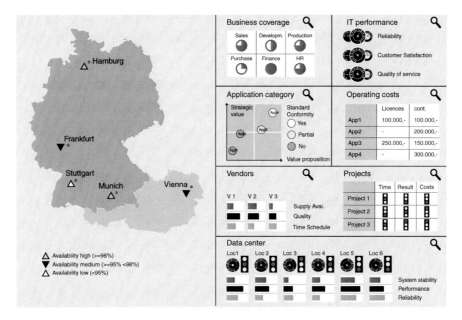

Fig. 6.23   Example of a cockpit for a CIO

such as SLA fulfilment and degree of business coverage to the individual sections of the business segment.

Once we get to enterprise board level, yet another set of indicators are relevant. IT aspects are here in part presented in consolidated form. Figure 6.25 gives an example: IT performance in this case aggregates many IT indicators, and presents them in a variety of ways, in both numbers and graphics.

One type of indicator is the traffic light. A traffic light-type indicator maps values of performance metrics to colour signals. In practice, one finds either two-colour traffic lights (red and green) or three colours (red, amber and green). To determine the colour, the values of the metrics are clustered into ranges according to a specific scheme, e.g. high risk, medium risk or low risk. Each of these ranges can then be assigned a colour, making the information far easier for users to take in. Scales can also be used (such as 0, 25, 50, 75 or 100%) when no detailed figures are required. This too makes the salient information easy to identify at a glance. Another form of presentation is a portfolio – useful if there is a two-dimensional classification of control objects, e.g. strategy and value contribution.

Spreadsheets with diagramming functions are often used to compile and compose indicators. It is also possible to use OLAP, BSC or Cockpit tools.

When figures are presented in graphic form, users can take in and process information faster and better, because pictures make greater impact than text and numbers. Useful diagrams (see [Mar00]) include business charts such as bar charts or graphs, also portfolios for plotting multi-dimensional values, and tree diagrams, network diagrams and maps for presenting structures.

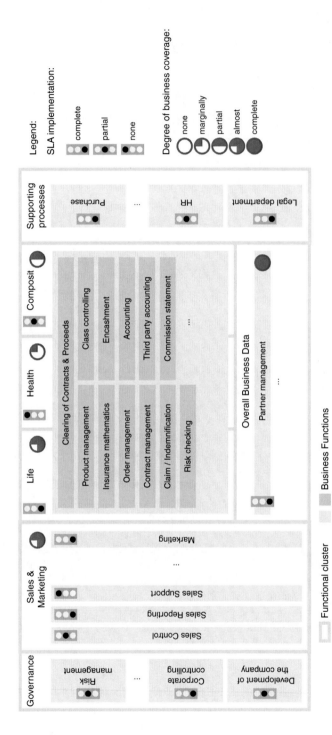

Fig. 6.24 Example of the IT control cockpit for a business segment manager

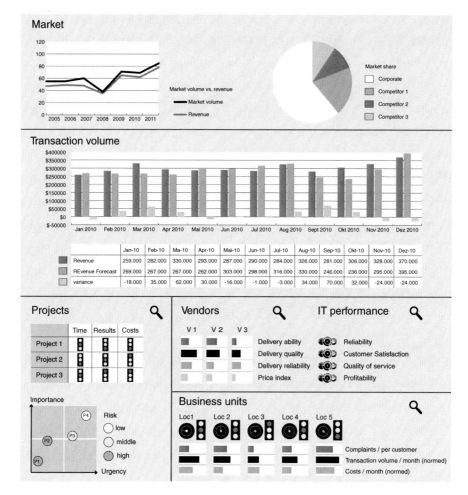

Fig. 6.25 Example of a cockpit for enterprise board

The purpose of the classic business chart is to present numeric values and the relationship that exists between them. Structural associations between information are commonly presented using tree-type diagrams such as organisational charts or decision trees. Spatial or topological associations such as the spatial distribution of business outlets are shown by maps (see [Ahl06]).

Fact file:

The control toolkit for each of the stakeholder groups must be designed in accordance with their goals and focus. The toolkit should be developed, agreed and also introduced over a manageable timeframe of no more than one year. This is the only real way to get management on side and to ensure the impact does not simply fizzle out.

The control toolkit must be practice-tested. Once the initial system has been established, it is essential to collect feedback from the stakeholders who use the tools, and to channel these improvements into refining the systems.

Introducing a Control Toolkit

Once you have defined the control toolkit, the next step is to get it ready for operation and then pilot-test it.

Key to operationalising the system is to feed real data into the indicators, which is what gives stakeholders access to up-to-date control information in the required quality. Performance measurement systems and cockpits have to be established. You may have to adapt your existing reporting or OLTP systems for this purpose and integrate the metrics into the new system.

Important:

Choose pragmatic methods, not over-sophisticated computing models!
Stick to important, obtainable indicators and control quantities.

You may also have to make a range of organisational adjustments to ensure data is collected reliably, and that reporting takes place regularly. What really takes time and effort is ongoing monitoring and post-hoc adjustment to verify that the data being channelled into performance management systems is up to scratch on quality.

Define standard reports or other automated procedures, and rigorously demand that they be kept available – since this will ensure people have prompt access to the information they need to steer the company and its processes. Incentivise the introduction of new measures of performance to ensure data will be collected with a commitment to quality.

At the end of the pilot phase the control toolkit must undergo a planned review, the objective here being to reduce the original set of indicators further. Check the following:

- Whether indicators make as meaningful a statement as originally assumed;
- Whether additional or different indicators are required;
- Whether the quality of measurement values is satisfactory;
- Whether the indicators remain stable even in the event of organisational changes.

What makes EAM governance a success:

- Enter into an intensive dialogue with the business. This enables you to build a relationship of trust with the business segments.
  What matters is to have clearly defined and established boards and roles on both the business and IT sides, and to institutionalise a regular exchange between the two camps.
- Make certain you have the backing of your executive board. A member of the executive management must be represented on the boards for strategic and operating-level control of IT.
- Define boards and decision processes for all IT decision areas.
  For each decision process, you have to make an authoritative definition of the processes themselves, the boards, roles and responsibilities on both the business and IT sides, with their decision, participation and execution rights and responsibilities.
  There is a direct correlation between the influence which IT has, and its integration into decision processes and boards.
- Choose the right form of IT organisation for the structure, organisation and culture of your company.
- Work out your performance potential and core capabilities. Define your future performance potential and core capabilities in the sourcing strategy.
- If your enterprise has international business activities, also take into account the principles of global IT.
- Work out your current position, and establish a change management programme that takes things from this point.
- Raise the qualification levels of your IT! Business expertise, communication skills and powers of persuasion are just as important as technology expertise.
- Work out your control tasks, and document them, also specifying who has overall responsibility in each case.
- Determine appropriate indicators for the control tasks, integrate them into your planning and control processes, and underpin them with obtainable metrics.
- Provide good tool support to assist strategic controlling. Only in this way can you establish a reporting system that delivers information when it's needed, in the right quality, with the perspectives that stakeholders need. Your goal is to provide the right information at the right time in the right place.
- Last but not least: get the control toolkit institutionalised in your organisation.

Literature

[Aie04]	Aier, S.; Schönherr, M. (Hrsg.): Enterprise Application Integration – Service-orientierung und nachhaltige Architekturen. 1. Edition. Gito, Berlin 2004
[Aie05]	Aier, S.; Schönherr, M. (Hrsg.): Unternehmensarchitekturen und Systemintegration. 1. Edition. Gito, Berlin 2005
[Ahl06]	Ahlrichs, F.; Knuppertz, T.: Controlling von Geschäftsprozessen. Prozessorientierte Unternehmenssteuerung umsetzen. 1. Edition. Schäffer-Poeschel, 2006
[All05]	Allweyer, T.: Geschäftsprozessmanagement. 1. Edition. Publisher W3I, 2005
[Bae07]	Bär, M.; Krumm, R.; Wihele, H.: Unternehmen verstehen, gestalten, verändern. Das Graves-Value-System in der Praxis. 1. Edition. Gabler Publisher, 2007
[Bal08]	Bals, L. (Author); Jahns, C. (Hrsg.): Sourcing of Services. International Aspects and Complex Categories. 1. Edition. Gabler, 2008
[Bas03]	Bass, L.; Clements, P.; Kazman, R.: Software Architecture in Practice. 2. Edition. Addison-Wesley Longman, Amsterdam 2003
[Ber03-1]	Bernhard, M.G.; Blomer, R.; Bonn, J. (Hrsg.): Strategisches IT-Management – Band 1: Organisation – Prozesse – Referenzmodelle. Symposion Publishing, Düsseldorf 2003
[Ber03-2]	Bernhard, M.G.; Blomer, R.; Bonn, J. (Hrsg.): Strategisches IT-Management – Band 2: Fallbeispiele und praktische Umsetzung. 1. Edition. Symposion Publishing, Düsseldorf 2003
[Bie07]	Biethahn, J.; Huch, B. (Hrsg.): Informationssysteme für das Controlling: Konzepte, Methoden und Instrumente zur Gestaltung von Controlling-Informationssystemen. 1. Edition. Springer Publisher, Berlin 2007
[Blo06]	Blomer, R.; Mann, H.; Bernhard, M.G. (Hrsg.): Praktisches IT-Management. Controlling, Kennzahlensysteme, Konzepte. 1. Edition. Symposion Publishing, Düsseldorf 2006
[Boa99]	Boar, B. H.: Constructing Blueprints for Enterprise IT Architectures. Wiley & Sons, USA 1999
[Bre06]	Brenner, W.; Witte, Ch.: Erfolgsrezepte für CIOs. Was gute Informationsmanager ausmacht. 1. Edition. Hanser Publisher, Munich 2006
[Buc05]	Buchta, D.; Eul, M.; Schulte-Croonenberg, H.: Strategisches IT-Management: Wert steigern, Leistung steuern, Kosten senken. 2. Edition. Gabler Publisher, Wiesbaden 2005
[Buc07]	Buchsein, R.; Victor, F.; Günther, H.; Machmeier, V.: IT-Management mit ITIL V3. 1. Edition. Vieweg+Teubner, Wiesbaden 2007
[Bur04]	Burke, B.: Enterprise Architecture or City Planning? http://techupdate.zdnet.com/techupdate/stories/main/Enterprise_Architecture_or_City_Planning.html
[Coe03]	Coenenberg, A.G.; Salfeld, R.: Wertorientierte Unternehmensführung – Vom Strategieentwurf zur Implementierung. 1. Edition. Schäffer-Poeschel, Stuttgart 2003

[Der06]   Dern, G.: Management von IT-Architekturen. 2. Edition. Vieweg+Teubner, Wiesbaden 2006

[Dic85]   Dickson, G. W.; Wetherbe, J. C.: The Management of Information Systems. Mcgraw-Hill Professional, New York 1985

[Die06]   Dietrich, L.; Schirra, W.: Innovationen durch IT – Erfolgsbeispiele aus der Praxis. 1. Edition. Springer, Berlin 2006

[DOD04-1]   Department of Defence Architecture Framework Working Group: DoD Architecture Framework Version 1.0, Volume I: Definitions and Guidelines. USA 2004

[DOD04-2]   Department of Defence Architecture Framework Working Group: DoD Architecture Framework Version 1.0, Volume II: Product Descriptions. USA 2004

[Dop02]   Doppler, K.; Lauterburg, C.: Chance Management. Den Unternehmenswandel gestalten. 10. Edition. Campus Publisher, Frankfurt 2002

[Fel08]   Feldbrügge, R.; Brecht-Hadraschek, B.: Prozessmanagement leicht gemacht: Geschäftsprozesse analysieren und gestalten. 2. Edition. Redline Wirtschaftsverlag, 2008

[Fer05]   Ferstl, O. K.; Sinz, E. J.; Eckert, S. (Hrsg.); Isselhorst, T.: Wirtschaftsinformatik 2005: eEconomy, eGovernment, eSociety. S. 627–646. 1. Edition. Physica-Publisher, 2005

[Fis08]   Fischermanns, G.: Praxishandbuch Prozessmanagement. 7. Edition. Publisher Schmidt (Götz), Wettenberg 2008

[Foe03]   Foegen, M.: Architektur und Architekturmanagement – Modellierung von Architekturen und technisches Architekturmanagement in der Software-Organisation. wibas GmbH, Darmstadt 2005. http://www.wibas.de/e20/e2695/e52/e915/architekturundarchitekturmanagement_de.pdf

[Foe08]   Foegen, M.; Solbach, M.; Raak, C.: Der Weg zur professionellen IT. Eine praktische Anleitung für das Management von Veränderungen mit CMMI, ITIL oder SPICE. 1. Edition. Springer Publisher, Heidelberg 2008

[Frö07]   Fröhlich, M.; Glasner, K.: IT-Governance – Leitfaden für eine praxisgerechte Implementierung. 1. Edition. Gabler, Wiesbaden 2007

[Gar05]   Gartner Research Publication, G00128285, Juni 2005; Audrey Apfel,Gartner Symposium/ITxpo 2005

[Gar08]   Gartner Research Publication, November 2008; Cannes, France, Symposium/ITxpo 2008

[GPM03]   GPM Deutsche Gesellschaft für Projektmanagement e.V.: Projektmanagement Fachmann. 7. Edition. RKW-Publisher, Eschborn 2003

[Haf04]   Hafner, M.; Schelp, J. et al: Technisches Architekturmanagement als Basis effizienter und effektiver Produktion von IT-Services. In: HMD 41 (237), S. 54–66, 2004

[Han09]   Hanschke, I.: Strategisches Management der IT-Landschaft. Ein praktischer Leitfaden für das Enterprise Architecture Management. 1. Edition. Hanser-Publisher, Munich 2009

[Hei01]   Heilmann, H. (Hrsg.): Strategisches IT-Controlling. 1. Edition. Dpunkt Publisher, Heidelberg 2001

[Her06]   Herzwurm, G. (Hrsg.): IT – Kostenfaktor oder strategische Waffe? Geschäftsziele und IT in Einklang bringen. 1. Edition. Lemmens Publisher, Bonn 2006

[Hor02]   Horn, E.; Reinke, T.: Softwarearchitektur und Softwarebauelemente. Eine Einführung für Softwarearchitekten. Hanser Publisher, Munich 2002

[Hru06]   Hruschka, P.; Starke, G.: Praktische Architekturdokumentation: Wie wenig ist genau richtig? In: OBJEKTspektrum 1, S. 52–57, 2006

[IEE00]   ANSI/IEEE Std 1471: Recommended Practice for Architectural Descriptions of Software-Intensive Systems. http://www.iso-architecture.org/ieee-1471/

[IFE05]	Institute For Enterprise Architecture Developements: Trends in Enterprise Architecture 2005: How are Organizations Progressing? http://www. ea-consulting.com/Reports/Enterprise%20Architecture%20Survey%202005%20 IFEAD%20v10.pdf
[IGI08]	IT Governance Institute: CobiT 4.1. http://www.isaca.org/cobit.htm (Download 2008-01-03)
[itS08]	itSMF und ISACA: Praxishandbuch. ITIL-COBIT-Mapping. Gemeinsamkeiten und Unterschieder der IT-Standards. 1. Edition. Symposion Publishing, Düsseldorf 2008
[Joh07]	Johannsen, W.; Goeken, M.: Referenzmodelle für IT-Governance. Strategische Effektivität und Effizienz mit COBIT, ITIL & Co. 1. Edition. Dpunkt Publisher, Heidelberg 2007
[Kag06]	Kagermann, H.; Österle, H.: Geschäftsmodelle 2010 – Wie CEOs Unternehmen transformieren. 1. Edition. Frankfurter Allgemeine Buch, Frankfurt 2006
[Kel06]	Keller, W.: IT-Unternehmensarchitektur. Von der Geschäftsstrategie zur optimalen IT-Unterstützung. 1. Edition. Dpunkt Publisher, Heidelberg 2006
[Ker08]	Kerth, K.; Asum, H.: Die besten Strategietools in der Praxis. Welche Werkzeuge brauche ich wann? Wie wende ich sie an? Wo liegen die Grenzen. 3. Edition. Hanser Publisher, Munich 2008
[Keu08]	Keuper, F.; Schomann, M.; Grimm, R. (Hrsg.): Strategisches IT-Management. Management von IT und IT-gestütztes Management. 1. Edition. Gabler, 2008
[Klu06]	Kluge, C.; Dietzsch, A.; Rosemann, M.: Conference Proceedings of the 14th European Conference on Information Systems, Göteborg, Sweden 2006. How to realise Corporate Value from Enterprise Architecture. http://www.bpm.fit. qut.edu.au/projects/refmod/ECIS2006%20-%20Kluge,%20Dietzsch,%20Rosemann %20-%20How%20to%20realise%20corporate%20value%20from%20Enterprise% 20Architecture_final.pdf
[Krc05]	Krcmar, H.: Informationsmanagement. 4. Edition. Springer, Berlin 2005
[Krc90]	Krcmar, H.: Bedeutung und Ziele von Informationssystem-Architekturen. Wirtschaftsinformatik 32 (5), S. 395–402, 1990
[Krü03]	Krüger, S.; Seelmann-Eggebert, J.: IT-Architektur-Engineering – Systemkomplexität bewältigen und Kosten senken. 1. Edition. Galileo Press, Bonn 2003
[Küt06]	Kütz, M.: IT-Steuerung mit Kennzahlensystemen. 1. Edition. Dpunkt Publisher, Heidelberg 2006
[Küt07]	Kütz, M.: Kennzahlen in der IT – Werkzeuge für Controlling und Management. 2. Edition. Dpunkt Publisher, Heidelberg 2007
[KüM07]	Kütz, M.; Meier, A. (Hrsg.): IT-Controlling. 1. Edition. Dpunkt Publisher, HMD Heft 254, Heidelberg April 2007
[Lei07]	Leitel, J.: Entwicklung und Anwendung von Bewertungskriterien für Enterprise Architecture Frameworks. Technische Universität Munich, Fakultät für Informatik, Masterarbeit 2007. http://www.matthes.in.tum.de/file/Publikationen/ 2007/Le07/Le07.pdf
[Luf00]	Luftman, J. N.: Assessing Business-IT Alignment Maturity. In: Communications of the Association for Information Systems 4 (2000), Dezember 2000
[Mai05]	Maizlish, B.; Handler, R.: IT Portfolio Management Step-by-Step. 1. Edition. Wiley & Sons, USA 2005
[Mar00]	Marty, R., Prof. Dr.: Wertorientierte IT-Governance. 1. Edition. Springer, Berlin 2000
[Mas05]	Masak, D.: Moderne Enterprise Architekturen. 1. Edition. Springer, Berlin 2005
[Mas06]	Masak, D.: IT-Alignment: IT-Architektur und Organisation (Xpert.Press). 1. Edition. Springer, Berlin 2006
[Mat04-1]	Matthes, F.; Wittenburg, A.: Softwarekarten zur Visualisierung von Anwendungssystemlandschaften und ihren Aspekten – Eine Bestandsaufnahme.

Technische Universität Munich, Fakultät für Informatik, Lehrstuhl für Informatik 19 (sebis), Technischer Bericht, 2004

[Mat04-2] Matthes, F.; Wittenburg, A.: Softwarekartographie: Visualisierung von Anwendungslandschaften und ihren Schnittstellen. Technische Universität Munich, Fakultät für Informatik, Lehrstuhl für Informatik 19 (sebis), Technischer Bericht, 2004

[Mey03] Meyer, M. et al.: IT-Governance: Begriff, Status quo und Bedeutung. Wirtschaftsinformatik 45, S. 445–448, 2003

[Min05] Mintzberg, H. et al.: Strategy Safari. Eine Reise durch die Wildnis des strategischen Managements. 1. Edition. Redline Wirtschaft. Heidelberg 2005

[MIT03] MIT Sloan School Center: MIT Sloan School for Information Systems Research (CISR), 2003

[Mül05] Müller-Stewens, G.; Lechner, Ch.: Strategisches Management – Wie strategische Initiativen zum Wandel führen. 3. Edition. Schäffer-Poeschel, Stuttgart 2005

[Nie05] Niemann, K. D.: Von der Unternehmensarchitektur zur IT-Governance. 1. Edition. Vieweg+Teubner, Wiesbaden 2005

[Ost03] Osterloh, M.; Fros, J.: Prozessmanagement als Kernkompetenz. Wie Sie Business Reengineering strategisch nutzen können. 4. Edition. Gabler Publisher, Wiesbaden 2003

[Pey07] Peyret, H.: The Forrester Wave^{TM}: Enterprise Architecture Tools, Q2 2007. http://www.metastorm.com/library/reports/AR_PV_Forrester_Wave_EA_Q207.pdf

[Por85] Porter, M.; Millar, V. E.: How information gives you competitve advantage. In: Harvard Business Review 63. Jg., 1985, 4, S. 149–160.

[Rog95] Rogers, E. M.: Diffusion of Innovations. 4. Edition. The Free Press, New York 1995

[Rom07] Romeike, F..: Rechtliche Grundlagen des Risikomanagements: Haftungs- und Strafvermeidung für Corporate. 1. Edition. Schmidt Publisher, Berlin 2007

[Rüt06] Rüter, A.; Schröder, J.; Göldner, A.: IT-Governace in der Praxis. 1. Edition. Springer Publisher, Berlin 2006

[Rup07] Rupp, C.; Queins, S.; Zensler, B.: UML 2 glasklar. Praxiswissen für die UML-Modellierung. 3. Edition. Hanser Publisher, 2007

[Sch01] Scheer, A.-W.: ARIS – Modellierungsmethoden, Metamodelle, Anwendungen. 4. Edition. Springer, Berlin 2001

[Sch04] Schönherr, M.: Enterprise Architecture Frameworks. In: Aier, S.; Schönherr, M. (Hrsg.): Enterprise Application Integration – Serviceorientierung und nachhaltige Architekturen. 1. Edition. Gito, Berlin 2004

[Sch07] Schönherr, M.: Erarbeitung von Blueprints mit Architekturframeworks. Technische Universität Berlin, 2007

[Sea03] Seacord, R. C.; Plakosh, D.; Lewis, G. A.: Modernizing Legacy Systems: Software, Technogies, Engineering Processes, and Business Practices. 1. Edition. Addison-Wesley, Boston 2003

[Seb08] Sebis: Matthes, F.; Buckl, S.; Schweda, C. M.: Enterprise Architecture Management Tool Survey 2008. 1. Edition. Sebis, 2008

[Sek05] Sekatzek, P: Visualisierung von IT-Bebauungsplänen in Form von Softwarekarten – Konzeption und prototypische Umsetzung. Technische Universität Munich, Fakultät für Informatik, Masterarbeit 2005

[Ses07] Sesselmann, W.; Schmelzer, H. J.: Geschäftsprozessmanagement in der Praxis. Kunden zufrieden stellen, Produktivität steigern, Wert erhöhen: Kunden zufrieden stellen – Produktivität steigern – Wert erhöhen. 6. Edition. Hanser Fachbuch, 2007

[Skk04] Schekkerman, J.: How to survive in the Jungle of Enterprise Architecture Frameworks. 2. Edition. Trafford Publishing, Canada 2004

[Sie02] Siedersleben, J. (Hrsg.): Standardarchitektur der Informationssysteme bei sd&m, Munich 2002

[Skk04] Schekkerman, J.: How to survive in the Jungle of Enterprise Architecture Frameworks. 2. Edition. Trafford Publishing, Canada 2004

[Sow92]   Sowa, J. F. L.; Zachman, J. A.: Extending and Formalizing the Framework for Information Systems Architecture. In: IBM Systems Journal 31 (3), S. 590–616, 1992

[Star08]   Starke, G.: Effektive Software-Architekturen – Ein praktischer Leitfaden. 3. Edition. Hanser Publisher, Munich 2008

[Ste05]   Müller-Stewens, G.; Lechner, C.: Strategisches Management. 2. Edition. Schäffer-Poeschel, Stuttgart 2005

[Tie07]   Tiemeyer, E.: Handbuch IT-Management. Konzepte, Methoden, Lösungen und Arbeitshilfen für die Praxis. 2. Edition. Hanser, Munich 2007

[TOG01]   The Open Group: Other Architectures and Architectural Frameworks. The Open Group 2001. http://www.opengroup.org/architecture/togaf7-doc/arch/p4/others/others.htm (Download 2007-05-07)

[TOG03]   The Open Group: TOGAF^{TM} (The Open Group Architecture Framework) Version 8.1 "Enterprise Edition". The Open Group 2003

[TOG07]   The Open Group: Downloading TOGAF^{TM} Version 8 "Enterprise Edition". The Open Group 2007. http://www.opengroup.org/architecture/togaf8/downloads.htm (Download 2007-05-07)

[TOG08]   The Open Group: TOGAF^{TM} Version 8.1.1 "Enterprise Edition". http://www.opengroup.org/architecture/togaf (Download 2008-01-03)

[TOG09]   The Open Group: TOGAF^{TM} Version 9. Van Haren Publishing, 2009

[Vah05]   Dietmar V.: Organisation. Einführung ind die Organisationstheorie und -praxis. 5. Edition. Schäffer Poeschel Publisher, Kornwestheim 2005

[Vog05]   Oliver, V.; Ingo, A.; Arif, C.; Edmund, I.; Uwe, M.; Thomas, N.; Markus, V.; Uwe, Z.: Software-Architektur. Grundlagen – Konzepte – Praxis. 1. Edition. Spektrum Akademischer Publisher , Munich 2005

[War02]   Ward, J.; Peppard, J.: Strategic Planning for Information Systems. 3. Edition. Wiley & Sons, USA 2002

[Wei04]   Weill, P.; Ross, J. W.: IT Governance – How Top Performers Manage IT Decision Rights for Superior Results. Mcgraw-Hill Professional, New York 2004

[Wei06]   Weill, P.; Ross, J. W.; Robertson, D. C.: Enterprise Architecture as a Strategy. Mcgraw-Hill Professional, New York 2006

[Win03]   Winter, R.: Methodische Unterstützung der Strategiebildung im Retail Banking. In: BIT – Banking and Information Technology 2, S. 49–58, 2003

[Zac08]   The Zachman Institute for Framework Advancement: Mission Statement und Zachman Framework. http://www.zifa.com (Download 2008-01-03)

[Zac87]   Zachman, J.: A Framework for Information Systems Architecture. In: IBM Systems Journal 26 (3), S. 277–293, 1987

[Zin04]   Zink, K. J.: TQM als integriertes Managementkonzept. Das EFQM Excellence Modell und seine Unterstützung. 1. Edition. Hanser Publisher, Vienna 2004

Glossary

Actuating variable   Variable that impacts on control objects. One or more indicators in the performance management system should have the desired target value. Actuating variables are not themselves indicators, but they can be directly related to one or more indicators. As a rule a change to an actuating variable impacts on several indicators.

Agility   The ability of an enterprise to adapt efficiently and effectively to all types of changes.

Analysis pattern   An established, generalised pattern for identifying and highlighting points where there is potentially a need for action or improvement in the IT landscape.

Application   Software or software package for associated functionalities which are logically and technically distinct from other areas of functionality, and which can be supported entirely or to a large extent by IT.

Application category   A particular type of applications, for example OLTP or OLAP.

Application cluster   A set of functionally related applications. Applications are considered to be functionally related when they share data, support the same business processes or come under the responsibility of the same business units. The formation of clusters is a useful way of identifying opportunities for optimisation – e.g. for close linkage or possible merging of applications.

Application domain   An application domain groups a number of applications with common criteria. Application domains are commonly used to organise the application landscape – and the responsibilities for landscape planning – into related units.

Application landscape   The sum total of all business applications in the company. The application landscape consists largely of applications, their data and interfaces.

Application landscape model   Documents the application landscape of the enterprise, i.e. the applications and their interfaces, including information flow via these interfaces. An application landscape can be organised into application domains, also known as landscape clusters.

Architectural domain   Structural elements used to group technical components in the blueprint.

Architectural pattern   (Also termed Architectural component) An established, generalised solution template to address a particular area of concern in a specific context. Example: "data access from a JEE application to a relational database".

As-is landscape   Describes the current productive status of the landscape, e.g. all business processes which are executed in this state, or all applications which are currently used in productive operation.

Balanced scorecard (BSC)   A management tool that uses "leading" and "lagging" indicators to investigate and present the vision and strategy of an enterprise, relevant internal and external aspects and how they interrelate.
The enterprise is viewed from several perspectives, ratings being provided by metrics in each of these perspectives. The perspectives of the Balanced Scorecard typically include "Finance", "Customer" and "Employees".

Basic infrastructure   This is composed of IT products which can be sourced unchanged from the market – for example, PCs and workstation software such as office and communication platforms and server infrastructure components.

Benchmark   Benchmarking is the process of comparing two companies or organisations on the basis of usually standardised metrics. Care must be taken to ensure that metrics are comparable. Often standards are set by using values from the strongest organisations as best practices and measures.

Business alignment   The process by which IT is brought into line with the requirements of the business. The primary focus of IT is to provide the best possible support for the enterprise strategy and goals.

Business architecture   Describes the major structures of an enterprise that essentially drive its business activities – for example its business processes, business functions, products, business objects and business units.

Business continuity management   A set of processes to ensure that critical business services continue to be available even in the event of a crisis or disaster. This is done by explicitly managing the risks, in other words determining the potential impact of each disaster scenario in financial and non-financial terms (e.g. also damage to the company's image), the probability of each scenario, and the measures to take in the event of occurrence.

Business domain   A business domain is a structural element that serves to group associated elements in the business landscape.

Business driver   The success factors for the business. As a rule, business drivers correlate with the strategic goals.

Business function   A distinct, cohesive set of business functionality such as "customer relationship management". The enterprise's capabilities are expressed in terms of the business functions it carries out. Business functions exist independently of their use in business processes – i.e. they can be used in multiple business processes.

Business function cluster   A set of business functions which are closely associated in functional terms. Business functions should be grouped into clusters when one of the following conditions is met:

- A set of business functions which are assigned more than once in this combination to a business process or a product.
- A set of business functions which are assigned more than once in this combination to a business unit, or the majority of which are under the stewardship of business units within a single organisational cluster.
- A set of business functions which are supported more than once in this combination by an application.
- A set of business functions which enact the same business goals.

Business landscape model   Describes the major functional units of an enterprise that essentially drive its business activities. The main elements of the business landscape model are business processes, business functions, products, business units and business objects.

Business mapping   Assignment of business landscape elements to other business landscape elements, e.g. business processes to business units, but also to applications.

Business model   A business model presents the implementation of the corporate strategy for a particular segment of business. It determines the "what" and "how" of a corporate strategy. The goals in a business model are generally expanded and elaborated by specifying particular products, customers and resources.

Business object   A business object represents a real-world entity – abstract or concrete – which encapsulates some part of the business activity of an enterprise (customers, for example, products or orders). Business objects can be associated with one another by relationships and are used by business processes. The specific data of an application, the information objects, can have a logical reference to a business object. For example, an application can be the master application for customer numbers and names, and can exchange this data with other applications.

Business process   A sequence of logically connected activities or sub-processes that contributes in some way to the enterprise's value-added. Each process has a defined start and end, is repeatedly performed and is expressed in terms of performing some action for customers.

Business requirement   Requirements, expressed in business language, which are broken down into IT-related aspects. Business requirements can be both operational level and strategic.

Business segment   An area which deals with a specific section of the business, such as the business processes in a value chain, or the business functions of a functional cluster.

Business strategy   A comprehensive description of the decisions taken by the executive board to safeguard and leverage future business opportunities. The business strategy is cascaded back from a vision of success which will materialise at some point in the future; it also stakes out the path for taking decisions in the present. The business strategy provides answers to the following essential questions: "where do we stand now with our company" (as-is situation)? "Where do we want to go?" (target and to-be) and "how do we get there?" (paths to this goal).

Business unit   Logical or structural units of the enterprise, such as departments, sites and plants; also logical user groups such as "field sales team" or "internal administration".

Business-relevant IT products   These are created by bundling individual IT services and products into packages which the business can use to advantage in a particular context. Example: provision of a package for new sales staff which comprises both the software itself and also connectivity services and hardware.

Chief information officer (CIO)   The role of the Chief Information Officer is specific to each enterprise, with differences in the overall mandate and responsibilities. The main tasks of the CIO are generally to align IT to the enterprise strategy, and to build and operate appropriate IT landscapes. In many enterprises, the CIO reports directly to the CEO (Chief Executive Officer), and can also be a member of the executive board.

Cluster analysis   A form of dependency analysis, cluster analysis is a method to identify functionally associated sets of functions, business processes, business objects and business units, applications, infrastructure units and projects.

CMMI   (Capability Maturity Model Integration) A quality management model for system and software development and for related fields; a successor of the well-known CMM (Capability Maturity Model), developed in the 1990s by the US Defense Ministry to standardise quality appraisals of software providers.

CobiT   (Control Objectives for Information and Related Topics) A reference model for IT governance that defines a set of control objectives for IT processes. In the current third version, the model identifies 34 IT processes which can be evaluated using 318 control and monitoring guidelines. Critical success factors, key performance indicators and other metrics provide managers with the input they need to ensure measurability in IT and to measure their IT environment in terms of the IT processes identified by CobiT.

Cockpit   A management control instrument offering a compact, structured presentation of key information via a set of control objects, usually in graphical form.

Commercial-off-the-shelf-product (COTS)   A COTS product is software or hardware which is used as bought, without modification. COTS products are relatively low-cost mass products. They are easy to install and work directly with existing system components. Most programs which a normal user will work with fall into this category, e.g. operating systems, word-processing programs, presentation software and e-mail clients.

Commodity   Originally goods sourced directly from nature which are easy to store and whose quality is easily compared. Purchase decisions are taken as a rule solely on the basis of the price, meaning that commodities are often exchange-traded goods.
In IT, a commodity is a product or service which can be supplied by a variety of providers in comparable quality, enabling customers to switch providers relatively easily. Example: data centre operation.

Compliance   Term denoting the self-imposed obligation of an enterprise or its managers to adhere to rules prescribed by legislative bodies, shareholders or supervisory boards. In many cases such rules concern ethical aspects of the corporate philosophy.

Configuration management database (CMDB)   A CMDB is a repository of the current information about the configuration items in the IT infrastructure (applications, clients, network, servers and storage) and the relationships between these items. It also stores the basic data for supporting the service management processes.

Control object   Some aspect which should be managed and directed in terms of accomplishing a particular goal. Control objects can be services, processes, products, applications, individuals, business units or projects.

Control quantity   Metrics such as goals, indicators and finance required for controlling and directing systems.

Controlling   Management function which comprises all activities to provide ongoing support for business planning and preparing for decisions.

Current landscape model   This comprises the as-is and planned landscape models. The current landscape model documents the current state of knowledge about the landscape.

Data cluster   A set of business objects which are closely associated in functional terms. Business objects should be grouped into data clusters when one of the following conditions is met:

- A set of business objects which are used more than once in this combination in a business process, product or business function.
- A set of business objects which are assigned more than once in this combination to a business unit, or the majority of which are under the stewardship of business units within a single organisational cluster.

- A set of business objects which occur more than once in this combination in the application landscape, i.e. either by being assigned to applications or exchanged via interfaces.

Data governance   Data governance ensures that the enterprise has appropriate organisational guidelines and standards in place to manage data quality and uphold compliance with external directives. Good practice in data governance also entails defining specific roles and responsibilities for data quality management.

Data master application   The application for a business object or information object which is the master for the object in question. Other applications can "source" the business object from the data master application. It is the task of the data master application to ensure adequate data quality.

Domain   Structuring according to predefined criteria. The landscape model, for instance, can be organised into application domains or functional domains.

Due diligence   In IT terms, a due diligence is the process of stocktaking and appraising a customer's products and services, IT landscape and processes.

Economies of scale   Economies of scale are achieved through the lower per-unit costs of high volumes. Economies can be achieved through purchasing power (e.g. when buyers are negotiating on greater volumes) or when a company or provider specialises in a particular type of product or service.

Enterprise architecture   A fully integrated collection of models and documents that cover business, information, applications and technology.
An enterprise architecture describes the interactions between all the key IT and business elements. It creates an overall view of IT in the enterprise, forging links between particular business structures and the structures in IT. This enables the impact of business decisions on IT to be analysed, providing a strong basis of evidence for taking investment decisions.

Enterprise architecture framework   A framework for creating and maintaining the enterprise architecture. It provides a basic set of structures which users can assemble into an architecture reflecting their own enterprise. Frameworks differ in terms of their focus: some set more store by structures, others on development of the architecture.

Enterprise architecture management (EAM)   Comprises the complete set of processes for planning and directing the enterprise architecture.

Flexibility   The ability to adapt IT systems rapidly to changing business requirements and external constraints.

Functional correlation   An object is considered to have a "functional correlation" to another object, e.g. to a process cluster, when it supports a large number of business processes in a particular cluster, or exclusively the processes in a particular cluster. The principle is the same for business functions and products.

Functional reference model Structures the landscape model according to functional criteria. Applications are categorised into the functional reference model by grouping them according to functional criteria. This forges connections between the business (through the functions executed by the applications) and IT.

Goal A future state which presents a changed, desirable status compared to the present. As such, the goal is a defined as a desirable endpoint of a process, usually human activity. The goal often marks the success of a project or undertaking which entails some level of effort.

Guideline Guidelines are mandatory frames which define the scope for IT decisions. Any departure from guidelines must be explained, with the reasons why the choice has been made. Guidelines make it more likely that actions will be taken in accordance with objectives, and help drive through such objectives.

Inconsistency Designates a state in which two elements, both of which can be considered valid, cannot be combined with one another. To correct the inconsistency is a major undertaking. Inconsistent data can have a negative impact both in business terms and on image equity, e.g. when incorrect price data is used in customer orders.

Indicator Shows in numerical or diagram form what is being investigated to check or measure progress towards goals. Indicators must be formulated as precisely as possible and must make a statement of the planned or actual state of a control object at a particular point in time.
An indicator can be an absolute number, e.g. an investment sum or project runtime, or be expressed in relation to other items of information, e.g. degree of innovation or completion.
Often a target value will be specified for each indicator, e.g. cost reduction by 30%, also with a threshold at which some intervention is required.

Information landscape model Comprises the agreed enterprise taxonomy (business objects) and application-specific information objects, the links that exist between two information objects, and their use in process and application landscapes.

Information management Systematic, method-supported planning and control of how business intelligence is provided. The value-added in every segment of the company hinges in no small part on the quality of information processing and business intelligence received.

Information object An application-specific term. Information objects are used by applications in different ways (e.g. CRUD), and are transported by interfaces. Information objects are linked by relationships with the business objects which represent real-world entities.

Infrastructure element Infrastructure units such as hardware or networks on which applications are run.

Infrastructure landscape model   Documents at a high level of granularity the infrastructure elements of the enterprise.

Infrastructure systems   Infrastructure systems generally provide services which can be used by other infrastructure systems or applications. Unlike applications, infrastructure systems do not deliver any direct business support – in other words they do not implement any business functions. For this reason, they are typically not included in an application landscape. One example of an infrastructure system is portal infrastructure.

Insourcing   In-house production/provision of services or products which were previously sourced from outside the company. Insourcing entails bringing more of the value chain in-house, the objective being to reduce costs and also to build the capabilities to serve new business segments.

IT architecture   This comprises the static and dynamic aspects which define the fundamental structure of a system. An IT architecture consists of various views:

- Conceptual view: context, core content and interaction with immediate environment
- Logical view: logical, functional and technical components, and their interaction.
- Technical view: implementation units, i.e. code structures and mapping of implementation units to logical components and to the deployment units
- Infrastructure view: mapping of the deployment units to the operating infrastructure and operating view (to ensure operationally-relevant requirements are met).

IT audit   Reporting directly to executive management, IT audit checks the organisational units and process flows to verify compliance with rules and directives. Audit criteria include compliance, risk, security, economic viability, sustainability and fitness for purpose of the areas and items under investigation. As part of the company's internal audit, the IT audit focuses on investigating IT systems and infrastructures, IT service provision and IT-supported workflows.

IT commodity   See commodity

IT consolidation   Optimises the deployment of people, processes and technologies to ensure more efficient and effective operation. The goals of IT consolidation are to optimise IT resources in order to reduce costs, raise service levels and thus make the enterprise more flexible.

IT governance   IT governance is the set of principles, procedures and methods which ensure that the organisation's IT is actually aligned with corporate goals, that resources are being deployed responsibly and risks adequately monitored.

IT landscape   The sum total of all the enterprise's IT systems, e.g. applications and operating infrastructure.

IT landscape management   IT landscape management brings transparency to the IT landscape and forges links between the structures in business and those in IT.

An enterprise architecture pulls together disparate information from business and IT and creates associations between elements such as business processes (from the business) and applications (from IT). It creates a unified picture of IT in the enterprise, and renders explicit the interdependencies and impacts of changes in business and IT. IT landscape management creates a transparent picture of the as-is and to-be status, and of the implementation roadmap.

IT management   A catch-all term for IT-related management tasks which impact directly on the success of the business by raising the value-added of IT in terms of what it delivers to the company, and at the same time minimising attendant risk and cost.

IT product   Software and/or hardware elements produced as a cohesive entity through in-house development or bought or licensed as third-party software.

IT project portfolio   The enterprise's IT project portfolio comprises all its active IT projects, from approval through to completion.

IT service charges   These are the fixed set of charges billed to users or customers for IT services. Products and services are precisely specified, and costs are defined and calculated in advance for a particular period.

IT strategy   The IT strategy stakes out a formal, authoritative frame for the various segments in which IT operates. It codifies planning assumptions and guidelines for the evolutionary development of IT over a timeframe of several years. Integral to the corporate strategy, a robust IT strategy will set out a vision and draw a trajectory from the existing "old" landscape to the necessary new elements in the future. The IT strategy is reviewed regularly and adjusted if necessary. It can also comprise many sub-strategies, e.g. for infrastructure, applications, innovation, sourcing and investment.

IT system   Technical information processing units are termed IT systems. IT systems can be applications (e.g. SAP R/3), database management systems (e.g. Oracle) without or in conjunction with operating systems (e.g. Unix) and hardware/network components.

ITIL   (Information Technology Infrastructure Library) A non-proprietary collection of best practices for IT service management. ITIL has become the de facto standard for IT service management.

Interface   An interface defines a dependency between two information systems. A direction can in some cases be defined for the interface. Interfaces can take the form of information flows or control flows. In the context of IT landscape management, the term interface is taken to mean an information flow between applications.

Key performance indicator (KPI)   KPIs measure accomplishment or progress toward key objectives within an organisation, or determine critical success factors. KPIs deliver an at-a-glance status overview and show up the points where action is required. However, unless they are broken down to specific figures at operational level, they do not offer an adequate basis for taking decisions.

Landscape diagram   Many enterprises use landscape models to present their existing and planned IT landscapes in graphical form. Alongside portfolio diagrams, the landscape diagram is the key tool to help the enterprise move ahead on its business and IT goals. The diagram forges the links between business structures such as business processes, products, business functions, business units and business objects, and IT structures such as applications, interfaces, blueprints and infrastructure.

Landscape model   An instance of an enterprise architecture, i.e. for a particular company. The model takes in all perspectives of the entire architecture or part of it – such as the business, application, technical and operating infrastructure architectures. A landscape model populates the structures which are defined by the enterprise architecture.

Legacy   "Software systems become legacy systems when they begin to resist modification and evolution."([Sea03])

Lifecycle   The entire life of an object, complete with all the states and state transitions which the object undergoes along this path.

Maturity level   Describes the degree of maturity of an enterprise. This evaluation model was developed on the basis of the Capability Maturity Model (CMM).

Medium-term strategy   A medium-term strategy typically maps out the to-be landscape model for an extended period of time, but not too far into the future. A horizon of three to no more than five years is customary. Accordingly, the medium-term strategy is a milestone on the road to the to-be landscape model.

Merger & ac-quisitions (M&A)   Corporate transactions (particularly involving large organisations) in which companies merge or change ownership.

Method   Basis for an orderly, consistent series of actions, or the manner in which actions are executed.

Migration strategy   Planned, organised procedure for replacing one IT solution with another. Before going ahead with migration, it is essential to appraise the time, cost/benefit and risks of implementation.

Mission   The purpose of an organisation, and what justifies its existence. Ultimately the mission is the answer to the question "what do we do, and for whom?"

Modelling guidelines   Determines granularity, structuring and the nature of mapping of objects in documentation or landscape data.

Multi-project management   With IT projects being so functionally and technically complex – and often mutually dependent – it is difficult to regard them in isolation. Decisions in one project can have a knock-on impact in others.

The purpose of multi-project management is to take account of these mutual interdependencies.

Need for action   "Need-for-action" points are the points where changes must be made in the business or IT.

Offshoring   The moving of IT services to low-wage countries such as India (offshore) or Romania (nearshore) in order to save labour costs. The likely savings in each case is a matter for individual company estimates. Offshore development centres are also common. IT functions are moved to low-wage countries and external resources bundled in a separate company or joint venture.

Operating infrastructure   Comprises the hardware and network units on which applications are run.

Operating infrastructure landscape model   Describes the hardware and network units on which applications are run.

Operational excellence   The ability to support business processes through IT quickly, reliably and cost effectively.

Opportunity costs   The cost of not going ahead with a particular course of action, i.e. the cost in terms of lost revenue because opportunities to use resources are not taken.

Organisational cluster   A set of business units which are closely associated in functional terms. Business units should be grouped into organisational clusters when one of the following conditions is met:

- A set of business units which execute associated business processes, e.g. processes which share a common value chain (common parent).
- A set of business units which execute the majority of functions in a functional cluster, or the majority of business processes in a process cluster.
- A set of business processes which are responsible for the majority of functions in a functional cluster, or for the majority of business processes in a process cluster, or for the majority of business objects in a data cluster.

Organisational structure   The way a company is organised, e.g. by business units such as departments, by locations or plants.

Organisational unit   The structural units of a company – departments, for example, also plants or locations. Organisational units can also be specific parts of an enterprise's organisational structure.

Outsourcing   Using external resources and moving IT processes to an external provider with the objective of cutting costs, particularly by benefiting from the economies of scale which an external provider can frequently offer.

Owner   The owner of a landscape element is responsible for this element in terms of what business functionality it comprises. For example, a business process can be the data owner for a business object.

Performance measurement system A performance measurement system comprises a set of metrics which can be calculated in relation to one another. One of the best-known performance measurement systems is the Balanced Scorecard. A performance measurement system gives a snapshot of the planned or actual status of a predefined set of control objects. Data can be qualitative and quantitative.

Planned landscape The planned status of a landscape model at a particular point in time. A planned landscape model describes one step on the trajectory from the as-is model to the to-be landscape model, or one step between two planned landscape models. It is possible for multiple planning scenarios to exist simultaneously. Each of these scenarios will represent one possible route to the to-be status of the landscape.

Planning scenarios Alternative planned landscape models, each of which presents one possible snapshot of the landscape at a future point in time.

Policies Policies are a specific kind of principles. They are essentially binding, and there must be good reasons for any non-compliance. Principles are in themselves enduring; they are not impacted by rapid pace of change in technology or products.

Portfolio Originally from the world of stocks and shares, a portfolio in IT landscape management is a two-dimensional presentation which plots various objects such as projects, applications or processes according to their values for each of the dimensions. The portfolio presents an overall picture of how objects are classified in terms of the selected dimensions.

Principles Principles are a set of independent statements which establish a general direction for selecting or designing solutions, and set an authoritative scope within which decisions must be taken.
Examples: "service orientation" or "best-of-breed".

Process cluster A set of business processes which are closely associated in functional terms. Business processes should be grouped into process clusters when one of the following conditions is met:

- A set of business processes which are the data owners for the majority of business objects in a data cluster, or, if no data owners are modelled, use virtually the same set of business objects.
- A set of business processes which are supported more than once in this combination by an application.
- A set of business processes which enact the same business goals.
- A set of business processes which are assigned more than once in this combination to a business unit, or the majority of which lie in the responsibility of business units within the same organisational cluster.

Process landscape model A process landscape model documents the enterprise's as-is and to-be business processes. The number of process levels differs depending on the company. The process landscape provides the basis for appraising the processes using the CMMI method.

Product The outcome or deliverable of an enterprise's service process. Products can be either material (e.g. goods such as cars or computers) or immaterial (services).

Product cluster A set of products which are closely associated in functional terms. Products should be grouped into clusters when one of the following conditions is met:

- A set of products which are assigned more than once in this combination to a business unit.
- A set of products which are supported more than once in this combination by an application.
- A set of products which enact the same business goals.
- A set of products which are assigned more than once in this combination to a business unit, or the majority of which lie in the responsibility of the business units of the same organisational cluster.

Program This term is often used instead of project, when the project has strategic or overarching significance. In many cases, enterprises will also speak of a programme when they are staging a range of larger-scale projects.

Project A project is essentially a one-off activity overall, e.g. in terms of its objectives, restricted timeframe, funding, personnel and other parameters, and its clear demarcation from other projects. In addition it will often usually also have a separate organisation (see [GPM03].

Project cluster A project cluster is considered to exist when the majority of changes conducted across the project impact on the same business units or the same business processes and functions, products, business objects, applications, technical components or interfaces plus the attendant infrastructure, and the changes are made in project timeframes which at least in part overlap.

Project portfolio The project portfolio of the company is the sum total of its active projects, from approval through to completion. The project portfolio can include projects for organisation, strategy, software engineering, architecture or infrastructure. With projects being approved, reprioritised, discarded and completed all the time, the IT project portfolio is in a state of constant flux. The purpose of IT project portfolio management is to ensure the right projects are staged at the right time in the right context.

Proposal for solution Part of the to-be or planned landscape comprising one possible way – in IT terms – to enact a business or IT requirement.

Ramp-up A phase in the life cycle of new software or new software publications which follows completion of the development and precedes general market release. The software is installed with a few selected customers, where – managed by the manufacturer – it undergoes productive tests.

Reference architecture   Pattern-type description of the architecture of an application or part of an application in a particular category, e.g. web-based applications. A reference architecture utilises technical components from the standardisation catalogue and sets down the rules for how these components are to interact.

Risk   An event that could potentially jeopardise the accomplishment of a goal.

Runtime environment   Technical infrastructure for executing an application.

Service and product portfolio   The sum total of the IT services and IT products which an enterprise can offer to its IT customers – e.g. application hosting, infrastructure provisioning, also support processes for business process modelling.

Service IT   Comprises the delivery of all IT commodity services such as IT operation or provisioning of peripheral equipment.

Service level agreement (SLA)   An agreement between the service provider and service client on the quality and quantity of services to be delivered (demonstrable and auditable). An SLA includes definitions on service content, service times and response times.

Service level management   Process which ensures service delivery is in accordance with the service level agreement. This is done by providing a series of checkpoints for the service client. Service level management is based on service monitoring and reporting.

Service management   The sum total of activities for establishing, managing and expanding service activities provided to the customer – service and support of applications and infrastructure, and also consulting services. The reference model for service management is ITIL.

Shared service centre   Centralisation of IT services in a separate unit with standardisation of IT systems and processes, the objective being to reduce cost through economies of scale.

Site   A physical location of service delivery. Examples: buildings with a room number, factory, plant or plant section.

Sourcing strategy   The sourcing strategy sets the cornerstones for the enterprise to find the right mix between make or buy. The choice of sourcing strategy depends very much on the company's own capabilities, i.e. the extent to which it is able to perform services for itself.

State of health   This can be seen both in functional and technical terms. The functional state of health describes the degree or quality of coverage of business requirements. The technical state of health is determined by technical quality requirements. These determine whether, for example, it makes economic sense to adapt a system to new business requirements and maintain it afterwards. If the architecture is not right, or if poor design is barring the way to further development, both the underlying system itself and the vendor relationships are in jeopardy.

Strategic planning The process by which goals are defined, and the strategies laid out to accomplish these goals. At the end of each planning activity, a decision is taken on which goal is to be attained in which period of time.

Strategies Measures to secure the long-term success of an enterprise, i.e. the courses of action selected to help the company achieve its strategic goals. The catalogue of possible measures can be highly varied, and there is a correspondingly wide variety of strategy types. Different strategy types are appropriate for different levels of the company. Strategy is a medium to long-term course of action.

Strategy Definition according to the St. Gallen General Management Navigator ([Ste05]):

A strategy is a precise plan of one's own course of action is which serves to achieve a goal, and into which one factors other aspects which can impact on one's own course of action.

Supplier management The set of processes for developing and managing a portfolio of vendors to fit with the enterprise's make-or-buy policies (i.e. which services the company can perform for itself, and what sort of sourcing strategy it operates). Supplier management involves selecting, appraising and controlling the supplier portfolio.

Synchronized plan Consolidated plan which comprises various other plans, e.g. of projects, and takes both content-related and chronological interdependencies between projects into account. Synchronisation usually takes place at the key milestones of the projects.

Technical blueprint Defines the standards for hardware, networks and software infrastructure both on the application level (e.g. SAPx) and technical level (e.g. EDIFACT). The blueprint can be utilised in the application landscape, i.e. its components serve as the "building blocks" for defining the landscape.

Technical component Provides information on technical implementation of applications or interfaces. Technical components are standardised by technical standardisation processes. The result is a catalogue (named technical blueprint) of standardised technical "building blocks". As well as the standardised components, it might be necessary in documenting the as-is landscape to include non-standardised technical components as well.

Technical landscape model Sets out the objectives for technical implementation of applications, interfaces and parts of the infrastructure. The technical landscape model can include reference architectures and architectural patterns, as well as IT products, components and tools, and can be organised into architectural domains.

Technical standardisation This comprises the sum total of processes for planning and directing technical standardisation in order to raise the flexibility and quality by ensuring the architecture is appropriate for the purpose, and to reduce costs by standardising on particular technologies (principles, standard architectures, tools, blueprint and best-practice examples).

Third party IT product Third-party IT products are software and hardware solutions which are sourced straight from the market without any customising for the enterprise. Such products typically include PCs, PC workstation software such as office or communication platforms and server infrastructure components.

To-be landscape The to-be landscape is the vision for the future, the target status in which the business and its goals will be implemented. It is documented either without any statement on times and schedules, or, if times are included, they are in specific steps, e.g. 2015 and 2020. The to-be landscape is the optimal landscape. Implementation is uncertain, because parameters, constraints and business requirements can easily change over time.
What the to-be landscape does is stake out a general direction: it creates an authoritative scope within which the enterprise moves towards implementing the landscape. The to-be landscape is where we find general strategic statements which technologies, manufactures or IT products should be used. These statements are enriched by principles and guidelines. Alongside the strategic goals, the as-is landscape information, and the action points identified on strategic and operational level, are all key input for establishing what the to-be landscape is to look like.

To-be scenario Visionary scenario for all or part of the landscape, presenting one possible future landscape for the area under consideration.

Traffic light A type of indicator. A traffic light-type indicator maps values of performance metrics to colour signals. In practice, one finds either two-colour traffic lights (red and green) or three colours (red, amber and green).

Utilisation In terms of IT landscape management, utilisation is an expression of the links which exist between one landscape model and another. For example: when developers are working with the application landscape model or with landscape planning, they will utilise elements from the technical landscape model, and link these to applications or interfaces, in order to show how applications, interfaces or other elements will be implemented in technical terms.

Value chain The sum total of primary and secondary processes which contribute to creating value in a company (See [Por85]). In specific terms, the value chain is the path taken by the entire product or service beginning with the source, continuing with the provider or manufacturer, right through to the end customer

Vertical integration The more vertically integrated an enterprise is, the more processes it performs in-house. However, many enterprises are increasingly focusing on their core competencies (and outsourcing non-core activities) as a way of enhancing their value-added.

Vision Long-term goal or objective toward which all enterprise activities are aligned. A vision is an idea of what the company would like things to be like. It also takes the present situation into account, meaning that it is essentially an attainable scenario.

Abbreviations

ADM	Architecture Development Method (TOGAF)
CIO	Chief Information Officer
CMDB	Configuration Management Database
CMMI	Capability Maturity Modell Integration
CMS	Content Management System
COTS	Commercial-off-the-Shelf-Product
CRAMM	CCTA Risk Analysis and Management Method
CRUD	C – Create, R – Read, U – Update, D – Delete
C4ISR	Command, Control, Communications, Computers, Intelligence, Surveillance, and Reconnaissance
DMS	Document Management System
DoD	Department of Defense
DoDAF	Department of Defense Architecture Framework
EAI	Enterprise Application Integration
EAM	Enterprise Architecture Management
EPC	Event-driven Process Chains (Context ARIS process modelling see[Sch01])
ERP	Enterprise Resource Planning
ESB	Enterprise Service Bus
HW	Hardware
ITIL	IT Infrastructure Library
JIT	Just in Time
JRE	Java Runtime Environment
LOC	Lines of Code
M&A	Mergers & Acquistions
NW	Netware
OLAP	Online Analytical Processing
OLTP	Online Transaction Processing
PoC	Proof of Concept
SCM	Supply Chain Management
SLA	Service Level Agreement

SOA	Service Oriented Architecture
SRM	Supplier Relationship Management
SWOT	Strength, Weakness, Opportunity, Threats
TAFIM	Technical Architecture Framework for Information Management
TOGAF	The Open Group Architecture Framework
VR	Virtual Reality

Index

segment managers, 304–305
    perspective, 303
status analysis, 152
strategy, 3–4, 66, 107, 134, 159–160,
    165–166, 178
transformations, 5, 159–162, 171–172
unit, 14, 71–72, 81, 91, 125, 267–268, 281

C
Capability analysis, 287
Central IT organisation, 266–268, 270
Changing the IT organisation, 283–285
Cherry-picking principle, 28
Chief information officer, 322
CIO, 5, 13, 47, 97, 99, 140, 193–194, 198, 206,
    209, 277, 281–283, 290, 306–307
Cluster
    analysis, 147, 152–153
    information flow diagram, 83–84, 143,
        145–146
CMDB, *see* Configuration management
    database
CMMI, 16, 50
CobiT, 16, 92, 194, 262–264, 271, 283
Cockpit, 45–47, 95, 289, 306–310
Commercial-off-the-shelf-product, 323
Commodity, 11–12, 14, 20, 75, 246, 248–249,
    254–255
Common language, 2, 48, 55, 112, 206, 264
Compliance, 2–3, 10–12, 36, 45–47, 52, 83,
    97, 114, 222, 228–231, 242, 259,
    286, 291, 298, 304
    analysis, 152
Configuration management database, 85
Constituents
    of the best-practice enterprise architecture,
        70
    of IT landscape management, 115–125
Content of an IT strategy, 43–45
Control
    indicators, 292–303
    object, 32, 52, 263, 289, 294–300, 306–307
    quantity, 132, 323
    toolkit, 9, 11, 45–46, 59, 186, 197, 208,
        285–311
Controlling, 2, 5, 9, 53, 75, 82, 94–96,
    149–150, 174–176, 187, 271, 275,
    278, 282–283, 285–289, 311
Core data, 119, 123–124, 129, 136, 212, 229
Cost-benefit analysis, 98, 166
Cost savings, 17–18, 72, 112, 172, 222,
    246–251, 258, 287
COTS, 119

Criticality analysis, 152
Current
    landscape model, 118, 157–158, 164, 166,
        168, 178, 181, 191, 192, 201
    performance potential of IT, 11, 15–16, 53

D
Data
    architecture, 62, 65, 67
    cluster, 323–324
    dependency analysis, 152
    governance, 94
    master application, 118, 137, 142, 155
    providers, 99, 101–103, 134, 136, 210,
        214, 261
    provision, 132–133, 135, 139–140, 157,
        208, 212, 261
    strategy, 32
Decentral IT organisation, 266–267, 270
Decision
    areas, 277–282, 311
    boards, 197, 261, 276–283
    -making groups, 303–311
Decoupling strategy, 30
Deduce implementation scenarios, 158,
    177–185
Degree
    of automation, 123, 138, 297–298, 305
    of compliance, 228, 231
Deriving IT goals, 22–26, 51
Design principles, 28, 173
Directing compliance, 47, 234, 240, 242
Divide & conquer principle, 29
Documenting the IT landscape, 130–140, 198
DoDAF, 61–62
Domain, 2–3, 7, 66, 76, 81–82, 91, 116, 118,
    147, 162–163, 223–225, 227–228,
    231, 233, 238, 256
Due diligence, 324

E
E2AF, 62
EAM, 4–5, 58–59, 97–99, 129, 140, 208,
    261–311
EAM Governance, 261–311
Early adopters, 236
Early-majority, 236
Economies of scale, 18, 141, 172, 222,
    246–247, 250, 258, 267, 271
Efficiency analysis, 152
Elements of application landscapes, 115–125
Employees, 21, 44, 46–47, 50, 274, 277, 287,
    294, 296
Enacting standardisation, 234, 240–242